The Thinking Computer

A Series of Books in Psychology

Editors: Richard C. Atkinson
Jonathan Freedman
Gardner Lindzey
Richard F. Thompson

THE THINKING COMPUTER
Mind Inside Matter

Bertram Raphael

Stanford Research Institute

W. H. Freeman and Company
San Francisco

Library of Congress Cataloging in Publication Data

Raphael, Bertram.
　The thinking computer.

　Includes index.
　1. Computers.　2. Problem solving—Data processing.　3. Artificial
intelligence.　I. Title. QA76.R268　　　001.6'4　　　75-30839
ISBN 0-7167-0722-5
ISBN 0-7167-0733-3 pbk.

Printed in the United States of America

9 8 7 6 5 4 3 2 1

To Glen and Kathy

Contents

Preface

The computer is a tool, like the lever or the wheel, whose continued improvement, and subsequent expanded application, can be of immeasurable benefit to mankind. One might imagine many ways in which computers could be improved. Computer scientists and engineers try to make their machines faster, cheaper, more reliable, and easier to use. In addition, a few specialists in a growing field called "artificial intelligence" are devoting their professional careers to trying to make computers more intelligent. This book is an attempt to explain why such an effort is important, how far it has already progressed, where this work is headed, and what seem to be the principal obstacles along the route.

Amid frequent reports of space satellites, test-tube babies, miracle drugs, telepathy, organ transplants, and so on, even the scientist has trouble today distinguishing between fact and fiction. Computer stories in the newspapers, on television, in pulp magazines, and in erudite journals and philosophical papers, come to the attention of the public and leave myriad paradoxical and frequently misleading impressions: computers are mysterious, incomprehensible, stupid, frightening, slavish, and so on.

This book is an attempt to clear up the confusion by presenting, in simple terms, some of the most interesting and novel capabilities of computers today and in the next few years. The presentation is focused on discussions of goals, current approaches, and difficulties, rather than specific solutions and descriptive case studies—although, of course, some case studies are used as examples. Therefore, although my own prejudices clearly shine through, readers are encouraged to make their own judgements about the feasibility and value of the methods being tried, and their own projections for the future of smarter computers.

The book is intended to fill the gap between the superficiality of popular expositions of its subject matter and the imposing complexity of the formal technical literature. Any reader with a good high-school mathematics education should be able to enjoy it. The casual reader, and the reader with no scientific background, can skip the more-technical sections—especially parts of Chapters 3, 4, and 5—and still follow the general flow of the presentation. However, enough technical "meat" is included to provide the serious student with a firm basis for launching into more advanced text and journal presentations.

Some familiarity with the basic nature of computers would provide useful but not essential background for the reader. Chapter 1, although necessarily superficial, offers enough computer basics to enable any reader to appreciate the rest of the book. Since some of the material there is somewhat unorthodox, however, I hope even the computer-sophisticated reader will at least scan this chapter.

I have not tried to be comprehensive. My goal is to stimulate the reader, not exhaust him. For the interested reader, a list of reference books and periodicals covering the general subject of the book appears on page xiv. Brief bibliographies at the end of each chapter point to more-thorough, more-technical material covering the specific topics featured in the chapter.

As a text, this book could be used as the basis for a new lower-division course in a university or junior college, or as supplementary reading for a variety of existing courses. It might be used in the second (and perhaps final) course about computers in a general college curriculum, following a more conventional introduction to computers or data processing; alternatively, it might be used in an early course of a more-specialized, technical sequence. The book may also be of interest to the general public, and to the nontechnical professional who is curious about the potential impact of computers on his field.

Most of this material was prepared in Vienna under the support of a Fulbright-Hayes Senior Lectureship, with the cooperation and assistance of the Austro-American Education Commission and the Technische Hochschule of Vienna. I am also indebted to Stanford Research Institute, especially the SRI Artificial Intelligence Center and its principal sponsor, the Advanced Research Projects Agency, for providing a stimulating environment responsible for many of the ideas and much of the research presented in the following pages.

A great many individuals helped me, directly or indirectly, to complete this book. I believe it all began back in 1957 when David B. Meyer launched my computer career by losing a chess game. A few years later, Hartley Rogers, Jr., introduced me to the wonders of predicate calculus, and Marvin L. Minsky awoke my excitement over the concept of intelligent computers. The friendship of Dori and Larry Burger certainly enhanced the pleasures of my stay in Vienna while I was preparing this manuscript. My wife Anne provided the extra patience, persistence, and confidence I needed to complete this effort. Numerous typists in Vienna and California struggled with various illegible drafts. Finally, I received a great many valuable suggestions from the following people who all carefully read at least a portion of an earlier draft of this book: R. V. Andree, N. Chapin, R. O. Duda, P. E. Hart, D. C. Lynch, N. J. Nilsson, C. Raphael, and C. A. Rosen. The remaining errors, omissions, and other flaws are probably due to my laziness or obstinacy in failing to follow some of their well-founded recommendations.

August 1975   Bertram Raphael

General References

Artificial Intelligence, An International Journal (quarterly). North Holland Publishing Co., Amsterdam, 1970–

Bobrow, D. G., and A. Collins. *Representation and Understanding.* Academic Press, New York, 1975.

Feigenbaum, E. A., and J. Feldman. *Computers and Thought.* McGraw-Hill Book Co., New York, 1963.

International Joint Conferences on Artificial Intelligence, held every two years since 1969. *Advance Papers of the Third Conference,* 1973, may be available from the Artificial Intelligence Center, Stanford Research Institute, Menlo Park, California. *Advance Papers of the Fourth Conference,* 1975, may be available from the Artificial Intelligence Laboratory, Massachusetts Institute of Technology, Cambridge, Massachusetts.

Jackson, P. D. *Introduction to Artificial Intelligence.* Petrocelli Books, New York, 1974.

Meltzer, B., and D. Michie (eds). *Machine Intelligence* (annual). American Elsevier Publishing Co., New York, 1966–1973. 7 vols.

Minsky, M. D. (ed.). *Semantic Information Processing.* MIT Press, Cambridge, Mass., 1968.

Nilsson, N. J. *Problem Solving Methods in Artificial Intelligence.* McGraw-Hill Book Co., New York, 1971.

SIGART Newsletter, (bimonthly). Special Interest Group on Artificial Intelligence, Association for Computing Machinery, New York, 1966–

Slagle, J. R. *Artificial Intelligence: The Heuristic Programming Approach.* McGraw-Hill Book Co., New York, 1971.

About Computers 1

About this book

In the mid-1940's the first experimental computers consisted of rooms full of equipment that cost millions of dollars, were available only to a few elite scientists, and constantly broke down. Today, in the mid-1970's, machines with similar computational speed and precision can be purchased in any department store for about $100, fit in the palm of your hand, and work reliably for years. Today's large computers are many millions of times more powerful than the legendary ENIAC, JOHNIAC, and WHIRLWIND machines of less than thirty years ago. Clearly computers are evolving at a rapid rate. They are becoming faster, more accurate, more reliable, physically smaller, and about twenty-five percent less expensive every year. But are they becoming any smarter? How does one go about trying to educate a computer, anyway? And why would anyone want a computer to be smart? This book will attempt to answer such questions.

By 1950 the feasibility of computers had been well established in the laboratory and the world's first commercially produced computer, UNIVAC 1, was purchased by the Census Bureau of the United States government.[1] Even as the world was just beginning to discover the existence of computers, a few dreamers were thinking about the distant

---

[1]Coincidentally, the first widely used punched card system, invented by Hollerith in the 1870's, was also developed for the United States Census Bureau.

future of such devices. In a famous paper published in 1950,[2] A. M. Turing, a British mathematician, wrote,

> We may hope that machines will eventually compete with men in all purely intellectual fields. But which are the best ones to start with? Even this is a difficult decision. Many people think that a very abstract activity, like the playing of chess, would be best. It can also be maintained that it is best to provide the machine with the best sense organs that money can buy, and then teach it to understand and speak English. This process could follow the normal teaching of a child. Things would be pointed out and named, etc. Again I do not know what the right answer is, but I think both approaches should be tried.

Since that day, computers have permeated our society. No large bank, insurance company, research laboratory, or educational institution can survive today without using computers. More than 100,000 computers are now in use in the United States. Most of these computers are still being used in essentially the same way the UNIVAC 1 was used: to mechanize the drudgery of routine arithmetic calculations. A small number of computers, however, serve as experimental systems in laboratories with extravagant-sounding names like "Artificial Intelligence Center," where scientists quietly pursue Turing's dream.[3]

During the past quarter century both approaches suggested by Turing—the application of machines to abstract, formal activities like playing chess, and the development of machines that can see, hear, and understand—have been tried. So have other approaches, such as the development of complete robot systems. Most of the scientists engaged in these studies today are motivated by much more immediate goals than Turing's academic interest in machines that "will eventually compete with men in all purely intellectual fields." Rather than machines competing with men, these researchers believe that machines can and should help men, in all fields; just as mechanical machines have helped men in their physical activities for over a hundred years, computing machines should help men in their intellectual activities—and perhaps combined sensory, computer, and mechanical machine systems should help men in many of their complex perceptual and problem-solving activities. Certainly, with all the problems facing mankind today—energy, pollution, inflation, international tension, and so on—men need all the help they can get, from any likely source, and soon.

Progress toward making computers smarter has been slow, and some critics have urged that this research be abandoned—although whether these critics are motivated by a belief that the work is wasteful

---

[2]A. M. Turing, "Computing machinery and intelligence," *Mind,* 59(1950); 433–460. Reprinted in Feigenbaum and Feldman, *Computers and Thought,* McGraw-Hill, 1963.

[3]The term Artificial Intelligence is widely used as the name of the branch of computer science that studies how to make computers smarter.

because it is doomed to failure, or by a fear that it will succeed and produce dangerous results, is not always clear. The goals of this book are to explain some of the obstacles to making machines smarter, and how these obstacles are being attacked; to describe some of the successes that have already been achieved, and some that lie in the near future; to show that smarter computers are already beginning to move from the laboratory to important posts in society; and, most important, to point out that smarter computers are not a dangerous threat, but rather a promising hope for the future of mankind.

There are hundreds of good books and college courses, with names such as *Introduction to Computer Science* and *Data Processing* and *Computers and Society*, that explain in great detail the physical construction of computers and how they work. This book has a somewhat different purpose; it will deal with the present and future uses of computers in a more abstract fashion. If you already know something about computers, you may be able to imagine precisely how some of the methods discussed in later chapters can be carried out by today's computer equipment. If you do not know anything about how computers work, I still want you to understand enough about them to appreciate what they can do, without any feelings of great awe or mystery. Later sections of this chapter therefore describe, at a superficial level, the basic mechanisms of computers: the physical equipment, or *hardware,* and the programs, or *software,* that make the hardware go through its paces. Before describing what a computer is, however, I want to clear away some misleading myths—some cliches that have created a false picture of the nature and the limitations of computers.

Misleading myths

Many people share the belief that computers are inherently stupid, and that even a suggestion that computers might be made smarter is ridiculous. This belief is so widespread that most people—scientists as well as laymen—never even consider the many ways in which smarter computers might help them. Misconceptions about a computer's limitations seem to be based upon two widely accepted but basically untrue premises. Let us examine these myths in turn. By pointing out some of their fallacies, perhaps I can open your mind to the fascinating prospects for smarter computers.

THE ARITHMETIC MYTH. *A computer is nothing but a big fast arithmetic machine.*

This myth seems to be based upon the following erroneous reasoning.

1.   Computers were originally needed to do the kinds of large arithmetic calculations that arose in the tasks of aiming ballistic weapons and of producing approximate solutions to equations of nuclear physics. [True.]

2.   Therefore, the designers of computers intended them to be only big, fast arithmetic calculating machines. [Doubtful. The basic design and operations of computers are much more general, as we shall see below.]

3.   Therefore, computers are nothing but big fast arithmetic machines. [False! Although the intentions of the original designers of computers are subject to wide interpretation,[4] when we study the capabilities of today's machines objectively we find much more powerful, more flexible systems.]

Computers are arithmetic machines, certainly; virtually every computer has wired into it the ability to add and subtract. But are they "nothing but" arithmetic machines? Certainly not. Take the reference manual for any computer, and scan through its "instruction set": the collection of basic operations it has been designed and wired to perform. You will see a few, perhaps as many as ten or twenty, operations that bear some close resemblance to arithmetic—e.g., ADD, DIVIDE, FLOATING SUBTRACT, MULTIPLY STEP, and so on—but you will also see many, perhaps one or two hundred, operations that have relatively little to do with arithmetic—e.g., STORE, LOAD, TEST, SHIFT, READ, WRITE, REWIND TAPE, SKIP, MOVE, MASK, MATCH, TRANSFER, and so on.

To see why computers must be able to perform so many nonarithmetic operations, consider as an example the simple task of preparing the pay checks for a business firm. This is a common job for a computer. But is it a job for a "big fast arithmetic machine"? If a human accountant did the job, he might sit down with the record books, time cards, check forms, and a small calculating machine. In a simple case, he would use the machine to multiply each employee's hourly salary by the number of hours the employee had worked and write the answer on a check.

Now suppose we want a computer to do a similar job. What *program*—sequence of elementary operations—must we give it? The program will have to do everything that both the accountant and his calculating machine did when the job was done by hand. True, the computer will have to do an occasional MULTIPLY operation, just as the calculator did; but it will also be very busy doing all the things the accountant did: looking up an employee's name, looking up his hourly salary, noting the salary in a convenient place, checking whether the employee was

---

[4]I am reminded of the story of the little old lady who walked up to Wernher von Braun, the rocket expert, at the end of his lecture and asked, "Dr. von Braun, why do people want to fly to the moon? Why don't they sit home and watch television, like the good Lord intended?"

listed as away on vacation or sick leave and if he was not then looking for the record of his time card, finding where the total hours worked was noted, copying that total in a convenient place, supervising the MULTI-PLY calculation, finding and positioning the next blank check (if the book of blank checks is empty then starting another book), copying the employee's name onto the check, dating the check, copying the calculated pay onto the check, imprinting a facsimile of a signature on the check, and moving the check to the "done" pile. Even in this trivial job a computer would have to spend almost all its effort doing what a man would do, and very little doing what a calculator would do.

Almost all the time that a computer works on the problem just described, and in fact much of the time that any computer works on any problem, the computer is positioning, comparing, moving, choosing, copying . . . , but it is not doing arithmetic. Rather than calling a computer "nothing but a big fast arithmetic machine," it is much more accurate to say that a computer is *a big, fast, general-purpose symbol-manipulating machine*. With this definition as a foundation, we can progress in later chapters to an appreciation of how it is possible to develop flexible, decision-making, problem-solving, perceiving computers—in short, smart computers.

THE STUPID COMPUTER MYTH. *A computer is an obedient intellectual slave that can do only what it is told to do.*

This second myth is even more persistent than the first one, and even more damaging in the way it tends to constrain our thinking. Suppose I gave you the pieces of a jigsaw puzzle and told you, "by the way, these pieces cannot be fit together." Would you try very hard to fit the pieces together? Why should anyone try to build a smart computer, if he is told over and over again that computers are inherently stupid?

The stupid-computer myth has been repeated and generally accepted for more than a hundred years. In 1842, after Professor Babbage of Cambridge designed his Analytical Engine, a large-scale mechanical digital computer (which unfortunately was never completed), his friend Lady Lovelace wrote, "The Analytical Engine has no pretensions to *originate* anything. It can do *whatever we know how to order* it to perform." There is no question that Lady Lovelace's argument, and all the subsequent versions of the stupid-computer myth, are true, in a certain literal sense: a computer must be given its program of instructions, and it will always do exactly what those instructions tell it to do (unless, of course, one of its circuits fails). And yet this basic truth is not a real restriction on the intelligence of computers at all.

A couple of examples will resolve this paradox. One of the first scientists to challenge the stupid-computer myth was A. L. Samuel of IBM. In 1961, he developed a program to make a computer play checkers.

After practicing by playing against itself for a while on the new computers in the basement of an IBM manufacturing plant, the program could consistently beat Samuel, its creator. How was this possible? Samuel had figured out how to order the computer to learn to play a better game. (Chapter 5 has some further details about how this was done.)

In 1969 "Shakey," a computer-controlled robot at Stanford Research Institute, could find its way from room to room, avoiding or rearranging obstacles according to general instructions such as "Block Door 3 with Box 5," even though its program had never before considered that particular task or that particular arrangement of obstacles. How? Shakey's designers had figured out how to program a robot to find its own way around and to solve, for itself, a wide class of problems (See Chapter 8).

The claim that a computer "can only do what it is told to do" does not mean that computers must be stupid; rather, it clarifies the challenge of how to make computers smarter; we must figure out how to tell (i.e., program) a computer to be smarter. Can we tell a computer how to learn? To create? To invent? Why not? I'd bet even Lady Lovelace would have agreed that the task of figuring out "how to order" a computer "to originate" something would be a fascinating and meaningful research challenge.

Hardware

What is a computer? Peek through the glass doors of any large computer installation; what do you see? Rows of shiny cabinets covered with mysterious switches and dials; a desk-like operator's console, with hundreds of tiny blinking lights and more controls than a Wurlitzer organ; spinning disks, clattering printers, chattering card readers; a false floor that hides hundreds of cables; cabinet doors that protect thousands of circuit cards and millions of wires; and a few people scurrying about, answering the phone, transferring paper or equipment from one place to another, generally looking harried but still more or less in control of the situation.

What's going on? Data is being fed into the computer, and answers are being printed out. The computer system may be engaged in printing pay checks or solving a differential equation, or preparing next months' inventory orders, or measuring electrocardiograms, or any of a tremendous number of other activities. All these diverse tasks are done with the same collection of physical equipment, which is unglamorously known as the hardware of the computer installation.

BASIC HARDWARE

How can we describe the basic hardware components of a computer system? A computer is usually a collection of metal, plastic, glass, fiberboard, and special materials such as silicon. These elements have been made into such things as wires, transistors, electronic circuits, buttons, switches, lights, machinery, insulation, sheet metal cabinets, and paint. The complete system may cost less than $1000 or more than $100 million, weigh less than a pound or more than fifty tons, and fit in the palm of your hand or occupy several huge rooms.

To understand why the tremendous variety of such systems are called "computers," we must look at their components from a functional point of view: i.e., we must talk about what the major parts of a computer are supposed to do, rather than what they are made of or how they look.

The hardware of every computer can be divided into three functional parts: the *memory*, the *central processing unit* (CPU), and the *peripheral equipment* (Figure 1.1).

The *memory* is a physical device that can remember (or, in computer jargon, *store*) a large quantity—frequently millions—of numbers. A unique *address* labels each storage position in the memory (called a *memory location*, or a *word*) so that the number stored there can be easily identified and retrieved when desired. As a concrete analogy, think of a row of one million one-handed clocks. Each clock has a label, its "address," that numbers its position in the row; and each clock can "remember" one number between one and twelve, depending upon which

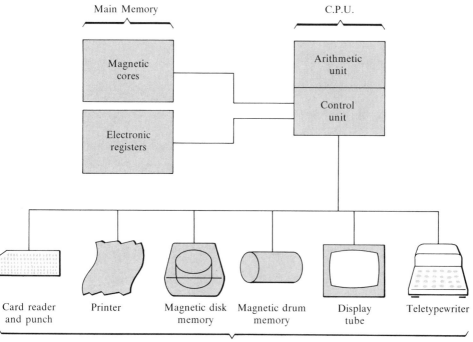

Figure 1.1 Main components of a typical computer system.

number on the dial its hand is pointing to. If a computer could reset any clock and read the number on any dial, then this collection of labeled clocks could serve as that computer's memory. (We assume the clocks are not wound, so that the setting on each clock—in computer terminology, the *contents* of each memory location—never changes spontaneously; it changes only when the computer commands it to change.)

In practice, a computer's memory is made up of magnetic or electronic devices, rather than clock faces. The devices of each memory location may contain a variety of different arrangements of electronic or magnetic indicators (like the clock-hand positions); however, the number of arrangements that each location can hold is usually not twelve, like the clock face. Typically, either a location can hold only two arrangements (like a simple switch that can only be either "on" or "off"), in which case the location is said to contain precisely one *bit* of information; or the location contains several bits which, as a group, can hold a larger number of different identifiable arrangements. A common grouping in a location —called the *word length*—is eight bits, whose indicators can be arranged in 256 different ways. The longest computer words in common use today contain 64 bits, which allow 4,294,967,296 arrangements.

To describe the contents of a location, we could give each arrangement a different symbol as its name; the two possible arrangements of a one-bit location could usefully be referred to as "zero" and "one," or "A" and "B," or even "Morris" and "Adella." But for larger locations, it is clearly more practical to number the arrangements than to name them. Therefore, when someone says (as I may later in this book) that a certain computer word (memory location) "contains the number 176," don't believe that it really contains a number; it just contains, for example, the 176th arrangement of magnetic fields according to some arbitrary ordering of possible arrangements, and therefore "176" was chosen as the symbolic name for that arrangement. The computer inherently doesn't know any more about decimal numbers than it knows about Morris.

The memory of a computer has three major uses.

1. To hold the data upon which the computer operates—the column of numbers to be added, the equations to be solved, and so on.

2. To serve as "scratch paper," a place for the computer to note intermediate results that will be needed for later calculations.

3. To hold the program of instructions for the computer.

One of the basic concepts of modern computers is that the program should be stored in the computer's memory right along with the data. The following very simple (although somewhat silly) example shows the reason that the entire program must be prepared and given to the computer before any computations are begun. Suppose we want a computer to print out a hundred thousand entries of the fives' multiplication table: $1 \times 5 = 5, 2 \times 5 = 10$, and so on up to $100,000 \times 5 = 500,000$. If we did not have a prepared program, a man would have to sit in front of the computer and type instructions meaning, "multiply one by five, print the answer, multiply two by five, print the answer, multiply three by five," and so on. Each instruction would take several seconds to present to the computer and only a few millionths of a second to perform; the machine would be idle, waiting for instructions, about 99.9999 percent of the time. Instead, we can now compose a special coded version of the complete instructions, "Multiply each of the numbers from one to 100,000 by five and print the answers." With this code (called a program) instantly accessible, the computer can carry out the entire process at high speed. Whenever it needs to know what to do next it need merely look at the next instruction in the prepared program.

Now, where in the computer should this prepared program reside? The program could consist of wiring arrangements in the basic structure of the computer; and in fact some special-purpose computers are built in just such a manner. But a computer with a wired-in program can do only one job—e.g., print out the fives table—until somebody physically tears into it with rewiring tools. A much more flexible approach, and therefore the approach used with all general-purpose computers, is to let the program be represented by a series of numbers stored in the computer's own memory. This permits the program, and therefore the behavior of the entire machine, to be changed as easily as any of the numeric data may be changed, simply by storing some new numbers into an appropriate part of the memory.

The CPU is the part of the computer system that does most of the work: it carries out the operations called for by the instructions in the stored program. The two principal parts of the CPU are called the *arithmetic unit* and the *control unit.* The arithmetic unit really is "nothing but a fast arithmetic machine," which calculates whatever the control unit tells it to. The control unit is the heart of the system, like a puppeteer who pulls the right strings to make everything happen on schedule. The control unit oversees the progress of the stored program. It looks at an instruction, figures out what it means, and does it—calls upon the arithmetic unit to do some calculation using data from a particular memory location, starts or stops some peripheral device such as the printer, prepares to get a new instruction from a different part of memory, or whatever.

The *peripheral equipment*, also known as *input-output* (I/O) equipment, is a collection of diverse devices that enable the computer to communicate with the outside world. Standard peripheral devices include card readers, for sensing the holes on punched cards; card punch machines, for creating newly punched cards to be used in some future computer operation; high speed printers, to produce large quantities of tabulated or other printed results; typewriter-like "terminals," for communicating between the computer and a human operator directly by typing; and magnetic drum, disc, and tape systems, which are really external extensions of the computer's memory—large quantities of data can be saved for long periods in disc and tape libraries, thereby freeing the computer's main memory for more immediate concerns.

OTHER HARDWARE POSSIBILITIES

The hardware described above is the basic equipment for the most common type of computer in use today: the *general-purpose stored-program sequential digital computer.* "General purpose" means that the set of instructions available in the machine is broad enough to be used for programs that solve many different problems, rather than being restricted to a single application such as, for example, the flight-control computer of a jet aircraft. "Stored program" means that the particular instructions the computer should obey are stored right in its memory along with the data they act upon, rather than, for example, being supplied by a specially wired panel. "Sequential" means that the computer always does only one thing at a time. "Digital" simply means that the computer works only with discrete symbols, usually identified by numbers (digits). Its memory stores numbers, its control unit manipulates numbers, its peripheral equipment represents alphabetic characters by number codes. Whenever I use the term "computer" in this book, I mean general-purpose stored-program sequential digital computer, because that is the best known kind of computer and the kind with which I am most familiar. However, since most of the alternative ways of organizing computers are equivalent in computational power (they differ primarily in speed or cost), the discussions of approaches to smarter computers later in this book apply equally well to all possible computers. Two widely mentioned alternative computer organizations are the analog (rather than digital) and the parallel (rather than sequential).

Analog vs. Digital. Instead of numbers (or numbered arrangements of magnetic fields), analog computers use physical quantities to represent data. Thus the magnitude of an electrical voltage, the velocity of a rotating mechanical shaft, or the brightness of a beam of light—rather than numbers that measure such quantities—are direct inputs to the computer. Furthermore, instead of doing arithmetic, an analog computer uses the physical characteristics of its data to determine answers. For example, addition is done in an electronic analog computer simply by arranging a circuit so that the output voltage is the sum of the two input voltages. One of the simplest analog computers, the slide rule, is based upon the trivial idea of adding two lengths by placing one next to the other and looking at the total length.

By making use of such properties of physical analogs, analog computers can often avoid much time-consuming arithmetic. On the other hand, they can never be extremely accurate. Physical quantities are always difficult to measure precisely, and tend to fluctuate somewhat with changes in temperature, humidity, degree of wear, and so on. Like a slide rule, most analog computers produce answers that differ from the true answer by about one percent of its value; rarely can the error be reduced below one-tenth of one percent. The precision of a digital computer is generally much better than that, and can usually be made as good as you wish simply by allocating memory space to hold additional significant figures in the numbers that represent quantities. Therefore the results of any analog operation can be achieved equally well or better by a digital computer, although possibly much more slowly.

Parallel vs. Sequential. It has been argued that computers cannot be made much smarter because they do only one thing at a time, where-as a smart computer—such as the human brain—must be able to consider a great many things "in parallel," i.e., simultaneously. Yet such arguments neglect to explain why parallelism is necessary, or to point out the complex relationships between parallelism and speed.

Today's computers can do about one million sequential operations each second. Suppose, instead of such a computer, we had one million computers hooked together, and that each required one full second to complete an elementary operation. Would we be better off? At the end of one second we would have the same million operations accomplished—but how would we find which computer had produced the best answer? In larger tasks, how would the performance of all the parallel computers be coordinated, so that they could cooperate in solving common problems? Wouldn't it be much harder to find errors in programs for a parallel machine?

For a variety of reasons, developments in computer design during the 1960's and 1970's have led to ever faster sequential machines, rather than parallel structures, but the speed of sequential machines is approaching a limit, determined by the time it takes electricity to flow along wires in the computer. Thus, designers are beginning to focus more attention upon parallel systems. The point to remember is that questions of whether computers should be parallel or sequential, as well as analog or digital, are questions of speed, cost, and convenience, rather than questions of inherent capabilities. For any proposed analog or parallel machine, I can describe a sequential digital machine that, if fast enough, will do precisely the same job. Progress toward smarter computers is limited only by our primitive ability to program and use whatever computers we now have, rather than by the lack of some special new type of computer.

SPECIAL PERIPHERAL EQUIPMENT

A computer is generally thought of as an isolated "brain"—a machine that sits quietly and cogitates, totally separated from the sights and sounds of the real world. Its only normal source of input consists of numbers read from conventional peripheral devices: the positions of holes on punched cards, or the code numbers of keys struck on a typewriter terminal. When we ask how to make computers smarter, we should immediately notice this sterile environment. It is well known that human children develop intelligence by interacting with their environments; babies must see and hear, and touch, and feel, and taste, in order to develop normally. How can we enrich the environment of the underprivileged computer? Can we enable a computer to experience for itself the sights and sounds of the world? Indeed we can. The first key ingredient is a set of *special peripheral equipment* that gives the digital computer a numeric representation of the physical phenomenon it is experiencing; some examples of such equipment are presented in the following paragraphs. The second ingredient, which is more difficult to obtain, is a set of programs by means of which the computer can make sense out of these numbers; the development of such programs will be the main subject of Chapters 7 and 8 of this book.

The acquisition of physical data by a computer usually takes place in two stages: first, the intensity of the physical sensation of interest is translated into an electrical voltage, by a device called a *sensor*; second, the magnitude of the voltage is measured and turned into a number by a device called an *analog-to-digital converter* (A/D converter). A/D converters are widely available. Precisely how they work is not of direct interest to us; however, it is safe to assume that we can usually find an A/D converter that has the speed and precision required for any particular application. Since the voltage produced by a sensor sometimes changes rapidly, a good A/D converter will remeasure it frequently and thereby feed a steady stream of numbers to the computer.

Let us turn now to the sensors that translate various physical phenomena into electricity. Suppose we want our computer to "see": i.e., to sense the presence or absence of light. One of the simplest visual sensors is the photodiode, a device that permits electricity to flow through it only when a sufficiently bright light shines upon it. In the most common applications a permanent light beam is focused upon the photodiode, which is in an electrical circuit that operates a switch. If something interrupts the light beam—e.g., if a person steps into it—then the photodiode shuts off the electricity, the switch throws, and something happens—perhaps a door opens (or, in some places I have seen, the toilets flush) until the path of the light beam is again clear. Although it is not a complete computer, some people might be willing to say that even such a simple electromechanical system can "see"; it senses the person's shadow, and carries out an appropriate action.

The quantity of electricity flowing through a photodiode depends upon the brightness of the light shining upon it. Instead of simply activating an on-off switch, this electric flow can be measured and its value used to control some apparatus that needs to "know" what the brightness is. Thus, for example, an automatic-exposure camera "sees" how bright the scene is and sets its lens opening accordingly. This automatic perception of brightness levels can occur extremely rapidly; modern electronic flash attachments for cameras actually "see" how much of their light is being reflected from a scene in time to turn themselves off before the picture becomes overexposed.

Operating an electric door or a flash unit does not require A/D converters and general-purpose computers; such operations are usually carried out by small, special-purpose, analog computers. But more complex visual sensing is another story. Consider a television camera: it is really a sensor that translates a visual scene into an electrical signal that lasts 1/30 second. (Since this operation repeats 30 times each second, a TV viewer sees new pictures so often that he thinks he is watching the scene continuously.) Variations in the magnitude of this signal are proportional to variations in light intensity across horizontal lines of the scene; in fact, 525 lines of brightness information are contained in the 1/30-second signal. In normal use, a TV system transfers pictures from the camera to the home set without ever needing to know what is in the picture; the home viewer can judge that for himself. But now, suppose a home viewer of the future asks her computer to monitor the transmission for her, and, "turn off the sound during commercials" or "ring a bell every time a handsome man comes onto the screen." How can a computer be made to gather the necessary data on which to base its decisions? The first step is simply to plug in a high-performance A/D converter, translating each picture into a sequence of thousands of numbers to be placed in the computer's memory. This makes the data available in a form appropriate for computer processing. The next step, how to program the computer to understand the significance of those numbers, then becomes possible in principle, although in practice it is an extremely difficult and still largely unsolved problem. (Some aspects of this problem are discussed in Chapter 7.)

So far I have talked only about sensors for light intensity. Actually sensors exist for almost any physical quantity you can imagine. For example, *pressure* can be sensed, i.e., translated to electrical voltage, by a special spongy material whose electrical conductivity depends upon how strongly it is compressed; *sound* is sensed by a microphone, of course; *distance* can be sensed by radar or sonar measurements, or by a device that uses similar principles with laser light to get highly accurate distance measurements; *color* can be sensed by comparing the intensity of light received through various colored filters, or by using a color TV camera; *rotational position* is sensed by devices called *shaft encoders; force* is sensed by devices called *strain gauges;* and so on. The magnitude of virtually any physical sensation can be made known to a computer with an appropriate sensor and A/D converter. How a computer can best make use of such knowledge remains to be explored.

We have here considered special peripheral equipment for *input*—the process of transferring data from the outside world to the computer. The inverse task, output of computer-generated data to the world, can also be accomplished in many different ways. Computers can output numbers to conventional peripheral devices such as printers; they can output commands to operate switches; and they can also output numbers to *digital-to-analog converters* (D/A converters), which translate a series of numbers into an appropriately varying electrical voltage that operates the output counterpart of a sensor, called an *effector*, which produces a physical effect. The most common effector is a motor, whose speed or rotational position is controlled by the computer. For example, a *plotter* is an output device consisting of computer-controlled motors that operate pens and paper, which enable the computer to draw graphs and pictures. The D/A-converted signal might instead control the motion of a light beam shining on photographic film, thereby producing permanent records on *computer-output microfilm;* the signal might control the beam of electrons in a TV-like *cathode-ray-tube* (CRT) display, silently and extremely rapidly drawing diagrams or displaying text for an operator to study; or it might control a system of audio speakers, producing computer-generated music or synthesized speech.

Often special peripheral input and output devices are used together. For example, one early computer use of photodiodes was in a device called a *light pen,* which is used in connection with cathode-ray-tube displays. While one part of the computer's program lights up various places on the display, another part watches through the light pen pointed at the display to find out when the light pen can see the illuminated spots. By coordinating the photodiode's electrical response with these two programs, the computer can find out where the light pen is pointing. As another example, suppose a computer could operate the pan, tilt, and zoom controls of its own TV camera. It could then decide for itself what it wanted to see, aim the camera in that direction, take a picture, analyze it, perhaps then reach out with its mechanical arm and—but wait! We shall return to the story of robots in Chapter 8. All I want to convey here is that the hardware of computers, augmented by special but easily obtained peripheral equipment, is fully capable of interacting with the physical world in a variety of reasonably smart ways. The question of how to achieve the more intelligent performance that this hardware makes physically possible, is a question of software—the subject of the next section and also, to a large extent, the subject of the rest of this book.

Software

It takes three things to make a fine painting: a blank canvas, some tubes of paint, and an artist's dexterity and diligence in properly distributing the paint over the canvas.

The hardware of a computer, with its fantastic complexity and sometimes incredible cost, is really no more than a blank canvas: although it can support masterpieces of achievement, by itself it has little significance. The hardware must first be given some data, which, like the artist's paint, is a building block that determines the direction or "color" of a computation. Then, most important, the hardware must be augmented by a program, often called the software. Like an artist's skill, the program really determines the effectiveness of the entire system.

As discussed in the previous section, a stored-program digital computer is usually thought of as having numbers in its memory. Part of the memory contains data numbers, and part contains numbers that constitute the program. Although the data numbers can be actual numeric data for some arithmetic task, they also can be simply numeric *codes* for letters of the alphabet, or words, or lists, or abstract symbols. The nature of the codes may be determined by the peripheral equipment (e.g., whenever the letter A is struck on a keyboard a teletypewriter may transmit the number 61) or the code may be just an informal understanding established by some programmer (e.g., that all the data about an employee is filed under his social security number).

Similarly, the program numbers are codes rather than arithmetic data; in this case, the codes represent basic machine operations, and their decoding process is built into the wiring of the hardware. For example, suppose the number 17 is the code, in the circuitry of some computer, for the operation "addition." Then the sequence of program numbers

$$17, \quad 239, \quad 185$$

might mean,

$$\text{Add 239 to 185,}$$

the two program numbers 239 and 185 being treated as pieces of data. More usually, the program tells where the data are to be found, rather than what the data are. In most computers, the instruction

$$17, \quad 239, \quad 185$$

would be taken to mean something like, "Add the number in the 239th memory location to the number in the 185th memory location," where locations 239 and 185 are in the data part of the memory. This indirect way of referring to the actual numbers to be added together is an important feature of computers; for example, it permits a single unchanged program to add any set of figures that is placed in the data memory.

When a programmer for the first computers wanted to place an addition instruction into his program, he had to learn or look up the code for addition, say 17, and then insert that number into the program part of the computer's memory: 17 was the symbol that meant ADD in the language of the machine's circuitry, and the programmer had to express his desires in the basic language of the machine.

Then some forgotten genius had an idea: the process of looking up an instruction word like "addition" in a table to find its code, 17, is a routine mechanical operation that even a stupid computer should be able to do. If the computer contains in its data the word ADD followed by its machine code 17, then a suitable program can replace the word by the number whenever the word is typed or otherwise acquired from the peripheral equipment. (Of course, the word ADD cannot actually be placed into the computer; only a numeric code for it can exist in the computer's memory. But since the coding and decoding processes are largely automatic, we can begin to think and speak as if the computer manipulates symbols rather than just numbers.)

Thus, programmers no longer had to remember to type 17 when they mean ADD. Instead, they could type ADD, and a special program called an *assembler* would translate programs from symbolic *assembly language* into the actual numeric *machine language* that is understood by the circuitry of the computer.

Let's take another view of what is happening. The basic computer hardware can operate only upon numeric data with numeric program instructions. We put a particular program—the assembler—into the machine, and presto! The computer now understands a symbolic instruction language. The software has made the machine behave as if its hardware had been transformed into a different machine: namely, one that can accept directly English words such as ADD as instructions. In fact, such software generally has the effect of disguising a machine so that it behaves like a different, usually more powerful, machine. Therefore, when I speak abstractly of a computer, as I shall frequently throughout this book, I usually mean a combination of computer hardware and software. Given the performance characteristics of such a combined system, the dividing line between the capabilities of the underlying hardware and the capabilities added by the software cannot be detected, and isn't very important anyway. In order to make computers smarter, it is therefore not necessary to fiddle with the wiring of any computer; designing programs that make standard, unmodified hardware into smarter computer systems is a sufficient and completely feasible solution.

The assembler was only the first small step in the evolution of computer-programming languages—but a giant step in pointing the direction toward smarter computers. Here are a few examples of further steps on the software ladder from machine language to more powerful, "higher-level" computer-programming languages.

Macro Assemblers. The first assembly languages were just like machine languages except that they used alphabetic symbols instead of numeric codes. Each basic instruction expressed in the assembly language corresponded to (and was translated by the assembler into) precisely one basic machine-language instruction. As programmers learned how to construct more-clever assembler programs, the assembly languages were made a bit richer and their strict correspondence to machine language was relaxed. For example, most assembly languages today allow their users to define abbreviations called *macro-instructions*. A programmer might define the macro "AVERAGE, X, Y" to be an abbreviation for the two-operation sequence, "ADD, X, Y" followed by an operation that divides the previous answer by two to obtain the average value. A machine whose hardware may know only how to add and divide has now been taught how to take averages. A new programmer who uses this augmented assembler uses "AVERAGE" as one of his basic instructions, and often doesn't know or care whether the assembler translates it into one basic machine instruction or several, as long as correct averages are eventually computed.

Problem-Oriented Languages. Many other features have been added to assembly languages, making them much more flexible and convenient to use than direct machine languages. Still, assemblers retain the general flavor of the underlying hardware. Each brand and model of computer has its own special assembler, whose main features are determined by how the hardware works rather than by what the users may want to accomplish.

The next big step in the development of smarter computers was achieved by taking an entirely different approach: to design programming languages purely from the point of view of the classes of problems they will be used for, without regard for the detailed nature of computers, and certainly without consideration of the hardware of any particular computer. Thus, computer experts invented the FORTRAN (FORmula TRANslator) language as a convenient formalism for scientists and engineers who need to perform many algebraic calculations; COBOL (COmmon Business-Oriented Language) with features especially well suited for business record-keeping operations; APT (Automatic Programmed Tools) for describing the detailed motions of an automatic machine tool such as a lathe; and so on.

The remaining problem was how to teach existing computers, whatever their machine languages might be, to understand these various "problem-oriented" languages. Fortunately, the appropriate software can make any general-purpose computer appear to understand any well-defined formal language.

A program that makes a particular computer capable of processing a language quite different from its own machine language is called a compiler or an interpreter. A *compiler* behaves much like a very clever assembler; it scans a program in the problem-oriented language and translates it into a machine-language program. For example, the FORTRAN compiler for an IBM 370 computer is a program that accepts any complete FORTRAN program as its input data, and produces as its result

that are stored in sequentially addressed memory locations. As many items (characters) as possible are packed into each location. For example, suppose each memory location has enough room to hold six characters. Then the string

"THIS IS A STRING."

would appear in the computer as a sequence of three consecutive memory locations containing the characters:

T	H	I	S		I
S		A		S	T
R	I	N	G	.	/

where spaces and the period each occupy a character position, just like any letter, and the special symbol "/" identifies the end of the string. (Note that when we write about a string, we usually show it within quotation marks.)

A *list* is also a sequence of elementary items, usually English words rather than characters, but with the following special property: associated in the computer's memory with each item of the list is the sequencing information needed to locate the next item, which is often not in the next-numbered memory location. Typically, each memory location in a list is divided into two parts: the left-hand part contains exactly one item of the list, and the right-hand part contains the address of the memory location that contains the next item. Since the purpose of this right-hand part is to "point" to the place in memory where the list is continued, it is often called a *pointer*.

Sometimes it is useful to diagram the actual arrangement of information within the computer. In such diagrams, the pointers are represented by arrows. For example, the list

(APPLES MILK BREAD)

uses three memory cells arranged like this:

where the blank boxes really contain the addresses, whose precise values do not concern us, of the locations pointed to by the arrows, and "/" is the special symbol that marks the end of a list. (Note that when we write about a list, we usually show its items within parentheses, and we do not show the pointers at all.)

Lists use more of the memory space than strings, because of the space taken up by sequencing pointers. In return, lists are easier to modify, because insertions and deletions can be made by changing a few pointers rather than by moving large amounts of data. Moreover, an element (item) of a list can itself be a list, producing a useful kind of data called a *list structure*. For example, our shopping list could be expanded into:

(APPLES (3 QUARTS (NONFAT MILK)) (RYE BREAD)

which is structured in the computer's memory like this:

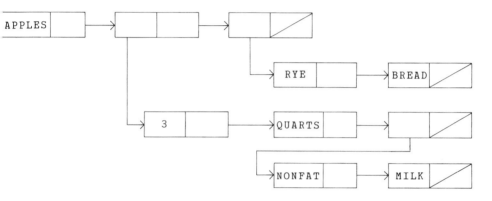

Note that this *hierarchical structure* permits us to scan the main list, for example, to examine the third item, the bread, with an amount of computational effort that does not depend upon how long and complicated the description of the second item (milk) becomes.

As we try to develop computer systems that can solve abstract problems, understand natural language, and perceive and affect the physical world, as described in the remaining chapters of this book, the role of symbolic rather than numeric reasoning vastly increases. It is therefore important to understand that no new breakthroughs are needed to make computers able to work with symbolic representations of concepts. Several programming systems for symbol manipulation are available and their use is increasing. The technology of automatic symbol manipulation is well understood and has been in practical use for some time.

In the next chapter we shall return to the uses of string and list-structure representations.

New Directions in Software. Any computer specialist will agree that programs written in just about any sufficiently well-defined programming language can be run on any sufficiently large computer, as long as someone is willing to develop an appropriate compiler or interpreter. On the other hand, almost all the programming languages that have been defined in the past are really constrained to be compatible with standard computer hardware in certain basic ways—e.g., because a computer only has one CPU, most programming languages permit only one thing to happen at a time, and because computer memory consists of a sequence of labeled positions, most programming languages access data in memory only by their locations.

Recent experimental programming systems have relaxed even these basic constraints. Programmers working in certain languages have been able to imagine a computer that runs several programs simultaneously; imagine that these programs can monitor and send messages to each other; imagine that data can be identified in memory in an "associative" manner, by giving a partial description of the appearance of the data even when they have no idea where it is located; imagine that programs can be identified by describing what they are supposed to accomplish, rather than by what they are named or where they are located; and even imagine that a program has the flexibility to start working, discover it has made an error, back up, and try another approach, all without any explicit directions. All these capabilities have been carefully defined in new formal programming languages. Interpreters and compilers for these new languages have been written and tested: the imagined capabilities, and more, already exist today on the computers in a few research laboratories. They do not yet perform very rapidly or with large amounts of data, but these pilot systems demonstrate the feasibility of producing the effect of almost any imagined machine organization on a standard computer, by means of an appropriate layer of software.

Many future computer users will not need to concern themselves with the details of how computers work. Instead, they will need only to be able to imagine how they would like computers to work, in order to accomplish any particular task; and software can then be developed by computer specialists, if indeed it does not already exist, that will make computers behave precisely as their users wish.

Summary

Computer technology is advancing at a rapid rate. Although computers are becoming more capable and less expensive, they are still usually thought of as merely big, fast, arithmetic machines. Actually a digital computer is a general-purpose symbol-manipulating machine. Its apparent intelligence is limited primarily by our current inability to program it to be smarter. The principal programming difficulties, and how they are being overcome, will be discussed throughout the rest of this book.

The hardware of a computer consists of a *central processing unit*, a *memory*, and *peripheral equipment*. In addition to the familiar card-, tape-, and paper-handling devices, peripheral equipment can include *sensors* and *effectors*. Such devices, when properly programmed, enable a computer to interact directly with its physical environment.

The software of a computer consists of sequences of instructions that may be expressed in a variety of programming languages. *Assembly language* is a convenient symbolic version of the *machine language* that is wired into the computer's circuitry. Special translators called *compilers* and *interpreters* enable computers to carry out programs written in many different problem-oriented languages. Symbol-manipulation languages are especially well suited for programs that process nonarithmetic data. Appropriate software can disguise the hardware of a computer so that it behaves like whatever machine the user would find most convenient.

SUGGESTED READINGS

Computers and Computation (Readings from *Scientific American*) W. H. Freeman and Company, San Francisco, 1971.

Dorf, Richard C. *Computers and Man.* Boyd & Fraser, San Francisco, 1974.

Rosen, S. *Programming Systems and Languages.* McGraw-Hill Book Co., New York, 1967.

Rothman, S., and C. Mosmann. *Computers and Society.* Science Research Associates, Chicago, 1972.

Sammet, J. E. *Programming Languages: History and Fundamentals.* Prentice Hall, Englewood Cliffs, N.J., 1969.

2 Representations

What is a problem?

You may think that asking so simple a question as "What is a problem?" is a silly way to begin a chapter; we all know what a problem is. However, our goal here is to study how computers can solve problems, what kinds of problems they can and cannot solve, and how they can be made to solve more kinds of problems. It is thus important for us to understand as precisely as possible what we mean by the term "problem." In fact, we shall see that the answer to "What is a problem?" is not at all clear, and we may have to accept an imprecise general understanding in order to proceed further with our study.

We wish to explore the characteristics of problems, so that we shall be able to state problems more clearly in terms a computer can understand. To begin, let us ask whether the following examples are problems:

(2.1)
$$
\begin{array}{r}
9567 \\
+\ 1085 \\
\hline
?
\end{array}
$$

Now this looks like a perfectly clear arithmetic problem. Almost all of you would say, "That is a simple arithmetic problem, and the answer is 10652," and of course you would be right. However, certain computer programmers, mathematicians, and people from the planet Og, where they have 16 fingers and 16 toes, are used to working with a different system of numbers. Instead of counting 1, 2, 3, 4, 5, 6, 7, 8, 9, 10, 11, 12, 13, 14, 15, 16, 17, 18, 19, 20, and so on, like the rest of us, these creatures count 1, 2, 3, 4, 5, 6, 7, 8, 9, a, b, c, d, e, f, 10, 11, 12, 13, 14, 15, 16, 17, 18, 19, 1a, 1b, 1c, 1d, 1e, 1f, 20, and so on, and they would also be perfectly correct, in their system, if they replied "The answer to problem (2.1) is a5ec."[1]

So we see that one of the characteristics of a problem is that everyone—the problem posers and the problem solvers—must have a common understanding of the meanings of the symbols used. In problem (2.1), this required an understanding of decimal integers and of the process of addition. If a computer is to be the problem solver, then the programmer who is the problem poser must be sure to express his thoughts in a terminology the computer understands.

Now consider the following problem:

$$
\begin{array}{r}
\mathrm{BEST} \\
+\ \ \mathrm{MADE} \\
\hline
\mathrm{MASER}
\end{array}
$$

(2.2)

I suspect that a few of you who are puzzle fans have already laid down this book and begun working on the problem. But most readers will be unfamiliar with this type of puzzle and will say, "Huh? What does this arrangement of symbols mean? Just what is the problem?" Therefore, I shall restate problem (2.2), or rather, state it more completely, as follows.

> The following is a problem from the class of puzzles called *cryptarithmetic*, or coded arithmetic. In these puzzles words represent numbers. Each letter of the alphabet that occurs in a cryptarithmetic problem represents a different decimal digit, but every occurrence of the same letter represents the same digit. The usual cryptarithmetic problem is to find what digits must be substituted for the letters in order to produce an arithmetically correct example. Usually there is only one possible solution. Now, in the cryptarithmetic problem
>
> $$
> \begin{array}{r}
> \mathrm{BEST} \\
> +\ \ \mathrm{MADE} \\
> \hline
> \mathrm{MASER}
> \end{array}
> $$
>
> what different digits must be substituted for A, B, D, E, M, R, S, and T, to make the sum come out right?

In this case, some important aspects of the problem have been explained in English, which presumably is a language understood by the intended problem solver. If we wanted to program a computer to solve cryptarithmetic problems, we would first have to determine how to express the complete explanation of the problem in a language that the computer could understand. Once the problem is understood, however,

---

[1]This number system, called *hexidecimal*, is used by most IBM computers.

it is easy for us to check the validity of any proposed solution—although exactly how to go about finding the right solution is another matter, which we shall take up in later chapters. (We leave the task of discovering a solution to problem (2.2) as an exercise for the reader.)

Games such as chess are a good source of well-defined problems, e.g.:

(2.3)

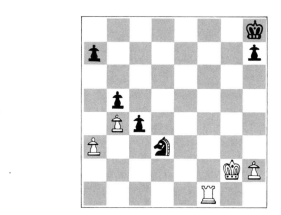

Black to play and win.

Here again there is considerable unstated knowledge that must be understood by the problem solver before he can proceed, and hence should be identified as part of the problem statement: e.g., that the diagram represents a chess board with certain pieces laid out on it, and that the standard rules for legal chess moves must be obeyed. Certain additional useful knowledge may be generally unknown except to a chess buff: e.g., that in chess problems checking the king before the final move is considered poor style. Once all the relevant information has been presented to define the problem, we may begin proposing solutions—in problem (2.3), sequences of legal chess moves—and testing their validity.

Is the following a problem?

(2.4)   How many angels can dance on the head of a pin?

This question occupied philosophers and theologians during the Middle Ages in endless, but absolutely serious, debate. Certainly it was a "problem" to them, and a rather important one. If (2.4) seems as strange to you as it does to me, perhaps it is because we do not have the proper auxiliary knowledge necessary to define the problem fully—like problem (2.3) for someone who knows nothing about chess, or problem (2.1) for a child who has no concept of arithmetic. Surely the theologians who attempted to answer (2.4) must have had some common set of background understanding, some way of evaluating their progress, some ideas about how to test the validity of a proposed solution. For those of us without these things, problem (2.4) becomes nonsense.

Let us turn to a much more concrete example. One of the most famous problems of modern mathematics is the so-called Traveling Salesman Problem. Yet, although many discussions of the problem appear in books and scholarly journals, a precise statement of just what the problem is can rarely be found. Here is one way of stating it.

(2.5) A traveling salesman must visit each of a number of cities. Each city is connected to every other city by roads of known length. The salesman must visit every city at least once. How can he find the route which will take him to every city and back to the city from which he started that traverses the shortest possible total distance?

Now, if we accept this as a definitive statement of the Traveling Salesman Problem, we may be puzzled over why it is of interest to mathematicians. After all, there is a trivial solution: simply list all the possible sequences in which the cities can be visited, add up the length of each of the corresponding routes, and select the sequence whose road length is shortest. If there are five cities, there are only twelve possible route lengths (Figure 2.1), so it is easy to list, measure, and compare them.

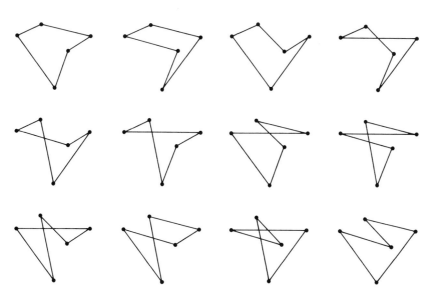

Figure 2.1 Routes for the five-city traveling salesman. Note that the length of the route does not depend upon which city the salesman starts from or which direction he goes around the route.

But note that the last sentence in the statement of the problem begins, "How can he find" rather than, "Determine." That is, we are not asked to find a route for a particular salesman, such as the best sequence in which to visit New York, Miami, Petaluma, Virginville, and Oshkosh; instead, the problem is to describe a method by which any salesman given any set of cities and corresponding distances can find his best route. Instead of simply a number or a sequence of symbols representing, say, cities or chess moves, the "answer" to this problem must be a complete description, in some mutually acceptable language, of how to calculate the desired route for any given set of cities and roads. For example, the solution might well be expressed in the form of a computer program that could subsequently be run on some computer to calculate the ideal route, whenever it was given a list of specific cities and their locations.

Unfortunately, the number of possible routes grows very rapidly as the number of cities is increased. It can be shown that the number of routes is $(n-1)!/2$ where n is the number of cities and "!" denotes the "factorial function": e.g., $m!$ is equal to the product of all the integers up to and including m. For 20 cities, the number of routes is 60,822,550,204,416,000, which is too many for even the fastest of today's computers to list in a thousand years.

Since the "trivial" solution is thus usually not feasible to execute, perhaps we should rule it out by changing the statement of the problem as follows:

(2.5′)   For the situation of problem (2.5), what is the best method for finding the desired route?

There are two flaws in the statement (2.5′).

1.   No criteria are given for the sense in which a method is "best." Is the best method the one that is more "elegant?" Can be expressed in the fewest symbols? Is preferred by the majority of salesmen asked?

2.   No obvious way is available for testing whether a proposed solution is indeed best, or even whether one solution is generally better than another.

Our final proposal for stating the travelling salesman problem is this:

(2.5″)   For the situation of problem (2.5), describe a method for finding the desired route, and prove mathematically that no other method requires fewer computational steps for finding routes with an arbitrarily large number of cities.

Statement (2.5″) is the problem that most authors probably have in mind when they refer to "*the* traveling salesman problem." Although many route-finding procedures have been proposed, none has yet been proved to be best in the sense of (2.5″). In fact, some of the proposed solutions might not even be valid candidates; even though they have worked efficiently on all test cases, it has not even been proved that they will always produce the shortest route. Although statement (2.5″) still has some weaknesses—the terms "prove mathematically" and "computational steps" are not yet fully defined concepts—it is sufficiently precise to constitute a problem that today's mathematicians worry about as intensely as yesterday's philosophers stewed over dancing angels.

Now consider common problems like the following:

(2.6)   Shall I wear a tie to work today?

This is indeed a serious problem for I must face it and solve it anew every day. It is on a par with the hundreds of problems that we all must solve every day of our lives—mundane, perhaps, but nonetheless requiring an immediate solution. Shall I walk, drive, bicycle, or take a bus to work? What shall I select from the restaurant menu? Shall I cross the street now, or wait for the light to change? When I get up in the morning, shall I wash my hands first, or brush my teeth first? Shall I go to sleep at night with the window open or closed? Some problems of this kind we solve once and for all, and the solution is retrieved automatically as a habit: "Insert left leg into pants before right leg." Some require little programs that adjust to special current conditions: "Walk to work if the weather is nice and there is no need to hurry." But usually, solving even these simple problems requires use of a significant amount of additional knowledge and constraints that are not apparent in the first, straightforward view of the problem.

Of course, a computer never has to worry about such matters as wearing a tie, selecting dinner, or brushing its teeth; but someday computers will control robot devices that will cross streets, obeying the traffic signals, and that will open or close windows at night. Since we want computers eventually to help man in all his day-to-day activities, we study even such trivial problems as deciding whether to wear a tie, and try to understand thoroughly what is involved in making every decision.

For example consider problem (2.6). Unless I evade the problem by establishing a habitual solution—e.g., always wear a tie, whether I need it or not—then considerations such as the following must be weighed anew every morning.

A tie is uncomfortable.
Wearing a tie is a mark of respectability.
Most people in my office do not wear ties.
My boss always wears a tie and may prefer that I do.
I think I make a better impression on people if I wear a tie.
I do not expect to meet anyone I want to impress today.
If I decide to wear a tie, I shall have to select one.
And so on.

Observe how much relevant data there is that needs to be brought out explicitly to complete the statement of the problem, before we can begin a systematic attempt to produce an acceptable solution. With problems like (2.6), we usually do not bother assembling all the relevant data. Instead, we quickly review those considerations that happen to come to mind first, and perhaps some irrelevant ones, such as "Did I wear a tie yesterday?," and allow ourselves to be influenced by "gut" feelings (which perhaps correspond to subconscious reviews of additional facts), and then make arbitrary, sometimes irrational decisions. These frequently may not be the best possible decisions, but that does not matter much with problems like this.

Problems like the following, though, matter a great deal.

(2.7)   Should the United States take action to protect the state of Israel?

This is a question of vital, worldwide importance. Its answer affects political, economic, social, and religious issues throughout the world. The answer could cause—or prevent—World War III, and with it possibly the destruction of civilization. Background knowledge includes all the details of several wars that have been fought in the past three decades, as the latest stage of more than 5700 years of relevant history.

Is (2.7) a problem in the sense of this chapter? Can questions of this complexity be solved completely and systematically, either by men or by computers?

Today such decisions are based upon the opinions of scores of experts employed by the State Department, Defense Department, and others, and are influenced in irrational ways by the "gut" feelings of the President and his closest advisors. I am not sure that the decisions that emerge by this process are always the best possible ones. Perhaps such decisions could be improved if the decision makers themselves—and perhaps the public—were more aware of precisely what facts they are considering in making the decisions, and precisely what criteria they are using to derive a decision from the facts. Perhaps guidance from a formal theory of problem solving, such as the ones computer scientists are beginning to develop and we shall hint at in the following chapters, can eventually be of some help to those who must make such decisions.

I hope you will excuse those computer scientists who appear to devote most of their energy to "playing" with "toy" problem domains like those of (2.2), (2.3), (2.5), and (2.6), rather than significant questions like (2.7). In fact, many of these scientists may really be working on issues like (2.7) by developing theories and techniques that will eventually be of direct use. Of course, we do not want to try out untested ideas on important questions, so first we test and refine them in the so-called toy domains. It has been suggested that the courses of action our politicians come up with are frequently untested, and therefore the events of the present that seem to be leading up to World War III should be recorded and stored deep in the earth, so that the next civilization will have an example to study of what can go wrong.

Choosing a representation

In the previous section we discussed some characteristics that problems must have before they are truly ready to be solved, by a person or by a computer. Now we move on to the next step. Given any problem, from any discipline, of any degree of difficulty, is there some general approach we may take in seeking a solution? For concreteness, we shall consider some specific illustrative problems:

1. Design the tail section for a supersonic jet transport.
2. Compute how long it would take for a cannonball dropped from the top of the Tower of Pisa to hit the ground.
3. Prove that alternate interior angles formed by a transversal cutting parallel lines are equal.
4. Suppose two diagonally opposite corner squares are removed from a standard 8 by 8 square chessboard. Can 31 rectangular dominoes, each exactly the size of two squares, be so placed as to cover precisely the remaining board? Prove your answer (See Figure 2.2).

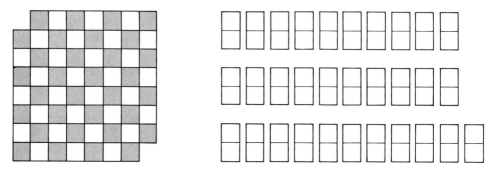

Figure 2.2 The mutilated chessboard problem.

Of course, these are not yet complete problem statements. As discussed in the previous section, we must also provide relevant background knowledge, determine criteria for testing a proposed solution, and so on. Let us now assume that that has been done, and we are facing fully defined problems. What is the next major step in the problem-solving process? To choose a representation.

In this section we shall consider some of the representations people use for their own convenience in solving problems. The next section will describe computer-oriented representation.

By a *representation* (sometimes called an *idealization*), is meant another data domain in which there exists an analogous well-defined problem that we shall attempt to solve, instead of attempting to solve the originally-stated problem.

Now this is rather peculiar. If we are given a problem, why should we arbitrarily go off and try to solve a different problem? The answer is that almost every real problem has certain features that make it very difficult or awkward to attack directly. By selecting an appropriate representation, however, the difficult features can be avoided. Moreover, if the representation has been well designed, its essential features correspond closely enough to those of the real problem that a solution to the idealized problem can easily be translated into a solution to the real problem. This final translation process is sometimes called *interpreting* the ideal solution.

Let us consider the examples. In 1, the essential requirement is to find a shape for the tail of the plane that will behave correctly when subjected to supersonic air flow. Perhaps the most natural way to solve the problem would be to propose a trial shape, have it built, fly the plane with it, and see what happens. This process would be extremely expensive, especially after several crashes. Instead, aeronautical engineers generally choose as a representation small scale *models* that can be observed in a wind tunnel. Here, with a file and a bit of putty, any number of shapes can be tested. The expense and awkwardness of building full-size test planes, as well as the dangers of flying them, have been avoided, while the essential feature of the real problem, to find a shape, has been preserved.

To solve the real problem 2 directly would require that we acquire a cannonball and a stopwatch, and then take a trip to Pisa. This approach is less convenient for most of us than it was for Galileo, who already lived in Italy when he conducted this experiment. On the other hand, a miniature model patterned after that used in problem 1—e.g., timing the fall of a marble from the top of a Lego tower—will not work, because the actual height of the Pisa tower is an essential parameter of the problem. Here, instead of a physical representation, we can use a mathematical representation. We know from elementary physics that a body falling from rest for t seconds covers a distance s feet, where $s = 16t^2$. Therefore our representation is an equation, and the solution[2] to the idealized problem is the mathematical formula $t = \sqrt{s}/4$ where s is the height of the Tower of Pisa, which we can look up in any encyclopedia. If we believe in the laws of physics, the solution to this problem is the same as the solution to

---

[2]Neglecting the effect of air resistance. The influence of air resistance could be added to our idealization by using much more complicated mathematical expressions.

the real problem—and we did not have to explain to airline guards why we were carrying a cannonball to Italy.

Problem 3 is an early theorem in Euclid's plane geometry. It already deals with mathematical objects, so a substitute mathematical representation problem is not necessary. What is necessary, for most geometry students (and even the computer program described in the article by Gilmore listed at the end of this chapter) is a diagram. The representation is the sketch shown in Figure 2.3 and the analog problem is, "In Figure 2.3, prove that angle A equals angle B."

The principal value of a diagrammatic representation is not that it leaves out distracting details (such as cannonballs), but rather that it focuses attention upon relationships that the problem solver might not otherwise have noticed; in this case, for example, that there exists an angle C that is a vertical angle of A and a corresponding angle of B. Such relationships are certainly present in the mathematical data that are relevant to the original problem, but only in the diagram of an appropriate representation do they gain the prominence necessary to suggest their usefulness for the solution.

Problem 4 is known as the Mutilated Chessboard Problem. This problem is a classic example of how important a representation can be in determining the difficulty of a problem. The straightforward approach to solving this problem is to take a chessboard, mask off the appropriate two squares, take a pile of dominoes, and begin trying to cover the board. This approach, or any mathematical representation of a similar approach, is doomed to failure, but the reason for the failure will be frustratingly elusive. Yet, if we represent the problem by another simple problem statement that is clearly equivalent but brings out an overlooked feature, the solution quickly becomes crystal clear. So as not to spoil your fun in thinking about this problem, I shall withhold its restatement for a few pages. (*Hint:* Think about the colors of the squares.)

As one last example, consider the following two-person game, which has been called Number Scrabble.

> Take nine slips of paper, mark them with the numbers from one to nine, and place them face up on the table. The first player must take any slip of his choice, then the second player must take one, and so on. As soon as either player has any three slips in his possession whose numbers add up to fifteen, he is the winner. The opportunity to go first should alternate in successive games.

Play this game for a while. Although most games will come out as draws, I suspect that you will lose occasionally, and that most of you will find it fairly difficult to play an "expert" game.

Now copy Figure 2.4. Play Number Scrabble again, this time using the figure. The first player should draw an X over each number he selects,

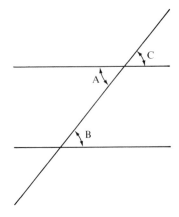

Figure 2.3 Alternate interior angles.

2	9	4
7	5	3
6	1	8

Figure 2.4 A representation of Number Scrabble.

and the second player should make an O around each number he claims. Do you recognize this game? Is it as difficult as you thought Number Scrabble was? What makes it so different?

Representations for computer problems

In the previous section we discussed the general problem of constructing representations to help solve problems. Now we shall look at particular representations that can be used within computers. Our first task for solving any given problem with a computer (unless it happens to be designed specifically as an exercise for a computer) will be to replace the real problem with an analogous problem of computation. This means that we must first represent the data of the real problem by some form of data that can be manipulated by a computer.

When computers were thought to be only number processors, they were used only for problems whose data could easily be represented by numbers. Now, however, as we saw in Chapter 1, computer systems can manipulate a variety of types of nonnumerical data, including list structures and character strings. To be sure, the types of data that computers can manipulate do not include all the types of data we might like to use for representations—e.g., no computer system can represent every detail of a physical structure such as a model airplane—and visual images, even simple line drawings like Figure 2.3, are not directly available as elementary computer-data types. However, the data types that are available can be used to represent a tremendous variety of objects with only minor coding effort by the human problem poser (whom we shall now call the *programmer*). Moreover, these data types can each be used for many different kinds of problems and each have well understood formal properties; that is, they can be constructed and modified only in certain known, standard ways. Special symbol manipulation programming languages and systems have therefore been developed to work with them. These systems greatly simplify the programmer's task as he develops the procedures by which the computer will solve the problem.

Most of the rest of this section deals with the use of standard types of symbolic data, especially strings and list structures, to represent the actual data for many different kinds of problems. Before getting into these approaches, however, I want to emphasize that we must always be on the lookout for special tricks that may have tremendous payoff in limited situations. Although we are beginning to understand how to design good representations, the ability to find or invent just the right computer representation for a new task is still largely an art rather than a science. The following example from a well-known game-playing program describes one representational trick that meant the difference between success and failure of a major programming effort. Even though it probably has no value outside of the special situation for which it was invented, this trick illustrates the power, and the importance, of finding just the right representation for each job.

> *Mutilated Chessboard Problem:* Can the mutilated board be covered by 31 dominoes that each must cover one black and one red square?

A TRICK FOR CHECKERS

In the mid-1950's, when Arthur L. Samuel began designing a program to play the game of checkers,[3] special symbol-manipulation systems were not available, and computers were considerably slower and had much smaller memories then than they have now. Dr. Samuel developed his program in assembly language on the IBM 700 series computers, whose

---

[3]We shall be concerned here with the game known in America as checkers and in Britain as draughts, which is played on a standard 8 × 8 chessboard. A similar game called checkers in most of Europe is played on a 10 × 10 board and is more complex. Therefore you can imagine the confusion when I first lectured about "checkers" to a continental audience.

memory locations contained 36 bits.[4] In order to experiment with many
checker positions in a reasonable amount of time, he needed to find a
good way to represent the positions of pieces on a checkerboard. He considered a representation "good" only if (1) a position could be represented in a small amount of memory space, and if (2) new positions that
can be reached from a given position by any legal move could be generated with only a small amount of computation.

Figure 2.5,*a* is a diagram of a checkerboard, with its 32 playable
squares numbered in the manner normally used by checker players, and
with five of the squares occupied by black pieces.

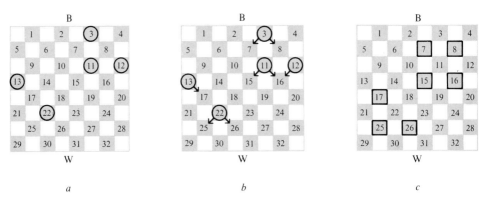

Figure 2.5   Checkerboard diagrams in standard notation. (*a*) Original position.
(*b*) Legal moves. (*c*) Potentially occupied squares.

The basic move rule is that pieces may advance to unoccupied,
diagonally adjacent squares. Black pieces move only to higher-numbered
squares, and white pieces (not shown in this example) must move to
lower-numbered squares. (For you checker experts, captures and kings
are beyond the scope of this discussion.) One straightforward representation for the position of the black pieces, using a 36-bit computer word, is
merely to mark with a 1 each numbered bit position corresponding to an
occupied square, mark with a 0 the position of each unoccupied square,
and ignore bits 33–36, as shown in Figure 2.6,*a*. Now consider all the
squares that can be reached from this position by legal moves of black
pieces (assuming no white pieces are in the way). The possible moves are
shown by arrows in Figure 2.5,*b*.
The resulting potentially occupied squares are shown in Figure 2.5,*c*, and
their corresponding representation by a computer word is shown in
Figure 2.6,*b*. Unfortunately, there is no easy computational procedure
by which the bit configuration of Figure 2.6,*b* can be generated from that

---

[4]Remember that a *bit* is a memory position that can store only two symbols, which we
call "0" and "1."

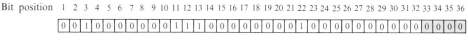

Figure 2.6 Computer word diagrams of checker positions. (*a*) Original position. (*b*) Potentially occupied squares.

of Figure 2.6,*a*. For some squares (e.g., square 22) an occupying piece may move to the two squares whose numbers are three and four higher; for some (e.g., 11) legal successor squares are numbered four and five higher; and for the side squares (e.g., 12 and 13) only four higher is a legal successor. It appears as if the squares must be divided into at least three groups, and different calculations performed for each group. Since this calculation of all possible successors lies at the heart of the subprogram that evaluates alternative moves and decides how to play, making it perform efficiently is crucial to the performance of the entire program.

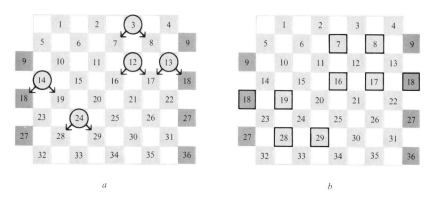

Figure 2.7 Checkerboard diagrams in Samuel notation. (*a*) Original position and legal moves. (*b*) Potentially occupied squares.

Dr. Samuel invented an alternative representation that is just as compact as the one described above—it still uses only one computer word for the positions of all the black pieces—but also greatly simplifies the calculation of possible successor positions. This simple yet elegant idea is a classic example of the usefulness of a clever representation. Here is how it works. Renumber the checkerboard, by adding four "phantom" squares off the edge of the board, as shown in Figure 2.7. The bits corresponding to the phantom squares 9, 18, 27, and 36 will be ignored in the computer representation, as shown in the top diagram of Figure 2.8. Now observe that the successor computation rule is uniformly: "Add both four and five to the current square number, and then ignore phantom squares." Since adding four to bit-position numbers is equivalent to shifting the bits to the right four places, the successor calculation for our example proceeds as shown in Figure 2.8. The bottom diagram is the desired result.

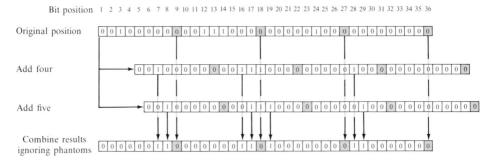

Figure 2.8   Computing successors in Samuel notation.

One sometimes hears that computer programming consists largely of balancing the tradeoffs between use of memory space and computation time. For example, a program that calculates logarithms could keep all the possible answers stored in a vast table, and therefore would need to do no calculation beyond looking up the answer, if its memory were large enough; or it could get along with no data in memory, if its users were willing to wait while it calculated each logarithm from scratch, using an appropriate mathematical formula. The checker representation example shows that computing is not just a matter of trade-offs; rather, an occasional smart idea can result in savings of both space and time.

The Samuel program, which contains many clever ideas besides the representation trick we have just studied, went on to become a master checker player, although never quite of championship caliber. It is still being improved occasionally at Stanford University and entered in tournaments. Because Dr. Samuel once had a major position within IBM, some people think the IBM 700 and 7000 series computers, which dominated the computer world for a decade, were designed with 36 bits to a word just because that many were needed for the representation of checker positions!

STRINGS AND LIST STRUCTURES

For any given problem, a programmer of the 1970's has considerably more latitude than Samuel did in his choice of data representation. If he decides that bits, or decimal numbers, or arrays of numbers are not convenient, he still has several symbolic data types available. Of these, strings and list structures have been the most widely used for the past decade, so they are to be preferred, because they have the most widely available and best-known programming systems associated with them. However, the adventuresome programmer might decide that the added convenience in his particular problem of such novel features as parallel processes makes it worthwhile to go to the trouble of using one of the new experimental systems.

The choice of a computer data type—the *medium* for the representation—is only the first part of the representation problem. The rest of the problem, which is at least as important, is designing the *method* of representation: i.e., the manner in which objects and concepts from the real task are to be represented in the selected medium. Below we shall look at some straightforward ways of representing the data for some typical nonnumeric computer problems. We should keep in mind, however, that the straightforward representation may not be the most effective one when the solution algorithm is constructed. On the contrary, a misleading representation can prevent an elegant solution from being found. For example, the straightforward way to represent the motions of the heavenly bodies is to use the simplest mathematical descriptions of their paths through the sky as seen from the earth. This obvious approach led Ptolemy to choose as his representation *epicycloids*, which are circular paths modified by small circular perturbations. Yet, if Copernicus had not moved the center of the representation from the earth to the sun, Kepler's much simpler laws defining elliptical paths, and Newton's subsequent theory of gravitation, probably could not have been developed. Even in "toy" problems like the mutilated chessboard, the method of representation can be the difference between success and failure. Since most of us are not as clever as Copernicus, we cannot always find the right representational method for every problem. We must always be on the lookout for clever representations to make problems easier. Luckily, not only are straightforward representations easy to construct, they are also usually adequate for solving most problems.

In the remainder of this section we shall consider how to represent data from several different problem areas by lists and strings. The construction of problem-solving programs that operate upon such representations will be the subject of future chapters.

For the following examples, I shall first identify a problem area in which computers might be helpful, but are not yet as widely used as they might be, and then show a typical specific piece of data in the printed representation usually used as the conventional noncomputer notation for the particular class of tasks. Finally, possible list and string representations will be shown. These are the kinds of representations usually used in the application programs to be discussed in the last chapter of this book.

Problem area. Symbolic mathematics, including algebra, trigonometry and calculus.

Example.
$$\frac{-b + (b^2 - 4ac)^{1/2}}{2a}$$

String representation. In order to represent a symbolic expression by a string, we must scrunch the entire expression down into a single line of printed characters. With the use of parentheses and the introduction of additional operator symbols such as "$/$" for division and "$\uparrow$" for exponentiation, any algebraic expression can be written unambiguously in a linear form such as:

$$\texttt{"(-b+(b}\uparrow\texttt{2-4*a*c)}\uparrow\texttt{(1/2))/(2*a)"}$$

Here a multiplication symbol, *****, has been introduced explicitly so that the intended reader, the computer, will not have to "know" how to recognize individual symbols—e.g., that "$\texttt{ac}$" does not stand for a single quantity, rather than "$\texttt{a}$ times $\texttt{c}$." This particular string representation does assume, however, that the reader knows about the relative priority of operators—e.g., that $\uparrow$ is "higher" or more urgent than $-$ or *****, so that $(\texttt{b}\uparrow 2 - 4 * \texttt{a} * \texttt{c})$ does not mean, "$\texttt{b}$ raised to the $(2 - 4 * \texttt{a} * \texttt{c})$ power."

In the string representation every character, including "$($" and "$)$", is stored in memory simply as part of a linear sequence of characters.

List Representation. The principal value of a list structure is that it divides the data it represents into major components, which may be accessed independently, and which may themselves be hierarchically structured. When we look at the original, mathematical representation of the example, we see the fraction line as its most prominent structural feature, and the numerator and the denominator as the major components. If we again use the symbol "$/$" to denote a fraction, and put it first to identify the type of the mathematical expression, a list-structure representation will have the form of a list of three items:

$(/$ [representation of numerator] [representation of denominator] $)$.

Similarly, the numerator is the sum of two terms, and might be represented by a sublist of the form

$(+$ [representation of $(-b)$] [representation of $(b^2 - 4ac)^{1/2}$] $)$

where the "**+**" is listed first to identify that the list represents a sum. If we systematically represent each component of the expression by a list whose first element identified its type—fraction, sum, or whatever—and whose remaining elements are the representatives of its subcomponents, then the complete expression will look like this:[5]

```
(/ (+ (- b)
      (↑ (+ (↑ b 2)
            (- (* 4 a c)))
         (/ 1 2)))
   (* 2 a))
```

where the indentations have no meaning to the computer, but should be of some help to the human reader in (recognizing ((the intended) groupings)).

In list representation, the parentheses are not stored as part of the data. They merely indicate the pointer structure of the actual computer words. Figure 2.9 is a diagram of the arrangement of computer locations and pointers corresponding to the above list structure.

Now, strings can certainly be thought of as single-level list structures; and conversely, list structures can be represented in the computer

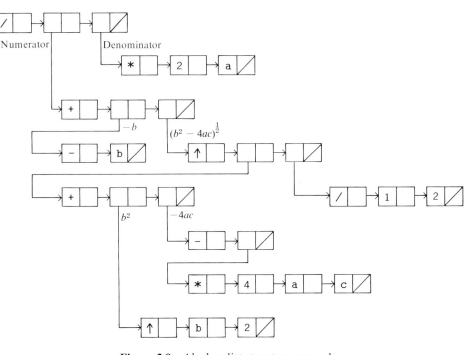

Figure 2.9 Algebra list structure example.

---

[5]Of course, there are many possible ways to represent a given algebraic expression by a list structure. The one chosen here is merely an example of a commonly used approach.

by strings of parentheses and other characters, just as they are on the printed page. This interconvertability is not generally of much interest. Each data type has its unique advantages; for example, strings are more useful for linear comparisons, and lists for structural access. Selection of a representation of a given type should be based on the applicability of the type's special features to the problem at hand.

Problem area. Board games.

Example. The following chess position.

String Representation. As a string representation, we can choose to construct a map of the board.

```
"W,   X,   X,   X,   X,   X,   X,   X,   X,
      X,  WB,   X,   X,   X,   X,   X,   X,
      X,   X,   X,   X,   X,   X,   X,  BP,
      X,   X,   X,   X,  BK,   X,   X,   X,
      X,   X,   X,  BN,   X,   X,   X,   X,
      X,   X,   X,   X,   X,   X,   X,   X,
      X,   X,   X,   X,   X,   X,   X,   X,
      X,   X,  WB,   X,   X,   X,   X,  WK"
```

After an initial symbol (**W** for White) identifying whose move it is, the items of the string represent the contents of successive squares of the board. Commas separate items, **X** marks an empty square, and the contents of occupied squares are represented by their standard chess abbreviations. (For you nonchess players, **W** and **B** stand for the White and Black players. Each piece is identified by the first letter of its name, except for the Knight. Since **K** stands for King, Knight is abbreviated **N**.) In some string-processing systems, we can access a particular element of the string if we know its position number. For example, the last square of the third row is known to be the twenty-fourth square and its contents would therefore be given by the twenty-fifth item in the above string. A request for the twenty-fifth item would evoke the immediate response, BP. In such systems the above representation allows us to find the contents of any particular square very rapidly. Even if no such special access mechanism is available, a simple program can scan the string, counting commas until the desired square is reached. This complete board layout is very useful for certain calculations. For example, we can look up the contents of all the squares a rook's move away from a given square by counting an appropriate number of positions forward and backward through the string.

Of course, such operations would be much more efficient if the representation were a two-dimensional array, so that each board square could be accessed by its integer coordinates in the horizontal and vertical directions. Unfortunately, most programming systems that make such arrays available allow only numbers to occupy cells of the array, so that the convenience of symbolic names is lost.

List Representation. A list representation can take advantage of the sparseness of pieces on the board to save a considerable amount of computer memory space. It can list the pieces on the board and tell where each is; the rest of the squares may be assumed to be empty by default. This technique of listing only positively known information and making uniform default assumptions about unlisted items is a common device in many list-structured representations. After identifying White (W) as the mover, the following representation contains lists of board pieces, grouped into White pieces and Black pieces:

```
(W (W (B QN7 QB1) (K KR1))
   (B (N Q5) (K K4) (P KR3)))
```

For each type of piece on the board, we use a sublist to give its abbreviation, followed by the squares on which pieces of that color and type appear. Instead of linear or array coordinates, the squares are here designated by standard American chess terminology. QN7 is the seventh square on the Queen's Knight column, and so on. As is conventional in the United States, the locations of the black pieces are given in relation to the black side of the board and the white in relation to the white side, rather than in relation to a universal coordinate system.

In addition to being quite compact in its use of memory, this representation makes the answers to certain data retrieval questions almost trivial—e.g., "list all the squares containing white bishops." On the other hand, answers to certain other questions—e.g., "what is on White's square KR6?"—are very difficult to determine from this list structure. If we had many questions similar to this one, we might construct another list representation organized primarily by board columns rather than by pieces, e.g.,

```
(W (QN (7 WB) QB (1 WB) Q (4 BN)
   K (5 BK) KR (1 WK 6 BP)))
```

Discussion. For an actual chess-playing program one would probably use an array or string-map representation and also several list representations that each make different features of a position easy to access. Each such representation may be viewed as a differently organized index to the same underlying information: the locations of the pieces on the board.

For a real chess-playing program, some historical information would be needed in addition to the current board position. For certain board positions, special moves like *en passant* pawn captures depend upon what the previous move was. For certain king and rook positions, castling may or may not be legal, depending upon whether the rook or king have moved before. Throughout the game, it is necessary to know whether each complete board position has occurred before, because the game is a draw if any position is repeated three times. This historical information itself provides an interesting problem of representation: how should the record of a game in progress be structured so that a program can find out, with a minimum amount of calculation, whether a given position has occurred before?

Storing many differently organized list-structure representations of the same basic data permits a program to answer many different types of questions efficiently. On the other hand, whenever the basic data is changed—e.g., when a move is made (or even contemplated) on the chess board—then all the representations need to be updated. How much computation should be done in preparing elaborate representations in order to reduce the computation that may be needed later to make use of the representations, is a familiar problem of efficiency in the design of list-processing programs. Its solution depends upon the nature of each particular program and thus varies from one application to another.

Problem area. Natural language analysis or translation.

Example. "This sentence will be our language example."

String representation. **"THIS SENTENCE WILL BE OUR LANGUAGE EXAMPLE."**

List representations.

1.   (THIS SENTENCE WILL BE OUR LANGUAGE
                                               EXAMPLE)

2.   ((THIS SENTENCE) ((WILL (BE))
                  (OUR (LANGUAGE (EXAMPLE)))))

3.   (SENTENCE
        (NOUN-PHRASE (ADJECTIVE THIS)
        (NOUN-PHRASE (NOUN SENTENCE))))

```
(VERB-PHRASE
  (VERB (AUXILIARY WILL) (VERB BE))
  (NOUN-PHRASE (ADJECTIVE OUR)
    (NOUN-PHRASE (ADJECTIVE LANGUAGE)
      (NOUN-PHRASE (NOUN EXAMPLE))))))
```

Discussion. By the term "natural language" we mean the ordinary languages that have evolved as the normal means of communication among people, such as English, German, Hebrew, and Swahili, rather than the formal or artificial languages that people have invented for special purposes, such as FORTRAN, Esperanto, arithmetic, and musical notation. The study of natural language is based upon observation and description, like biology or astronomy, rather than upon invention and definition, like mathematics, engineering, or computer science. Chapter 6 will deal with various ways in which computers are being used to help us study the nature of natural language. We are concerned in the present chapter merely with how to use strings and lists to represent the data for such studies.

Language normally occurs in linear sequences. In conversation, usually only one person speaks at a time, and because his vocal apparatus can usually produce only one identifiable sound at a time, spoken language is a string of sounds. Most written languages are basically phonetic —i.e., the symbols or characters represent individual sounds—and therefore written strings of characters represent spoken strings of sounds in a natural way.

Some written languages, such as Chinese, are basically pictorial rather than phonetic. Each written character represents an idea or a unit of meaning rather than a unit of sound. Such characters, which are frequently really stylized drawings, are usually quite complex and may very well require a two-dimensional description rather than just a string representation. The effect of the difference between phonetic and nonphonetic languages is striking. For example, most Englishmen can quickly learn to look at Spanish newspapers and figure out the correct sounds for every word, without having any idea of the meanings; most Japanese are familiar with the Chinese characters and can look at Chinese newspapers and understand the meanings of what they see, but have no idea what the sound of the spoken Chinese is. Since we are most familiar with phonetic languages, and in particular with English, we shall restrict ourselves to these more string-like natural languages in this book.

The string representation for our sample English sentence is straightforward: simply form a string of computer-readable characters—letters, spaces, and punctuation symbols—of the actual written sentence. This representation is almost identical with the sentence—the real data itself—and can be used for any basic linguistic processing. For example, we could write string-processing programs to look for particular letter combinations, to correct spelling errors, to separate verb stems from their endings, and so on.

In list representations, we usually treat the words, rather than the individual letters, as the elementary units, and so the elementary string operations just mentioned can no longer be performed. This is because in a computer each element of a list requires extra memory space for its pointer to the next element, and extra time to follow that pointer when any program tries to scan through the elements of the list. On the other hand, the list representation makes it easy to impose a higher-level structure upon the sentence string. We can show the results of *parsing* or *diagramming* sentence 1, according to some simple grammatical rules, as list structures 2. For a more complete structural description of the parsed sentence, we should also identify the role of each grammatical component of the sentence. List structure 3 does this by adding appropriate labels. It shows us that the sentence has two major components (the remaining two elements of the top-level list), a noun phrase followed by a verb phrase. The noun phrase consists of the adjective **"THIS"** followed by a noun phrase consisting of the single noun **"SENTENCE."** The verb phrase consists of a verb part, which itself has an auxiliary verb and a main verb, followed by another noun phrase, and so on. List-processing programs are well suited for grammatical analysis tasks such as transforming sentence 1 into its structural description (3). The linguistic analysis of English sentences by computer will be discussed further in Chapter 6.

Problem area. Picture processing.

Many different approaches to representing and analyzing pictures are possible. Since this subject will be discussed at length in Chapter 7, I shall not give any arbitrary examples here. Instead, let us just consider briefly what is meant by the "contents" of a picture.

It has been said that "one picture is worth a thousand words." We can test this adage in one technical sense, by figuring out the approximate information content of a typical picture and comparing it with that of a thousand words. Suppose we take the picture on a standard, well-adjusted American television screen as our typical picture. It is composed of about 500 horizontal lines of data, each of which can just barely be perceived if we look closely at the screen. Information is deposited along each line in a continuous manner, but because the system has been so designed that the resolution—the apparent "fuzziness"—is similar in the horizontal and vertical directions, it is fair for us to think of the TV picture as consisting of an array of about 500 by 500 points. Each point has some brightness on a scale between white and black, and it is generally agreed that the eye can perceive in the neighborhood of only thirty to fifty discrete shades of grey. Since there are in the neighborhood of thirty to fifty characters in the alphabet (counting the numerals and punctuation marks), we may say that each point in the TV picture carries about as much information as one letter. Therefore one picture can be represented by $500 \times 500 = 250,000$ letters. Since there are an average of about five letters to an English word, we see that to represent one picture by alphabetic characters we would need, not a thousand words, but rather

$$\frac{250,000 \text{ letters}}{5 \text{ letters per word}} = \text{about } 50,000 \text{ words.}$$

We must learn to distinguish between *information* and *knowledge.* The word "information" once had a perfectly good, generally understood meaning—a meaning that most of you probably still have in mind. Then the word was ruined by communications scientists, who gave it a very precise but somewhat different meaning for their own purposes: "information" is defined to be the amount of data that must be transmitted through a communication channel in order to convey a message, in all its detail, from one place to another. The resulting Theory of Information is of great value to engineers who design communications systems. It also provides the basis for arguments that lead to silly conclusions like the one above: that one (TV) picture is worth 50,000 English words, regardless of what the picture is a picture of.

We shall use the word "knowledge" to refer to what used to be called "information": to mean, roughly speaking, the data that must be transmitted through a communication channel in order to convey a message, not in all its detail, but well enough for the receiver to understand its meaning. However, we shall also be careful not to give "knowledge" a precise technical definition, and thereby ruin the word for future generations.

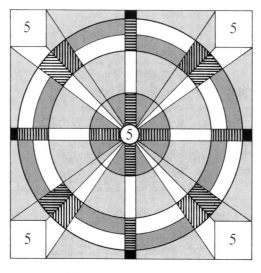

Figure 2.10   Test pattern.

Suppose my wife calls out from the next room, "What's on Channel 5 now?" and I turn on the TV set and see Figure 2.10. I could try to convey all the information in the picture, by explaining the precise placements and sizes of the numerals, the radii of the various circles, the arrangement and darkness of each line and band, and so on—but that would take about 50,000 words. Instead, I would probably convey my new-found "knowledge" of what's on Channel 5 with two words, "Test pattern." I might even try to get away with one word, "Nothing," but that would probably require further explanation about how I knew the receiver was not broken.

As another example, look closely at the wood grain on your desk, the linoleum under your feet, or the surface of the plaster on a nearby wall. Consider the details of the texture, the surface finish, the arrangement of ridges, the lines, the irregular patterns of light. You are certainly perceiving a considerable amount of raw data. In order to convey it to someone else, say over a telephone, you would need to transmit a great deal of information. But, how much useful knowledge have you gained?

Representations of knowledge

When we speak of the "representation problem," we usually think in terms of representing an object by another, more convenient object. Indeed, most of the fifteen-year history of attempts to develop smarter computers has been preoccupied with the notion of finding new and better ways to represent objects. Objects may be physical, like airplanes, or abstract, like mathematical expressions. Whether they were dealing with English words, chess positions, TV pictures, or algebraic sums, computer scientists have been oriented toward trying to identify the individual fixed entities that occurred in their problems and stuffing some representation for these entities into the computing machine. Only after this representation task was completed did they go on to try to develop programs that operated upon the modeled objects.

In the last section we began to talk about knowledge. Knowledge seems to be the real basis, or at least an important prerequisite, for understanding and intelligence. Common sense may be merely a matter of having some relevant knowledge, and being able to make use of it. One psychiatrist identifies an intelligent person as "the one who makes the most appropriate remarks." Such a person must have an appropriate store of knowledge.

If we wish to insert knowledge into a computer, what kinds of concepts must we represent? (1) *Objects*, certainly, but also (2) *relationships*, which establish meaningful links from one object to another; and, perhaps even more important, (3) *processes*, which govern the creation, destruction, transformation, and other behavior of objects.

We have discussed, earlier in this chapter, how various kinds of objects can be represented in a computer by symbolic data structures. Now we shall consider the representation of relationships and processes.

The *property list* (PL) is one commonly used mechanism for relating an object to various others. A property list is a list structure, associated with the computer representation of some object, that gives a symbolic description of that object. On the list are *attributes* of the described object, and after each attribute a corresponding *value.* The attribute may name a descriptive property, such as "color," in which case the corresponding value is the specific descriptor, such as "red." The attribute may also name a *relationship* between the described object and other objects. In this case, the value of the attribute identifies the other party or parties to the relationship.

For example, the relationships, "all men are mortal" and "Socrates is a man," are usually represented mathematically in the following way: MEN ⊂ MORTALS (the set of all men is included in the set of all mortal beings), and SOCRATES ∈ MEN (Socrates is one element of the set of all men). One natural way to put these data into a computer is to think of three objects: the set of men, the set of mortals, and the individual Socrates, and to associate with each of them a property list that describes its relations with the other two objects. For example,

PL of MORTALS:(SUBSET,MEN)
PL of SOCRATES:(MEMBER,MEN)
PL of MEN:(SUPERSET,MORTALS,ELEMENT,SOCRATES)

These PL's express the facts that MORTALS has a SUBSET named MEN, SOCRATES is a MEMBER of the set named MEN, and MEN has a SUPERSET named MORTALS and an ELEMENT named SOCRATES.

The symbols ∈ and ⊂ represent relations that each relate or connect two objects. In the above example we have split each of these two-way relations into two *unary* subrelations—i.e., subrelations that each apply to a single object. The attributes in a PL must always be unary, because they must apply to the single object that the entire PL describes. Of course, the value of the attribute may name another object or objects. In this case, ∈ has been split into ELEMENT and MEMBER, and ⊂ has been split into SUBSET and SUPERSET. These subrelation names identify not only the two-way relationship, but also which of the two elements of the pair is being described (e.g., SUBSET describes the second element, or right-hand side, of the ⊂ relation, and has as its value the first or left-hand element). It is always possible to decompose a two-place, three-place, or larger relationship into several unary subrelationships that may then be represented in the computer by property lists.

Another approach to representing a relationship is simply to associate with the name of the relation a list of the pairs (or triples for three-

way relationships, and so on) of objects for which the names relation
holds. For example, we might have:

⊂: ((MEN MORTALS) (TRIANGLES POLYGONS)
                                   (APPLES FRUITS))

For a large problem involving many relationships and many objects for
which various relationships are true, the selection of one of the above
ways of representing relationships, or the invention of some other way,
is a crucial part of the problem-solving process. The way in which the
relational data is stored in computer memory determines the speed with
which particular relational facts can be retrieved, and therefore the efficiency of operation of the complete program.

   Now let us turn our attention to the concept of *processes*. What do
we mean by a process? Informally, a process is a prescription for carrying
out some sequence of operations. Although the complete operation of
solving any problem may be thought of as a single process, it is frequently useful to divide a proposed solution into two or more separate
processes. Each process has an independent task to carry out, but must
also be sufficiently aware of the existence of other processes in order to
communicate with them effectively. In this way a group of cooperating
simple processes might be able to carry out a task more easily than a
single complex process could. Here is an example.

   Problem. Tell me which common four-letter English word ends
   with the sequence of letters, "ENY."

Most people who are given this problem approach it by thinking of
individual letters and then testing each letter they think of by inserting
it into the blank in "–ENY."[6] This approach can easily be viewed as
requiring two cooperating processes:
   1. *Generate* candidate letters to be tried.
   2. *Test* a candidate that has been generated, to see whether it
provides a solution.
   We can specify the external behavior and manner of communication of these two processes without any concern for their internal operation. We can then try various methods of internal operation for each
process, independent of its external behavior or the method of operation
of the other process. In this way the problem can be factored (separated)
into two (and sometimes, several) easier subproblems. Here is how the
factoring works in this particular example.
   External Behavior and Communication. The test process must ask
the generate process for a candidate letter, then wait until generate

---

[6]A few people think of the answer almost immediately. We do not understand the
thought processes of such exceptional individuals well enough to use them in our examples.

responds. When a letter has been provided, test must test whether the problem is solved. If so, it must report the solution. If not, it must ask generate for another candidate. Generate must produce a letter each time it is activated (called upon) by test. It must keep track of what it did in previous activations, so as not to repeat a letter it has previously generated. If it is activated and cannot find a letter, it must report failure.

Internal Behavior of Generate. Several generation strategies are possible. Many people make a few guesses at first, hoping for a quick solution, before settling down to a systematic generation procedure. One obvious procedure for generate is to generate letters in alphabetic order, and to remember the previous letter it generated between activations, to keep its place in the alphabet. Perhaps a better strategy would be to modify or reorder the alphabet in hopes of generating the right answer sooner. For example, the letters might be ordered for generation beginning E, T, N, R, O, A, I, S, D, L, H, C, P, F, U, and so on, which is the order in which letters most commonly appear in typical English text.

Internal Behavior of Test. Again, several strategies are possible. Most people merely "sound out" the generated words to themselves, until they come to the one that they know. Some will go to the trouble of writing down each candidate word, until they "recognize" the right one. As a last resort, test could look up each word in a dictionary; but, although perhaps necessary for a computer, surely such an awkward test procedure should not be necessary for an English-speaking person looking for a common word.

Surprisingly enough, many find this problem extremely difficult, and some might even deny that a solution exists. Have you solved the problem yet?

Now, one might argue that relationships and processes are themselves merely special kinds of abstract objects. A relationship is a structured object that has a name or description (e.g., "SUBSET") and two or more subobjects (e.g., "MEN" and "MORTAL") as components. A process is a complex object that can be represented by a sequence of instructions, such as a computer program, and that has special properties, such as the fact that it can be activated to produce some results. This view that anything can be thought of as an object is perfectly acceptable, so long as one is aware of the existence of these various special kinds of objects and how they can be used. The important thing is to recognize that there are different types of knowledge, and they can best be represented in different ways. For example, when a child learns to tie his shoe, he primarily does not learn a fact (that a shoe can be tied) or to recognize an object (the precise structure and appearance of a bow in a shoelace). Instead he learns a process: make a loop in one end of the lace, wrap the other end around it, hold the whole mess with your forefinger, and so on. When trying to give knowledge to a computer, a programmer should consider first whether some aspect of the real problem can best be thought of as a process, a relationship, or merely a simple object, and then how to fill in the details of a computer representation. The recently developed concept that knowledge can be represented in a computer by processes is causing a minor revolution in certain areas of current computer-science research, and promises to play a key role in the future development of more-intelligent computer programs. (See the discussion of Winograd's program, Chapter 6).

The precise way in which procedural knowledge can be represented in new computer-programming languages is too detailed to explain here. The important point is that factoring a problem's solution into separate processes, and then specifying the interprocess communication rules separately from the internal operations of each process, can be extremely helpful ideas; and several new programming systems make these ideas easy to use by providing special aids to the programmer who wants to think in terms of the activation, communication, and internal operations of a group of cooperating processes.

Summary

A problem is not fully defined or worthy of formal consideration unless it has the following characteristics.

    1.   The problem is expressed in terminology clearly understood by the potential problem solver.

    2.   The form and notation for the problem's solution is agreed upon.

    3.   The relevant data upon which a solution may be based is identified.

    4.   Some measure of the validity or acceptability of proposed solutions is agreed upon.

Although these characteristics are natural features of any problem-solving process programmed for a computer, they are easily—and frequently—overlooked in informal, human-problem-solving situations. One important reason for using computers to help people solve problems is that the process of describing the problem to the computer forces the human to endow the problem with the above-stated characteristics, thereby clarifying his own fuzzy thinking.

Problems are rarely solved in precisely the same terms in which they are initially expressed. Instead, it is common to choose some different form of data—called a *representation*—and then to construct an idealized problem that is analogous to the originally stated problem. The representation may consist of physical or abstract objects, and differ from the real problem in many ways including precision, size, and structure. Choosing a good representation may require considerable cleverness and ingenuity. Reasons for choosing a particular representation may include the following.

1. The real domain may not be practical because of the size, weight, expense, or inaccessibility of the objects involved.

2. Distracting features of the real domain that are not relevant to the problem may be omitted from the representation.

3. A mathematical or scientific theory may exist that can be applied effectively to an appropriate representation of the problem.

4. The representation may make apparent certain relationships among the data that are useful for the problem-solving process.

Once a problem has been solved in an idealized representation, the task remains of interpreting the solution with respect to the original problem, and proving that the obtained interpretation indeed solved the problem.

For a computer to solve a problem, the data of the real problem must be represented by some form of data that can be manipulated by a computer. Strings and list structures are the most widely used computer data types for nonarithmetic problems. Strings are more economical in their use of computer memory, and are efficient for storing and comparing linear sequences of symbols. List structures permit more flexible, hierarchical groupings of symbols to be used. When applying computer methods to a new problem area, the programmer's careful selection of a data representation can have a critical influence upon the success of the subsequent problem-solving programs.

Knowledge consists of data about objects, relationships, and processes. All three types of knowledge are useful in the course of representing and solving problems with computers. Objects can be represented by symbolic data structures such as strings and lists. Relationships may be represented by property lists or by other special list structures. Processes, represented by computer programs and by special features of new programming languages, provide a powerful way to factor certain problems into simpler subproblems. These different ways of thinking about, representing, and using knowledge in a computer have resulted in major advances in the development of automatic problem-solving systems.

SUGGESTED READINGS

Amarel, S., "On the Representation of Problems and Goal Directed Procedures for Computers." *Communications of Amer. Soc. Cybernetics,* Vol. 1, No. 2, 1969.

Gilmore, P. C., "An Examination of the Geometry Theorem Machine." *Artificial Intelligence,* Vol. 1, No. 3, 1970.

Polya, G., *Mathematics and Plausible Reasoning.* Princeton University Press, Princeton, N.J., 1954. 2 vols.

SIGSAM Bulletin (quarterly). Special Interest Group on Symbolic and Algebraic Manipulation, Association for Computing Machinery, New York City, 1965–

Wickelgren, W. A. *How to Solve Problems.* W. H. Freeman and Company, San Francisco, 1974.

Search 3

Choosing the search space

There is an old story about a man who was crawling around a lamppost on his hands and knees at midnight. A policeman came by, watched for a while, and then asked, "What are you doing?"

Man: "Looking for my glasses."

Policeman: "How did you lose them?"

Man: "I dropped them in that alley down the street."

Policeman: "Then why are you searching here?"

Man: "Well, I'd *never* be able to find them in that dark alley!"

Search is an important part of most problem-solving processes. Since, in order to make computers smarter, we must program them to master efficient search principles, we must first understand those principles ourselves. In this chapter we shall consider the general task of searching for solutions to problems. Search methods such as those explained in the following pages have been programmed for many computers and play key roles in various applications of smarter computers that are discussed in the later chapters of this book.

The first requirement for effective search is that the collection of places in which we are prepared to look—called the *search space*—actually contains a solution. Now this concept is not as silly as it may seem. For many problems, including the most important problems facing the world—e.g., how to prevent wars—we are not even sure that a solution is possible. We can merely construct compromises and approximations, hoping that the search space in which we are stumbling about not only contains at least one solution, but that we shall find one before it is too late. Perhaps some day political and social scientists, possibly aided by new theories of search and problem solving to be developed by computer scientists, will be able to prove that certain search spaces contain generally acceptable solutions to their (and our) most important problems. Such understanding of appropriate search spaces goes a long way towards actually finding acceptable solutions in the space being searched. Without such understanding, we may find ourselves looking under the nearest convenient lamppost and not even realizing that no solution can be found there.

The simple fact that a solution is known to exist in a given search space can be of tremendous help in solving a problem. The main reason for this is that the problem solver needs to have confidence in the approach he is taking. If he is not sure whether his approach will lead to a solution, he will easily be led to doubt its validity and to try to formulate different approaches that may explore different search spaces. Although such digressions may occasionally lead to useful changes in representation (see Chapter 2), a certain amount of perseverance within one approach is usually necessary to solve a difficult problem.

Early in their careers, most computer programmers go through a stage of overconfidence in their own abilities. When programs that they have written do not work properly, they decide too quickly that hunting for the source of the difficulty by looking for programming errors of their own is like looking under the lamppost; they believe no errors will be found, because they think their programs tend to be perfect. Instead, they change the search space by complaining to the hardware engineers that the computer has malfunctioned. More-sophisticated programmers have learned that they are themselves much more likely to make errors than the computer is. Armed wih this belief that the search space of their own programs contains a solution—the source of the difficulty—they are much more persistent and effective at finding it. The most frustrating programming jobs are those concerned with new or unreliable computers, where the appropriate search space for most difficulties is not known because both software and hardware are equally likely to cause problems.

Mathematics is another domain where knowledge of the existence of a solution to a problem is frequently of crucial importance. Some problems in mathematics are known to have solutions—e.g., the problem of finding the roots of a second-degree polynomial—and general formulas for the solutions have been worked out. Other problems—e.g., the problem of finding the roots of a fifth-degree polynomial—have been proven not to have any general solutions, even though one might expect such solutions to exist. In fact, in the 1930's logicians proved the existence of an infinite number of problems in higher mathematics that can never be solved. Moreover, one usually cannot tell whether any particular problem is unsolvable in this sense, or whether it is solvable but its solution has just not yet been found. For example, consider the problem of proving the following assertion from the branch of higher mathematics called number theory.

(3.1)   There do not exist any four integers x, y, z, and n for which x, y, and z are all greater than zero and n is greater than two, that satisfy the equation

$$x^n + y^n = z^n$$

Mathematicians do not yet know whether this assertion is:

(*a*)   False, but an appropriate set of numbers to form a counter example has not yet been found. For example, might there be a number x such that $x^{1,273} + (1,235,973)^{1,273} = (987,699,154)^{1,273}$?

(*b*)   True and provable within the normal system of mathematical reasoning, but the proof has not yet been discovered.

(*c*)   True but not provable within the normal system of mathematical reasoning.

Problem (3.1) would probably join the ranks of thousands of little-known open questions that fill the mathematics journals and are of little interest except as possible thesis topics for mathematics students, except for a peculiar discovery: in one of his last notebooks, Fermat, the famous seventeenth-century mathematician, made a comment in the margin to the effect that, "I have proven the assertion, but unfortunately do not have room here to sketch the proof." In effect, Fermat said to future generations, "A solution exists!" As a result, (3.1) is now known as *Fermat's Last Theorem,* and is perhaps the most famous conjecture in mathematics. In the course of three centuries many thousands of mathematicians have devoted themselves to trying to rediscover Fermat's proof, or to discover any other proof. In view of the lack of success of this extensive effort, some cynics have begun to believe that the theorem is not provable; either Fermat's proof had a flaw he did not notice, or his marginal note was a sly practical joke on posterity. We may never know.

Limiting the search space

It has been said that if a hundred monkeys typed at random on a hundred typewriters, eventually they would reproduce all the books in the British Museum, one of the world's largest libraries. Therefore the process of trying to generate a particular English sentence, for example, by either randomly or systematically generating all possible sequences of alphabetic characters and watching for the desired sentence to appear, has been called the British Museum Algorithm (BMA). No one would seriously propose using the BMA in a practical problem, because it would take longer than most of us can imagine to accomplish anything. However, the search space certainly contains the solution, and the search procedure is guaranteed to find it eventually, so the BMA is a concept that can be used as a "worst case" example with which other algorithms may be compared. For example, a BMA for our friend who lost his glasses might be to divide the surface of the world into six-inch squares, start at the North Pole, and look at each square in turn until the glasses were found. Since this approach will certainly find the glasses eventually (assuming they have not totally decomposed by then), this BMA approach is better than his original approach of limiting his search to the vicinity of the lamppost. Of course, he would do even better if he limited his search to the city, and even better if he limited his search to the alley where he dropped the glasses, and even better if he could determine in advance the particular six-inch square in which his glasses are lying. In fact, if he knew where the glasses were lying, he would not have to search at all; he would merely go and pick them up.

Suppose we are asked to find a positive integer x that satisfies the equation

(3.2) $$x^2 - 2x - 9800 = 0$$

(and we are told that a solution definitely exists). If we know very little about mathematics a BMA approach might seem natural, so we would try the positive integers, one at a time, testing each one:

$$1^2 - 2 \cdot 1 - 9800 = -9801 \neq 0$$
$$2^2 - 2 \cdot 2 - 9800 = -9800 \neq 0$$
$$3^2 - 2 \cdot 3 - 9800 = -9797 \neq 0$$
$$4^2 - 2 \cdot 4 - 9800 = -9792 \neq 0$$

and so on. After a while we would probably get discouraged and require reassurance that a solution exists in the search space, and so we should persevere.

A somewhat more sophisticated mathematician would look at the first few trials and notice that the values of the calculations, -9801, -9800, -9797, . . . , were slowly getting closer to the desired result, zero. He might try a big jump, say to $x = 500$:

$$500^2 - 2 \cdot 500 - 9800 = 239,200 \neq 0$$

Since 239,200 is greater than zero and -9801 is less than zero, and the problem deals with a well-behaved, "continuous" mathematical expression, he might guess that the solution is somewhere between $x = 1$ and $x = 500$, so he would try, say, $x = 250$:

$$250^2 - 2 \cdot 250 - 9800 = 52,200 > 0$$

Trying half way in between again, he gets

$$125^2 - 2 \cdot 125 - 9800 = 5,575 > 0$$

and then

$$62^2 - 2 \cdot 62 - 9800 = -6,080 < 0$$

He now knows that the solution is for x to be between 62 and 125, and he can proceed to "close in" by halving that difference and continuing in a similar manner. This approach of finding limits to where the solution might be and then looking halfway between those limits is much more efficient than the BMA because the search space is much smaller; instead of all the positive integers, the search space consists of a carefully chosen sequence of limiting positive integers, and yet it is guaranteed to contain the solution, because the limits keep getting closer to it.

Of course, someone who knows a little more mathematics would not have to search at all. He would merely remember that the solution to problems of the form

$$ax^2 + bx + c = 0$$

can be calculated with the formula

$$\frac{-b \pm \sqrt{b^2 - 4ac}}{2a}$$

so the answer can be obtained, without any search, by evaluating

$$\frac{-2 + \sqrt{(2)^2 + 4 \cdot 9800}}{2}$$

For most problems of interest nobody knows a formula that can produce the answer; we are forced to do some search through a "space" of possible answers. In fact, some kind of search operation is probably the most common basic ingredient in computer problem-solving programs. We need know only two things in order to construct a BMA for solving any problem: (1) a means for recognizing a solution if we stumble across it, and (2) a procedure for enumerating any class of items that contains a solution.

Fortunately, we usually have much more knowledge about a problem domain and this knowledge should be used as productively as possible. One way it can be used, as we have discussed above, is to limit the search space to the smallest possible space that we are still confident contains a solution. A second way to use knowledge in problem solving is to guide the search through the selected space so that candidate solutions are examined in an intelligent sequence rather than an arbitrary or random one. Most of the remainder of this chapter deals with how to order the search procedure.

Structure of the search space

Searching should be performed *systematically*. If I ask my five-year-old daughter to count a collection of seven buttons, she may come up with the answer five, or ten, or eight. She may overlook some, and count others several times. She has not yet learned to proceed through the collection systematically. My seven-year-old son, on the other hand, has learned that if he moves a button to one side of the table as he counts it, he will always know which buttons have been counted and which have not; in this way he can come up with a consistent total.

The elements of the search space must be arranged so that we can explore them in a systematic way, and not have to worry that we may re-consider the same element many times or may overlook some crucial elements. Some search spaces—e.g., the integers—have a natural ordering of their own. However, even in such cases we may not want to consider the elements of the space in their natural order; we may prefer to proceed in some other order, based upon knowledge of how to approach the solution faster (e.g., as in the "halving the difference" approach to the algebra problem discussed above). Furthermore, a problem-solving search should not consist of blindly considering elements of the search space until it trips over the solution, the way ignorant BMA searches do. Rather, the search should be directed toward the solution with the ex-amination of each element helping to suggest which other elements should be examined next.

As an example, we now return to the cryptarithmetic problem mentioned in Chapter 2,

$$\begin{array}{r} \text{BEST} \\ + \text{ MADE} \\ \hline \text{MASER} \end{array}$$

Remember, the problem is to find different integers for each of the letters **A, B, D, E, M, R, S,** and **T,** that will make the sum correct. We shall informally work out a search procedure to solve this problem, and then point out the important general characteristics of such a procedure.

First, a quick look at the straightforward BMA approach: we may select any eight of the ten digits 0, 1, 2, 3, 4, 5, 6, 7, 8, and 9, and assign them in any order to the eight letters that appear in the problem. It can be shown that there are 1,814,400 possible ways of making these assign-ments. If a man spent only ten seconds choosing a new assignment and testing whether it is a solution, he would have to work forty hours each week for more than two years in order to try all the possibilities. Since most people with any interest in this type of puzzle can solve it within a half hour, there must be a better way. If we want computers to be able to solve much harder problems than this one, we must understand the prin-ciples of more-efficient approaches. Let's see how some knowledge of arithmetic can help solve this probem.

In order to talk about the problem conveniently, we shall use the following terminology: the columns of figures will be numbered from 1 to 5 from right to left, and the symbols C_1, C_2, C_3, and C_4 will represent the number "carried" from the sum of a column to the next column—e.g., if the sum of column 3 is 10 or more, then $C_3 = 1$, otherwise $C_3 = 0$. (Figure 3.1)

	C_4	C_3	C_2	C_1	
		B	E	S	T
+		M	A	D	E
	M	A	S	E	R
Column number	5	4	3	2	1

Figure 3.1 Cryptarithmetic problem notation.

We shall begin our analysis with column 5, and then work more or less systematically to the right, combining and simplifying our partial results as we go, and using a diagram for bookkeeping purposes to keep track of our progress. From column 5 we can tell immediately that $M = 1$; it cannot be zero, because a leading zero would not have been written down, and it cannot be more than 1, because the most that two four digit numbers can add up to is less than 20,000. (9999 + 9999 = 19,998). Since M in column 5 is simply C_4 added to nothing else, we know that $C_4 = 1$ and that therefore column 4 must generate a carry. We begin noting our results on the diagram (Figure 3.2a).

Turning to column 4, we do not know whether C_3 is zero or one. Noting the two alternatives on the diagram (Figure 3.2,b), we shall consider them one at a time. First we assume that $C_3 = 0$, and proceed from there. Since $C_3 = 0$ and $C_4 = 1$, the column 4 sum must be $B + M = A + 10$, and since we already determined that $M = 1$, we have $B = A + 9$. Since B cannot be worth more than 9 (each letter must be a single digit), we have $A = 0$ and $B = 9$. We can now go on to the next column, where C_2 might be zero or one (Figure 3.2,c). The column sum is $C_2 + E + A = S$. For $C_2 = 0$, and we know $A = 0$, this means $E = S$. Since one of the ground rules was that two letters cannot equal the same number, we have shown that the choice of both $C_3 = 0$ and $C_2 = 0$ cannot lead to a solution, so we should abandon this "branch" of the search space (termination of the search in this direction is shown in Figure 3.2,c by an X).

We must now choose a new direction in which to search. Both the ($C_3 = 0$, $C_2 = 1$) combination, and the $C_3 = 1$ branch, are available for continued study and "growth." In the absence of any additional knowledge to help us decide which is more likely to lead to a solution, we may select one arbitrarily. At each point or *node* in this growing diagram, we consider the appropriate column sum from Figure 3.1, simplify it as much as possible using all the previously established information along the branches leading to that node, consider what alternative possibilities

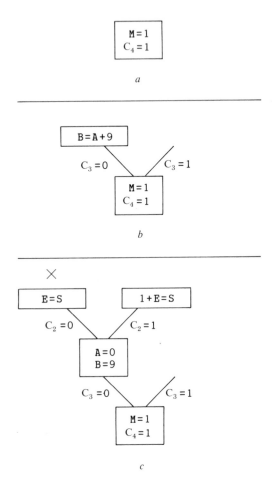

Figure 3.2 Growing a search space.

might sprout out of that node, and then choose a branch somewhere in the structure to pursue further.

Figure 3.3 shows a later stage of this analysis. At this stage all column sums have been considered, and all possible choices of the carry quantities except one have led to illegal assignments. Therefore we know that the solution must lie along the path marked with a double bar in Figure 3.3, and that $C_3 = 0$, $C_2 = 1$, and $C_1 = 1$. Also $M = 1$, $A = 0$, $B = 9$, $D = 8$, $1 + E = S$, and $T + E = R + 10 \geq 12$ (because R cannot be 0 or 1).

Before completing the solution to this problem, I want to point out that the general form of the structure in Figure 3.3 is that of a *tree* (see Figure 3.4), i.e., a structure that starts from a single *root* and grows with

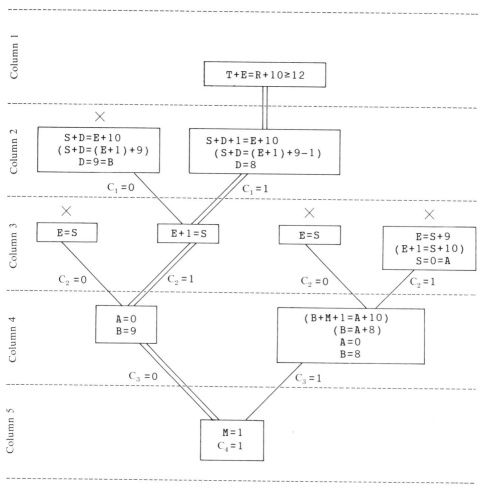

Figure 3.3 Expanded search space.

branches that may split or terminate at any level, but may never rejoin. This kind of conceptual structure is of wide use in computer science and parts of mathematics, and the terms *root, branch,* and *node* are used in the obvious way when referring to these abstract trees. However, people usually start reading or writing at the top of a sheet of paper and work their way down, whereas Nature starts her creations at ground level and grows up. Therefore our abstract trees will, hereafter, be drawn upside down; the root node will appear at the top of the tree diagram, and the branches will reach down toward the bottom.

Let us return to complete the cryptarithmetic example. Although many possibilities have been eliminated and some of the letter assign-

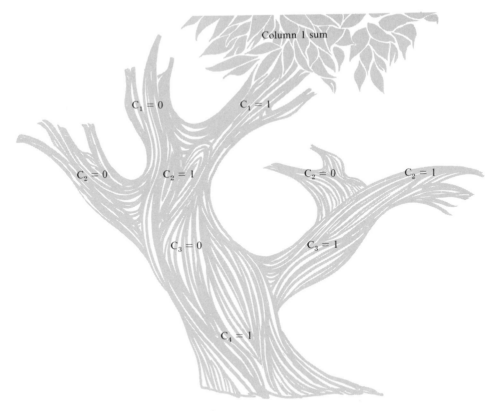

Column 1 sum

$C_1 = 0$ $C_1 = 1$

$C_2 = 0$ $C_2 = 1$ $C_2 = 0$ $C_2 = 1$

$C_3 = 0$ $C_3 = 1$

$C_4 = 1$

Figure 3.4 Tree structure of search space.

ments have been uniquely determined, we are still not finished; we must select assignments for **T**, **E**, **S**, and **R** from the remaining numbers 2, 3, 4, 5, 6, and 7, that satisfy the conditions

$$\mathbf{E} + 1 = \mathbf{S} \quad \text{and} \quad \mathbf{R} + 10 = \mathbf{T} + \mathbf{E} \geq 12.$$

This remaining problem is small enough, however, that rather than get a headache looking for clever mathematical explanations, I would not mind trying a BMA-type enumeration, at least to start, and see what happens. Since we seem to know the most about **E** (because it occurs in both conditions), we begin by "sprouting" the last node on the tree with all possible assignments to **E**. The resulting impossible requirements on **D** or **M** again quickly narrow the search, and a unique solution can be found. The complete solution tree is shown in Figure 3.5, where nodes are shown as circles and key results are boxed.

We have now solved the "**BEST** + **MADE** = **MASER**" problem, and incidentally have shown that our solution is the only possible one.

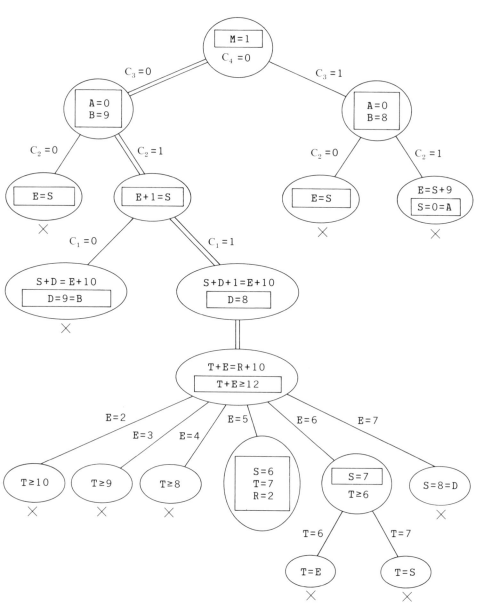

Figure 3.5 Complete search tree for cryptarithmetic problem.

Our method of solution, however, is certainly not the only possible one, and in fact there may be many more-efficient techniques for this particular problem. What we have presented is one frequently used general approach that is useful in many problem-solving situations. This approach has two key elements.

Systematic Exploration of a Structured Search Space. In the above example, the structure consisted of a tree whose branches represented hypotheses or "guesses" and whose nodes represented some of the conclusions from those hypotheses.

Frequent Use of Knowledge From the Original Problem Domain. In the above example, this knowledge included the constraints imposed by the problem statement, the ability to recognize a consistent solution, the rules of arithmetic, and some arithmetic intuition to guide decisions about which branches of the tree to extend further and what kinds of hypotheses to propose.

The first of the above elements, exploration of a structured search space, has been the subject of much intensive analysis and is the subject matter of a mathematical discipline called "Graph Theory." The second element, the use of knowledge, has been largely neglected, mainly because it is so difficult to approach in any systematic way. For years computer scientists had hoped that problems could be divided into two stages, in the first of which human programmers with an understanding of a problem domain could choose a good formal representation, and in the second a computer with no understanding could carry out such formal procedures as searching through structured spaces. These scientists are now realizing that in many of the most important and most difficult problems formal search and informal use of knowledge are intimately related processes, and they must constantly switch back and forth between them, just as we switched between tree searches and arithmetic calculations in the "toy" cryptarithmetic problem. Since we would also like computers to be able to search in a sensible manner, how to give a computer better "common sense" knowledge has become a major research topic. Some promising first steps in this direction have been made, and will be discussed in later chapters. In the following two sections of this chapter, we shall present the elements of a formal theory of search in abstract search spaces, and then return to how a computer can use additional knowledge to improve upon abstract search procedures.

Trees and graphs

An abstract search space often takes the form of a *graph*. A graph is an arbitrary collection of points called *nodes* and connections called *arcs* that go from one node to another. If we think of the nodes as representing locations in a search space, then we naturally think of the arcs as connections from each location to its *successors*—whichever locations might be considered next as we wander through the space. Now if exploration of location A suggests B as a successor, there is no reason to require that exploration of B must also necessarily suggest A; therefore, arcs are frequently one way or *directed.* The node at the tail of the directing arrow is called the *predecessor* of the node at the head of the arrow. However, since elements that are near each other in a search space may frequently suggest each other as successors, arcs may also be *bidirectional.* Figure 3.6 shows a typical directed graph.

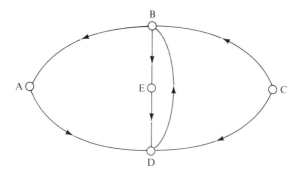

Figure 3.6   A directed graph.

If we begin at node A, it is possible to get to node E, for example, by traversing the intermediate nodes D and B; but it is not possible to get to C.

A *tree* is a special type of graph; namely, one that has the following properties.

1.   A tree has a unique *root*, or *top node*, that has no predecessors.
2.   Every other node of the tree has exactly one predecessor.

Figure 3.7 is an abstract tree with the same structure as that of Figure 3.5.

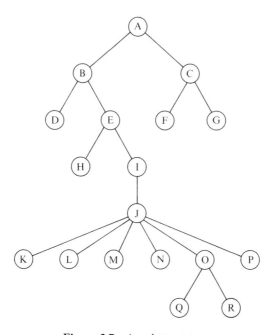

Figure 3.7   An abstract tree.

(We assume that every arc in a tree is directed downward, so arrows need not be drawn on the arcs.)

Trees are simpler structures to study than graphs. They have the nice property that there is at most one route or *path* that can get you from one node to any other node, and there can be no loops. In the graph of Figure 3.6, there are two different ways to get from C to A, for example, not counting loops. If we permit loops, there are an arbitrarily large number of ways—such as the path

C B E D B E D B E D B E D B A.

Therefore, although a graph may sometimes provide a more natural representation, we usually prefer to use tree representations. Moreover, if we are given a graph and a designated starting node of that graph to use as the root, we can easily begin to construct a corresponding tree. We may be required to copy parts of the graph many times and the tree may be infinite, but if the construction process stays one step ahead of the

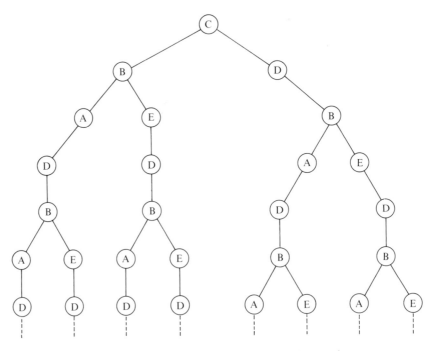

Figure 3.8   Partial tree representation of a graph.

search process this will not bother us. Figure 3.8 shows the graph of Figure 3.6 partially expanded as a tree from node C. We shall concentrate our study upon tree representation and search. Many of the following techniques can be extended to graphs, but the results are somewhat more complicated.

We first consider what kinds of things the nodes and arcs of a tree (or graph) may represent. I have said that the nodes represent locations of a search space, and the arcs suggest which other locations should be considered next. This general idea is rather vague and may be made more specific in a variety of different ways, each of which is useful in some class of problems.

1.   Nodes represent candidate solutions to be tested, and arcs represent rules for finding more nodes. The search for a value of x satisfying equation (3.2) was of this variety. The main goal was merely to find the right node, independent of the course of the search.

2.   Nodes represent tentative conclusions, and arcs represent additional hypotheses. This was the variety of tree we used in the "BEST + MADE = MASER" problem. Here each node represented all the information accumulated along the path from the root to that node, and our object was really to find a path that led to a complete, consistent solution to the problem.

3.   Nodes represent states of some process or computation, and arcs represent elementary actions that may be taken to change each state. In this important variety of tree representation, the identity of the goal node may be clearly known in advance, perhaps as part of the problem specification. The basic object of the problem-solving process is not to find the goal, but rather to find a path from the root to the goal. In some problems any path will do; in others, the path may be constrained in some way. This way of formulating problems has been called a *state-description* representation. One example of its use is in the traveling-salesman type of problem (see Chapter 2). Here each node can represent a city that the salesman may visit, and each arc can represent a road that the salesman may traverse to get from one city to another.

4.   Nodes represent complete descriptions of problems, and arcs indicate how different problems may be related to each other. Usually the root node represents the main problem for which we would like a solution, and the successors of each node represent separate subproblems or differently formulated problems whose solutions would contribute to the solution of the problem represented by that node. This approach is called a *problem-reduction* representation. The object of the search is to find some set of nodes in the tree such that the problem represented by each of the nodes in the set is easy enough that we can solve it quickly, and the combination of these solutions gives us a solution to the main (root) problem. For example, the "BEST + MADE = MASER" problem might have been begun with the problem-reduction graph of Figure 3.9.

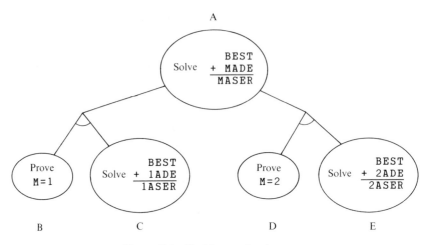

Figure 3.9 Problem reduction tree.

This tree shows that, in order to solve A, one must solve either both B and C or both D and E.

Thus the concept of searching through a tree-structured space for a path from the root node to some goal node, is useful for a variety of problem-solving approaches. In the following section we consider this abstract problem.

Finding a path in a tree

Before discussing particular procedures for searching for paths in trees, we must define the kinds of trees we are thinking of more precisely than we have thus far. By definition, every tree has a unique root or top node, and every other node in a tree has a unique predecessor—the node directly above. The *tree-searching problem* is the problem of finding a path in a tree from the root node to a designated goal node. We shall here consider path-finding situations with the following characteristics.

Trees may be defined implicitly as well as explicitly. An *explicit* definition is a diagram or similar presentation of the complete tree—e.g., Figure 3.10. An *implicit* definition of a tree is a rule that describes how to generate the tree; i.e., how to construct the successors of any node. For example, the tree in Figure 3.10 is defined implicitly as follows.

Node number 1 is the top node.

For $1 \leq n \leq 26$, each node n has three successors whose numbers are $3n - 1$, $3n$, and $3n + 1$, respectively.

No node whose number is equal to or greater than 27 has any successors.

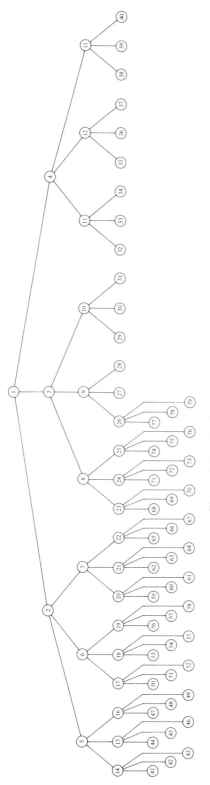

Figure 3.10 Explicit presentation of a tree.

This implicit definition is clearly more concise and possibly more useful than the corresponding explicit description, Figure 3.10.

Each node has only a finite number of successors. The number of successors—nodes immediately below a given node—may vary from node to node, however.

The depth of a tree may be infinite. The depth of a node is the number of nodes on the path from the top node to it (not counting the node itself). The depth of a tree is the maximum depth of any node in the tree. In Figure 3.10, the depth is 4. The depth of a root node is always zero. Figure 3.8 shows the top of a tree of infinite depth. Although only one infinite branch is necessary to give a tree infinite depth, the tree whose top is shown in Figure 3.8 has an infinite number of infinite branches. Of course, any tree of infinite depth must be defined implicitly.

The arcs of a tree may have costs associated with them. These costs will be represented by real numbers (numbers possibly including fractions or decimals). In many problems it is convenient to use these cost numbers as measures of the difficulty of traversing various arcs. For example, in a traveling-salesman problem where an arc represents a road between two cities, its cost might represent either the mileage length of the road or the dollar cost of gas and tolls for taking that route. If no costs are given for the arcs of a tree, we shall assume that every arc has a cost of one unit. The cost of a path is the sum of the costs of the arcs on the path.

Several nodes of the tree may be designated as goal nodes. For example, if the tree has been derived from a graph, like the tree of Figure 3.8, then one node of the graph can occur in many places in the tree. If that graph node were the goal, then all the corresponding tree nodes would be acceptable goals. The problem we shall concentrate on will be the problem of finding a path from the top of the tree down to any goal node.

Now we shall look at some commonly used procedures for solving the tree-searching problem. First, let us note the three conditions with which we shall judge the effectiveness of a tree-searching procedure.

1. *It should find a solution.* If a solution path—a path from root to goal—exists in a tree, a search process is not much good unless it is guaranteed to find it eventually.

2. *It should find a good solution.* The best solution path is a minimum-cost one, i.e., one whose cost is less than the cost of any other solution path. We would like a procedure that can always find it.

3. *It should find a good solution efficiently.* One procedure can be considered better than another if it can find just as good a solution in less time—e.g., by exploring a smaller part of the tree.

Now, let us look at some commonly-used tree-searching procedures, and evaluate them with respect to the above conditions.

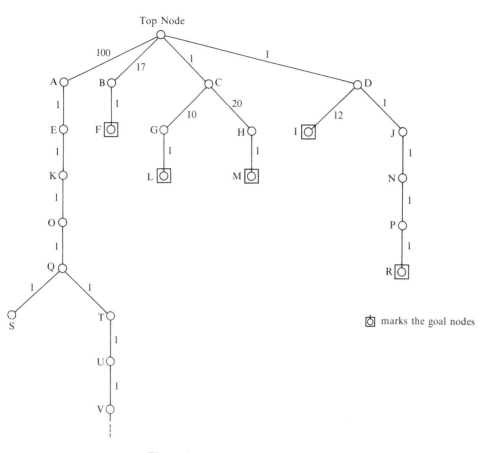

Figure 3.11 Tree search example.

BREADTH-FIRST SEARCH

This procedure examines each of the successors of the top node to see if it is a goal node. If not, it then examines all the successors of these successors, and so on. In Figure 3.10 this procedure would examine the nodes in their numerical order. In effect, it looks first for solution paths of length one, then of length two, and so on until it finds a solution. *Breadth-first* search is the easiest procedure to program in many programming systems, and is not too bad by our judgment criteria: it is guaranteed to find a solution if one exists, and the solution found will be the solution path of minimum length. If all arcs have the same costs—e.g., unity—then the minimum-length solution will also be the minimum-cost solution. Of course, in general, breadth-first search until a goal is found will *not* find the minimum-cost solution. In Figure 3.11, breadth-first search will proceed in alphabetic order and first find the solution path to F, whose cost is 18 and length is 2. If we modify the procedure to complete the examination of all paths of a given length, it will find the better path to I (cost 13). The only way to ensure that a solution found by a breadth-first search is the best one is to continue searching until the cost of each partial path explored is found to be greater than that of the best solution found thus far. For Figure 3.11, this would require exploring all paths up to length five.

DEPTH-FIRST SEARCH

Imagine you are a spelunker (an amateur cave explorer) going down a limestone tunnel hoping to find some unexplored territory, and you come to a branch point. You take the left-hand fork, climb up a waterfall, crawl through a narrow muddy passage, lower yourself by rope 43 feet into a pit, and discover three new passages at the bottom. A determined breadth-first searcher would now turn around, climb up the rope, through the mud, down the waterfall, and try the right-hand fork until it too reaches another branch point. But any spelunker I've ever known, most of whom have never heard of formal search procedures, would pick one of the new choices at the bottom of the pit and keep right on going, without considering going back up the rope until he had thoroughly explored the bottom of the pit, or until his strength or light or rope threatened to give out. In some computer-programming systems it is also desirable to avoid the amount of backing up and retracing necessary for breadth-first search; consider the bookkeeping needed to successively explore nodes N, O, P, Q, and R, in that order, in Figure 3.11. Therefore *depth-first* search is commonly used for searching trees. In this procedure just one branch, say the left-most, is chosen and followed until it ends. If it terminates without a goal node, the procedure backs up as little as possible, to the closest branch point, chooses another alternative, and continues. In Figure 3.11, depth-first search would explore nodes in the following order: Top, A, E, K, O, Q, S (back up to Q), T, U, V, and so on, examining everything below V before returning to consider B. If the branch below V were infinite, no solution would ever be found. Clearly, depth-first search is not desirable as a general procedure. Still, it is useful in many cases, especially if the tree is known to be small or to have many goal nodes, and if backtracking is expensive.

PROGRESSIVE DEEPENING

The *progressive deepening* strategy is a compromise between breadth first and depth first. It begins as a depth-first search with a level bound: i.e., a number indicating the maximum depth that is permitted. Even though a branch may continue beyond that depth, it is assumed to end and the search backs up. However, if the entire tree has been explored to the permitted depth and no solution has been found, the level bound may be increased by some predetermined increment and the search continued.

Note that if the level bound is initially set as one and its increments are one, progressive deepening is the same as breadth first. If the level bound is initially set as a million, then for all practical purposes progressive deepening is the same as depth first. For certain intermediate values, though, we get interesting intermediate strategies. In Figure 3.11 with the level bound set as two, we explore nodes A, E, (return to Top), B, and F, getting solution path BF rather quickly. If we continued searching for better solutions, we would explore nodes C, G, H, D, I, and J, finding the solution path DI. If the level bound were then increased to four, the goal nodes L and M (but not R) would also be found.

The progressive deepening strategy is guaranteed to find a solution, and the solution's path length will be within the level-bound increment of the length of the shortest solution; but, of course, we have not yet considered the costs of the solution paths.

OPTIMUM SEARCH FOR MINIMUM-COST PATH

By now the astute reader is probably muttering to himself, "Obviously the minimum-cost solution path in Figure 3.11 is the one to node R. Why is the author belaboring those stupid strategies that can't even see it?" I have two answers to this very reasonable mutter. (1) Breadth-first, depth-first, and progressive-deepening search strategies have been widely used by many persons who were not fully aware of their shortcomings, so it is worth pointing them out. (2) Although the best solution may seem obvious by "inspection" of Figure 3.11, it is not obvious what process went through your mind to enable you to decide that the path to R is best. Moreover, suppose that you could not quickly scan the entire tree, but instead, like the computer, you could look at only one node at a time. Imagine that the tree in Figure 3.11 covered ten sheets of paper and had more than 2000 nodes, instead of only 22. Then imagine looking at the figure through a low-power microscope, so that you can only see $\frac{1}{4}$ square inch of paper at a time. How can you gather enough information to find the minimum cost path, with the smallest amount of fiddling with the position of the paper or the microscope controls, and the minimum amount of straining your memory or scribbling on scratch paper? This roughly corresponds to how the computer sees the problem.

We shall now consider a procedure for finding the minimum-cost path in a tree. I shall dignify this procedure by calling it an *algorithm*, because it will consist of a complete, precise set of rules that could easily be translated into a computer program; and the algorithm has a name, A^T (Algorithm for Trees), so that we may refer to it later. First, we need a little more terminology.

With every node n we shall associate a number called $g(n)$, which is the total cost of the path from the top node to n. Of course, $g(n)$ may not be known for a node in a position of the tree that we have not yet examined.

Every node will have exactly one of the following three designations.

Closed, meaning it has been examined and is no longer of current interest.

Open, meaning it is a candidate for immediate further exploration.

Unknown, meaning it has not yet had a $g(n)$ calculated or been considered otherwise.

The algorithm A^T can be applied to both explicitly and implicitly defined trees. It will begin by focusing its attention upon the top node, and then systematically move down through the tree, examining or generating the deeper nodes as necessary.

Algorithm A^T

1. Initially all nodes and all $g(n)$ values are unknown. Open the top node (i.e., designate it as open) and set g(top node) $= 0$.

2. Select the open node whose value of g is smallest. Call it N. (After step 1, only the top node will be open so it will be the first N. However this step 2 will also be carried out after step 4, at which time there may be several open nodes, or none at all.) If N is a goal node, the path to N is the minimum-cost path, its cost is $g(N)$, and the problem is solved. If no open node exists, there is no solution path in the tree. If two or more nodes have equally small values of g, check whether any is a goal node. If so, choose it and terminate; otherwise choose one arbitrarily to be N.

3. Close node N. Generate all the successors of N and mark them as open. For each successor S of N, calculate $g(S) = g(N) +$ (cost on arc from N to S).

4. Go back to step 2.

Figure 3.12 shows the sequence of steps carried out as A^T is applied to the tree of Figure 3.11.

It can be proved that A^T will always find the minimum-cost path. Moreover, A^T is an optimum algorithm, because it does as little work as possible, in the following sense: no other algorithm that will always find the minimum-cost path can do so by closing fewer nodes that A^T does, except for certain tie situations of little interest. We can see that "number of nodes closed" is a reasonable measure of the calculation effort required by an algorithm, because each time a node is closed we must generate some successors and calculate some values of g.

Adding knowledge to tree search

A tree, with its nodes, arcs, and costs, can conveniently represent certain aspects of a problem. The algorithm A^T is the best algorithm we can ob-

Action	Open nodes	g(Open node)	Closed nodes	Known tree
Open top node		0		
Close top node Open A, B, C, D	A B C D	100 17 1 1	Top	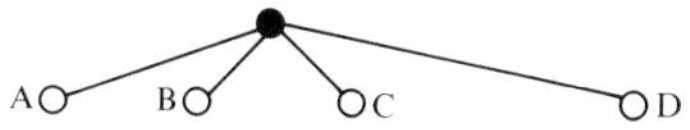
Close C Open G, H	A B D G H	100 17 1 11 21	Top, C	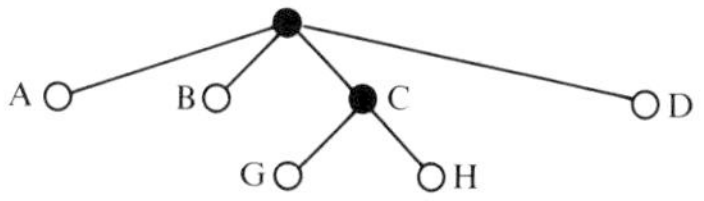
Close D Open I, J	A B G H I J	100 17 11 21 13 2	Top, C, D	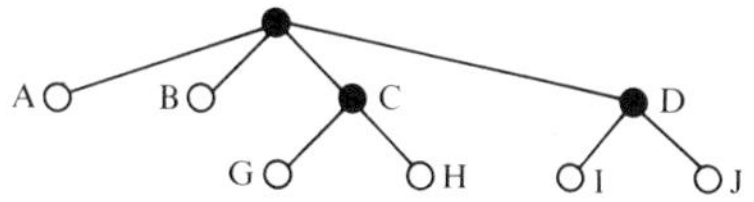
Close J Open N	A B G H I N	100 17 11 21 13 3	Top, C, D, J	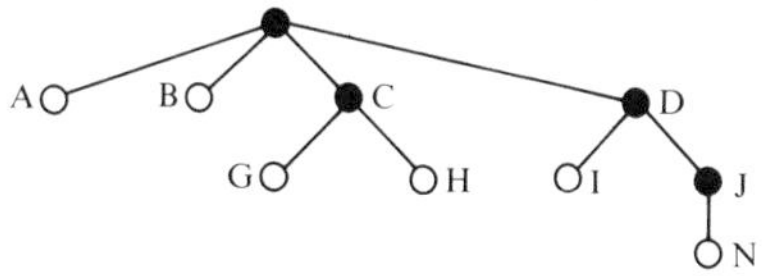
Close N Open P	A B G H I P	100 17 11 21 13 4	Top, C, D, J, N	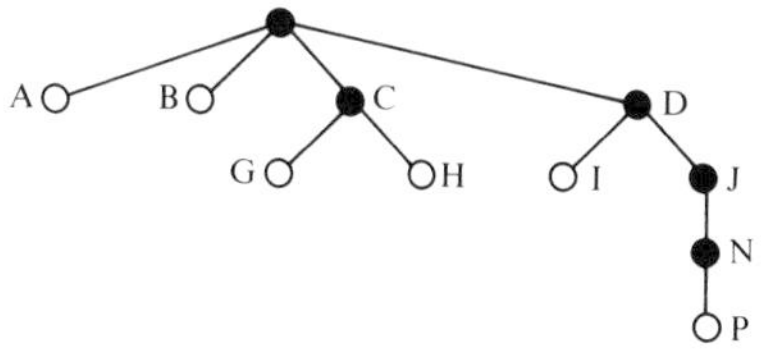
Close P Open R	A B G H I R	100 17 11 21 13 5	Top, C, D, J, N, P	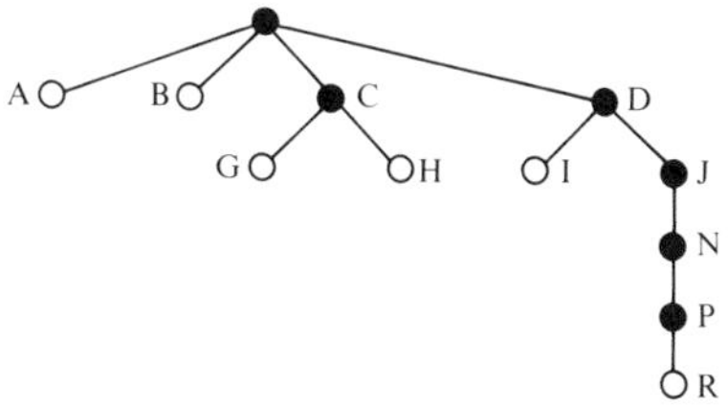
Select R Discover goal				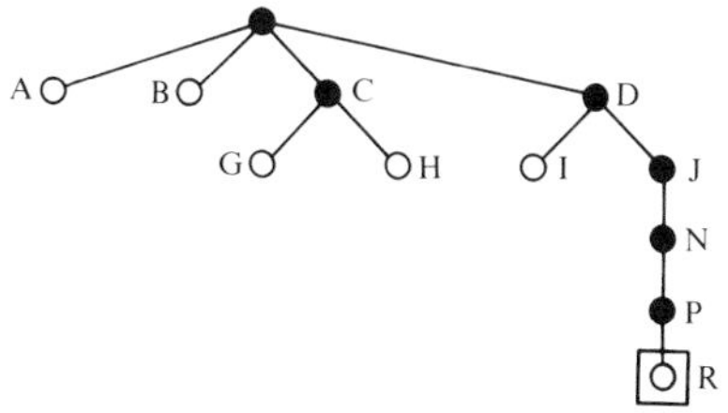

Figure 3.12 Tree search using A^T.

tain for searching the tree while using only the information in the tree itself. Sometimes, however, we have additional knowledge, based upon our understanding of the real problem situation, that is highly relevant to the problem at hand. Until the late 1960's, such a situation gave computer programmers only three choices: (1) ignore the additional knowledge and use a systematic general method such as A^T to search the tree; (2) ignore the tree and try to find a special *ad hoc* solution to the problem based upon the additional knowledge; or (3) try to design a more complex tree representation that builds the extra knowledge into the structure or into the cost values in the tree.

A fourth choice is now available. A new theory permits a certain kind of frequently available additional knowledge to be used to guide the tree search, resulting in a generally useful algorithm that is just as successful and often considerably more efficient than A^T. This algorithm, which we shall call A^{KT} (Algorithm for Knowledgeable Tree search) uses the additional knowledge to supply one number for each node. This number, called $\hat{h}(n)$, is an estimate of the total cost of the minimum-cost path from node n to a goal node. Thus $\hat{h}$ is a guess at the cost of a path that has not yet been discovered. For example, let's look again at the tree of Figures 3.11 and 3.12. After the first step of applying algorithm A^T, we knew that the paths from the top node to C and D both had the same cost, $g(C) = g(D) = 1$, and A^T then picked C arbitrarily as the next node to close. Now suppose instead of picking arbitrarily, A^T could ask an outside expert, "Which node is closer to a goal, C or D?" and the expert replied, "Well, I can't say exactly, but I think it will cost about 10 units to get from C to goal node, and it will cost only about 5 units to get to a goal node from D." That is, the outside information tells us that $\hat{h}(C) = 10$ and that $\hat{h}(D) = 5$. Then a smart algorithm would use this information and decide to pick D rather than C, and eventually find the solution path to R without ever having to open nodes G and H. Note also that even if the outside expert told us that $\hat{h}(B) = 1$, we would not want the algorithm to turn its attention to B, because getting from the root node to B was already too costly ($g(B) = 17$). To formalize all this a bit, let $\hat{f}(n) = g(n) + \hat{h}(n)$, the cost from the root to n plus the estimated cost from n to a goal: $\hat{f}$ estimates the cost of the minimum cost path from the root, to a goal, through node n. If the estimates are any good, we certainly should continue searching the tree from the node with the smallest $\hat{f}$, rather than just the smallest g. More precisely, the algorithm, which is very similar to A^T, may be stated as follows.

Algorithm A^{KT}

1. Initially all nodes and g, $\hat{h}$, and $\hat{f}$ values are unknown. Open the top node, set $g(\text{top node}) = 0$, use additional knowledge to calculate $\hat{h}(\text{top node})$, and set $\hat{f}(\text{top node}) = g(\text{top node}) + \hat{h}(\text{top node})$.

2.   Select the open node whose value of $\hat{f}$ is smallest. Call it N. If N is a goal node, the path to N is the minimum cost path, and its cost is $g(N)$. If no open node exists, there is no solution path in the tree. If two or more nodes have equally small values of $\hat{f}$, check to see if any is a goal node. If so, choose it and terminate; otherwise choose one arbitrarily to be N.

3.   Close node N. Open all the successors of N. For each successor S of N, calculate

$$g(S) = g(N) + (\text{cost on link from N to S}).$$

Use additional knowledge to calculate $\hat{h}(S)$. Let $\hat{f}(S) = g(S)$ and $\hat{h}(S)$.

4. Go back to step 2.

The properties of A^{KT} can be understood as follows. Let $h(n)$ be the cost of the minimum-cost path from n to a goal node: $\hat{h}$ is an estimate of h, which of course is initially unknown. If $\hat{h}$ were a perfect estimator (i.e., if outside knowledge made us so omniscient that we knew precisely what the cost of the path would be) then A^{KT} would be a perfect search routine (i.e., it would close only those nodes that were on the shortest path to a goal).[1] At the other extreme, if we had no outside knowledge we should make $\hat{h}(n) = 0$ for all nodes n (i.e., estimate that we might be just about at a goal node at any time). In this case A^{KT} reduces to precisely A^T. In between $\hat{h} = 0$ and $\hat{h} = h$ we have an interesting range of algorithms. It can be shown that, as long as $\hat{h} \leq h$, A^{KT} is guaranteed to find a minimum-cost solution. Moreover, the closer $\hat{h}$ is to h, the fewer nodes A^{KT} has to close. Also, A^{KT} is optimally efficient in the sense that no other generally successful algorithm can do less work, (i.e., close fewer nodes) unless it has access to better outside knowledge (i.e., can calculate $\hat{h}$ values closer to h).

If $\hat{h} > h$, A^{KT} is no longer guaranteed to find a minimum-cost path. However, if it finds any solution path, A^{KT} will do so in this case with very little work, and the path found may be good enough for many applications.

In order to get a feeling for the usefulness and power of A^{KT}, we shall look at a simple puzzle as an example. The Tower of Hanoi puzzle may be described as follows.

> There are 3 pegs—A, B, and C—and 64 discs of 64 different sizes. The discs have holes in their centers so that they may be stacked on any of the pegs. Initially all the discs are on peg A in size order, with the largest on the bottom and the smallest on

---

[1]Note that it is easy to become omniscient: simply let the "outside knowledge" that produces $\hat{h}$ be gained by doing a complete A^T search to determine the precise minimum-cost path, and use its cost as $\hat{h}$. But this trick simply hides the computation costs in the calculation of $\hat{h}$, instead of reducing them. What we need is an easy way to make a good guess at $\hat{h}$.

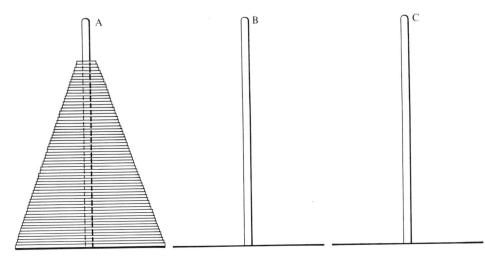

Figure 3.13   Tower of Hanoi puzzle.

the top. The problem is to transfer all the discs from peg A to peg C using peg B as an intermediary. However, only one disc may be moved at a time, and no disc may ever be placed on top of a disc smaller than itself. (See Figure 3.13.)

The name of this puzzle is derived from the legend that some monks in a monastery near Hanoi are working on the puzzle, and the day they complete it the world will come to an end. We need not worry, though, because if they make perfect moves of one disc per second it will take them close to a trillion years to finish.

Since we do not have that much time, we shall simplify the puzzle slightly: instead of 64 discs, suppose there are only 2. If we look at the discs from the side, the problem is to transform

into

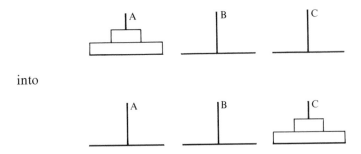

First we must represent the problem by a tree. We shall use a *state description representation.* Each node will represent a legal arrangement of discs, and each arc will represent the action of changing the position of one disc. We shall assume that all actions are equally difficult, so that every arc will have a cost of 1; therefore, the minimum-cost path will be the minimum-length path, i.e., the path consisting of the smallest number of moves.

Figure 3.14 shows the tree as explored by an A^T search. All nodes that appear on the figure have been opened, and those that were subsequently closed are shaded.

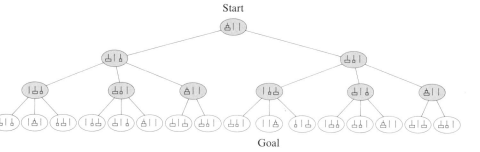

Figure 3.14 A^T search of Tower of Hanoi tree.

Now let us see what we know that might be of use as we traverse the tree. At each node, A^{KT} requires us to estimate the minimum number of steps from any position to a solution, and we would like to be able to make the estimate without a lot of extra computation. Knowing how the puzzle works, we can tell quite a bit just by looking at what is on peg C, the one to which we are trying to transfer the discs. If it has the two discs on it, we have finished, i.e., we are in a goal state. If it is empty, at least two more moves are necessary—one for each disc that must be transferred to it. If the large disc only is on C, we are at least one move away from a solution. Finally, if the small disc only is on C, it will have to be removed before the two discs can be put on in the right order; we are therefore at least three moves from a solution. Thus we can pick $\hat{h}$ just by looking at peg C.

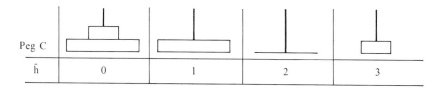

With these values of $\hat{h}$, the search tree for A^{KT} reduces to that of Figure 3.15.

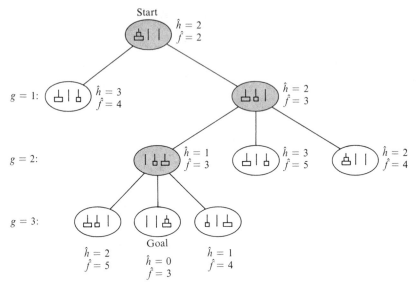

Figure 3.15 A^{KT} search of Tower of Hanoi tree.

Finding paths in general graph structures

Early in this chapter we decided to restrict our representations to tree structures. This restriction permitted us to explore some interesting algorithms, and did not hinder our problem-solving abilities very much. However, it did introduce the following awkward situation: a node representing the same physical situation may occur many times on a tree, and there is no convenient way of letting one occurrence of it know what has been learned by studying the other occurrences. For example, note how many times the configuration

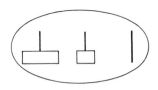

occurs in Figure 3.14; yet there is certainly only one "best" move from this situation no matter what historical developments led up to its occurrence. If we now relax the tree restriction and allow arbitrary graph representations instead, we can completely describe the two-disc Tower of Hanoi puzzle by the state-representation graph in Figure 3.16. As in the tree representation, each node represents a configuration and each arrow represents a legal move by one disc. However, arrows may now go either way; many paths may connect the same nodes, and we must be careful not to follow arrows around in circles while trying to find efficient paths.

Luckily, there is a generalization of the A^{KT} algorithm that works for graphs. It is called the A* (A-star) Algorithm, and it differs from A^{KT} in only one respect: as we go around a graph, we may find alternative ways of getting to the same place. If we find a new way of getting to a

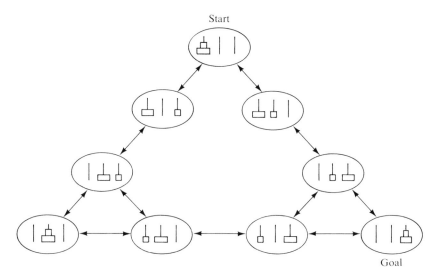

Figure 3.16 Tower of Hanoi state graph.

previously opened node, we must make sure that only the best route to that node is used as the basis for further analysis. This means that sometimes the algorithm should not open successors. Here is the full algorithm.

Algorithm A*

1. Initially all nodes and g, $\hat{h}$, and $\hat{f}$ values are unknown. Open the start node, set $g(\text{start}) = 0$, calculate $\hat{h}(\text{start})$, and set $\hat{f}(\text{start}) = \hat{h}(\text{start})$.

2. Select the open node whose $\hat{f}$ value is smallest. Call it N. If N is a goal node, the path to N is the minimum cost solution path and its cost is $g(N)$. If no open node exists, there is no solution path in the graph. If two or more nodes have equally small values of $\hat{f}$, then if any of them is a goal node, the path to it is the minimum cost solution. Otherwise choose one arbitrarily to be N.

3. Close node N. For each successor S of N, calculate

$$g'(S) = g(N) + (\text{cost on link from N to S}).$$

If S were previously opened and has a previous value $g(S) \leq g'(S)$, then ignore S. Otherwise open S and set $g(S) = g'(S)$. Calculate $\hat{h}(S)$, and $\hat{f}(S) = g(S) + \hat{h}(S)$.

4. Go back to step 2.

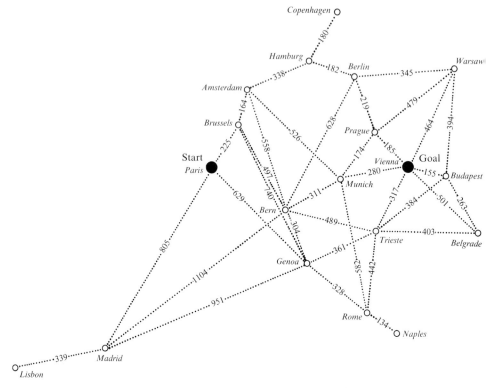

Figure 3.17 Approximate European road distances.

As another example of the power of embodying extra knowledge in the $\hat{h}$ functions, consider the graph of Figure 3.17. Each node of the graph represents a major European city, and each arc represents a major highway route between two cities. The costs on the arcs represent road distances expressed in miles. We may use algorithm A* to find a minimum-cost path—i.e., the shortest road connection in this highway network—between any two cities: for example, from Paris to Vienna. If we assume no extra knowledge—i.e., use $\hat{h} = 0$ for all nodes—then we must consider all roads leading away from Paris, in all directions, for distances of at least 1195 miles, the minimum distance to Vienna along roads in this network. In fact, the search would actually "close" all the following nodes—Paris, Brussels, Amsterdam, Genoa, Bern, Hamburg, Madrid, Copenhagen, Berlin, Munich, Rome, Trieste, Naples, Prague, and Lisbon—before concluding that the minimum-cost path reaches Vienna by way of Brussels, Amsterdam, and Munich. Moreover, considerable additional effort would have been devoted to exploring Portugal, Southern Italy, and Scandinavia, if we had been inconsiderate enough to include more roads in those regions.

Table 3.1   Estimates ($\hat{h}$)

City	Air Distance to Vienna	Air Distance + 20%
Paris	634	760
Brussels	560	672
Madrid	1110	1332
Genoa	435	522
Amsterdam	575	690
Bern	408	490
Munich	220	264
Hamburg	461	553
Trieste	172	206
Rome	475	570
Berlin	322	386
Prague	155	186

Of course, we "know" that one gets from Paris to Vienna by going generally east, so it is futile to look for a shorter route by way of Madrid or Copenhagen; but how can this "knowledge" be embedded in the formal algorithm? Easily, it turns out. Let $\hat{h}(n)$ be the airline distance from city n to Vienna. If we move to a city closer to Vienna, $\hat{h}$ will go down while g goes up, keeping the value of $\hat{f}$ fairly constant. If we move away from Vienna, however, both g and $\hat{h}$ will increase, making $\hat{f}$ much larger and therefore reducing the chances of closing nodes, i.e., exploring further, in those directions. Also, since $\hat{h}$, the airline distance, is certainly always less than h, the actual road distance, we can be sure that A* will find the best (minimum-cost) solution.

Table 3.1 is a chart of approximate airline distances to Vienna. By using these estimates as $\hat{h}$, A* closes only the following nodes: Paris, Brussels, Amsterdam, Genoa, Bern, Munich, Trieste, and Hamburg.

Finally, we can improve the search even more by "knowing" that road distance is always at least 20 percent longer than air distance, so that 1.2 times air distance would be a "better" $\hat{h}$—i.e., an $\hat{h}$ that is larger than our previous $\hat{h}$, but still less than h. With these values, given in the last column of Table 3.1, the search proceeds even more efficiently, closing only Paris, Brussels, Amsterdam, Genoa, and Munich. In fact, the only node closed that is not on the solution path is Genoa, which is on a reasonably competitive alternative route.

I have just presented some of the basics for a theory of how to solve real problems with the aid of formal graph structures. In concluding this section, I mention briefly some additional modifications or variations of this evolving theory that have been studied, but whose details are beyond the scope of this presentation.

g versus $\hat{h}$. In our presentation of A* we set $\hat{f} = g + \hat{h}$, giving equal weight to g, the cost incurred along the path thus far, and $\hat{h}$, the estimated cost yet to be expended. In fact, g and $\hat{h}$ may be given different weights.

A* is guaranteed to find some solution if we use $\hat{f} = wg + (1 - w)\hat{h}$ with any positive value of w up to one: $w = 1/2$ is equivalent to the equal weighting system we have used; w closer to zero emphasizes the $\hat{h}$ part of $\hat{f}$, thereby concentrating on the remaining costs and neglecting past investments, like the good poker player who pays much less attention to what he has put into a pot in the past than to what he can expect to get out of it in the future; w closer to one emphasizes the g part, and is much more concerned with finding the best solution than with reducing the amount of effort needed to find some solution.

Partial Closures. We have always treated the operation of "closing a node" as one step, in which all the successors of the node must be enumerated and their $\hat{f}$'s calculated. An alternative theory, which has not yet been fully developed, should permit only one or a small number of successors to be enumerated at a time, and the resulting partial graphs to be explored before returning to generate more successors.

Costs. The only costs considered thus far in our theory are the costs explicitly stated on the arcs. Some provision should be made for weighing in the effort costs of closing nodes and calculating $\hat{h}$'s.

Bidirectional search. In looking for a path through a bidirectional graph, significant savings can sometimes be achieved by treating both ends of the path as starting nodes and "growing" subgraphs until they join. More generally, if some intermediate nodes are known to be on the solution path, they may be used as stepping stones to help direct the search. In such cases the joining conditions are rather subtle and one must be careful that the extra effort required to recognize a path when one is found is not more than the effort saved by using bidirectional techniques.

Game trees

No book about smarter computers would be complete without some discussion of games and how computers can play them. Games are enjoyed by people of all ages and cultures. They provide a never-ending source of entertainment and intellectual stimulation. The oriental game of Go has been played for about four-thousand years. Although its rules are simple enough to explain in a few minutes and novices can quickly enjoy playing it, the strategies are so subtle that a lifetime of study is needed to become an expert. Although only about four-hundred years old, the game of chess is much more widely known in the western world. Most people would agree that anyone who has developed the ability to play chess well deserves our respect for his demonstration of at least certain aspects of intelligence and powers of concentration. One philosopher (and computer critic) believed the effective formulation of chess knowledge was an ability so uniquely human that a few years ago he said, "No computer can play even an amateur-level game of chess." (Shortly afterward he was beaten in across-the-board play by a computer at MIT.)

Naturally, computer programmers find the goal of developing competent game-playing programs an exciting challenge, but there are much more practical motivations for our interest in games. Games have been found to be a useful model for much of human behavior. The problem of deciding what move to make next while striving toward some goal, in competition or in cooperation with other people, arises every day—in business, in politics, in the courtroom, on the battlefield, even in romance. Perhaps if we understood the processes of making such decisions well enough to enable a computer to become, say, the world's champion chess player, we would learn how to program computers to help us more broadly in our thinking about more practical problems (although we should probably prefer to leave computers out of romance).

We shall use a very simple game to introduce the basic approach of analyzing two person games. The game, Last One Loses, is played with a single pile of chips. The two players, A and B, take turns removing chips from the pile. At each move, a player must take at least one chip, and he is permitted to take two or three if he wishes. The player who picks up the last chip loses. Suppose we begin with seven chips in the pile, and player A goes first. He has three possible moves: to pick up one, two, or three chips. If we represent the possible moves by arcs, we can show all possible moves in the game by the tree structure of Figure 3.18.[2] This *game tree* differs from the trees we discussed in the previous section in one important respect: at alternate levels of depth in the tree, alternate players choose which move to make. Moreover, the two players are trying to achieve two different, in fact two opposite, goals. Instead of trying to find a single path to a single kind of goal, we must analyze a game tree by constantly switching viewpoints to represent the decisions likely to be made by the opposing players. Each depth level—called a *ply* of the game tree—in Figure 3.18 is labeled with the name of the player who has the next choice at that level. If there are no chips left in the pile when a player's turn comes up, that player has won; therefore, Figure 3.18 gives the name of the winning player at the end of each possible sequence of moves.

Game trees are best analyzed from the bottom up, because at the bottom we have the most information; in this case, who has won. We would like to use this knowledge to calculate what the best move is at the top of the tree—i.e., from the initial position. Look first at the extreme

---

[2]The numbers on the arcs show the number of stones picked up, rather than indicating a cost as in our previous tree examples. The number in each node shows how many stones are left.

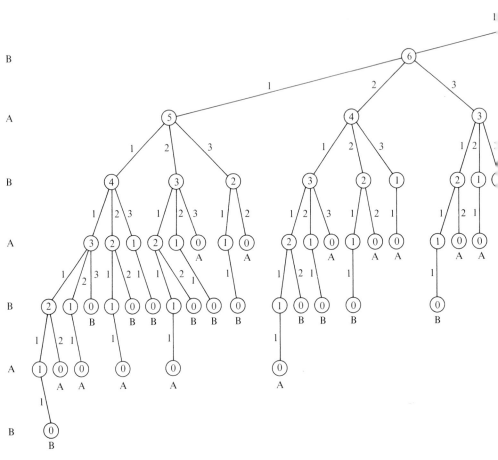

Figure 3.18 Game tree for Last One Loses.

left-hand branch, representing the move sequence in which each player always picks up just one stone. At the bottom of the branch, we see that B wins. Moving up one ply, we see that A had no choice at his move; there was only one chip available, and he had to pick it up, permitting B to win. Therefore that node of the tree may also be identified as a position from which B must win. Going back one more level, we see that at B's move he has a choice of whether to pick up one or both of the remaining chips. If he picks one, he puts A into the "B wins" position; if he picks both, then A wins. Assuming that B plays sensibly and wants to win, he will always pick one chip when there are two left and it is his move. Therefore this situation can also be marked as a "B wins" position:

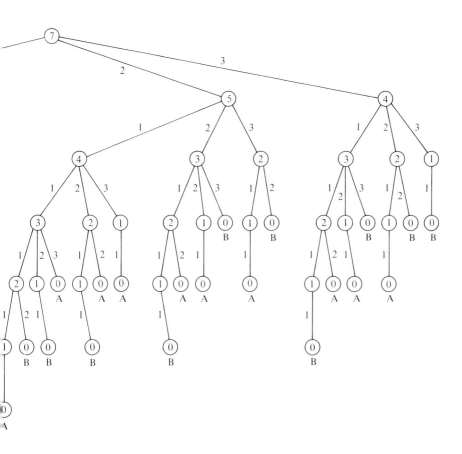

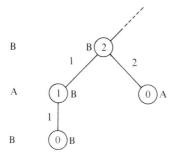

In general, if it is B's move and any successor position is marked as a win for B, then B can choose a winning move, so the current position may

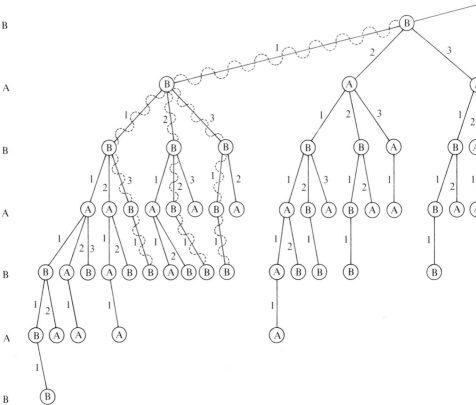

Figure 3.19 Backed-up game values.

also be marked as a win for B. However, if all successors are wins for A, then anything B does will lose, so the current position is marked as a win for A. Similarly at an A move, if any successor is marked with an A, the current position should be so marked; otherwise the current position is marked B.

Figure 3.19 shows the game tree after all terminal values have been "backed up" to the top. Since the top node is marked with an A, we now know that the game Last One Loses with an initial pile of seven chips can always be won by the first player, but only if he picks up two chips on his first move, as shown by the dark lines on Figure 3.19. If he picks up one or three, the second player can seize control by maintaining his winning options (wavy lines on Figure 3.19).

The technique of "looking ahead" by growing the game tree, and then "backing up" the terminal values in order to analyze the current

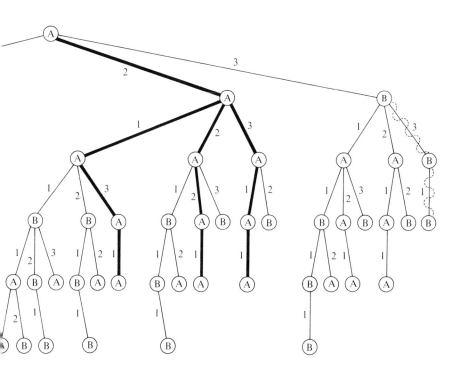

---

position, has been the basic tool for computer game-playing programs. It works perfectly for simple games like Last One Loses or Tic Tac Toe, but for most games that people find interesting, the game tree is much too large for even the best modern computer to explore. The technique must be modified and adapted to special situations. We list here some of the most important modifications that have been developed.

TRUNCATED LOOK-AHEAD AND EVALUATION

In our Last One Loses example, we followed every possible move sequence until the game was over, and we could see who had won. In more complex games, it usually is not necessary to go to the bitter end; one can follow a line of play for a while and decide that, "A is so far ahead he is sure to win" or "A is in serious trouble," even though the technical end of the game is not yet in sight. If we could be more precise, we might assign to each position a number that indicates who has the advantage and how great the advantage is. For example, suppose we let $+1$ mean that player A has a sure win, -1 mean that B must win, and 0 mean that the game is exactly even. The $+.5$ would mean that A is doing fairly well, $-.9$ that B has a huge advantage, $+.01$ that A has a very slight advantage, and so on.

We can try to design a program that will calculate such numbers. Such a program is called an *evaluation function*. It takes as its data some measurable characteristics of the game position. For example, in a game such as checkers or chess where the number of pieces a player has is of major importance, one simple evaluation function might calculate:

$$\frac{(\text{number of A's pieces}) - (\text{number of B's pieces})}{(\text{number of A's pieces}) + (\text{number of B's pieces})}$$

The important thing about evaluation functions is that they are rarely perfect. A perfect evaluation function could simply look at the alternative moves available and reliably tell which one is best, without needing any look-ahead. For very simple games such strategies may exist, but we would not dignify them by the name "evaluation function." After all, they have nothing to evaluate. They just calculate the right choice.[3]

When, as is usual, no perfect strategy is known, we design the best evaluation function we can think of. Then we assume that the closer the game is to the end, the more accurate the evaluation function will be, because even a crude evaluation should be able to recognize a clear win or loss. Therefore, the basic game-analysis strategy is to look ahead as far as space and time permit, evaluate each of the positions at the tips of the game tree's branches, and then back up those values to get a value (and playing strategy) for the top node. The backing-up procedure is only slightly more complicated than the one presented for Last One Loses: when it is A's move, assign to a position the largest of the values of its successor positions (since that is surely the move that A should choose); when it is B's move, assign the smallest of the successor position's values. This is sometimes called the *minimax* procedure. (If we let the value of every A terminal node be $+1$ and that of every B be -1 in Figure 3.18 then the backed-up results in Figure 3.19 are exactly the same as would be produced by minimaxing.)

TERMINATING CONDITIONS

The earliest game-playing programs that used a minimax strategy simply set some depth limit—e.g., seven plys—and then looked ahead along all

---

[3]In fact, such a strategy exists for Last One Loses: pick as many chips as necessary to make the number left in the pile a number that can be written $4n + 1$ for some integer n equal to or greater than zero, and you will win. If that is not possible, make any move at all; you will lose unless your opponent makes a mistake.

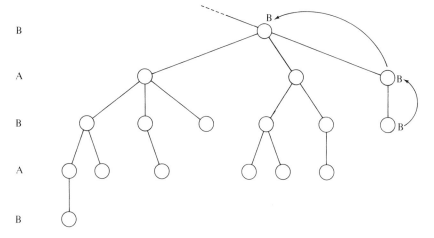

Figure 3.20   Tree pruning, by propagating value from one branch up the tree.

possible move sequences to precisely that depth. This sometimes led to applying the evaluation function to some peculiar situations for which it was ill suited. For example, suppose the evaluation function is similar to the piece-advantage measure given above, and the depth limit happens to cut off the action in the middle of an exchange. If a major capture is about to take place, then measuring piece advantage at the current position will give a false impression of the situation. Current programs generally look ahead to different depths along different lines of play, trying to find "quiet" positions in which the evaluation function is most likely to yield accurate information.

TREE PRUNING METHODS

Refer to the extreme right-hand branch of Figures 3.18 and 3.19. If we begin backing up from the B win at the tip of the right-hand branch, we quickly see that the top node of that branch, a B move, can achieve a B win (Figure 3.20). Therefore the rest of this branch need not be explored, for surely no additional information is needed to help B decide on his move. Similarly, if we had decided to explore the center branch of the complete tree first—the A-picks-two move, which happens to be the best move—we would have discovered that the top position (seven chips, A to move) is a win for A, without even considering the other two moves. In fact, it is a common property of the minimax procedure that information gained from exploration of part of the game tree makes it unnecessary to explore other parts of the tree.[4] This reduction in effort is most effective

---

[4]The formal procedure that makes optimum use of such information to reduce the amount of effort needed in evaluating a game tree has been called the "α–β principle," because it depends upon the use of two key parameters that have been named α and β.

if the part of the tree explored first has the best path in it. If the best move sequences happen to be the last ones explored, little savings can be realized and the entire tree may have to be examined. If the best move sequences are pursued first, then most of the tree will turn out to be ignorable, and the effort that would have gone into exploring the ignored nodes can instead be used to look ahead about twice as deep along the preferred path. The extended look ahead, in turn, makes the resulting move choice more accurate because the evaluation function is applied much closer to the end of the game. Even more important, note that a game tree is usually given implicitly by an initial position and a definition of legal moves. If the tree is partly grown in the direction of the right moves, a quick minimax evaluation may show that the rest of the tree need not even be generated, thereby saving considerable computation. Therefore considerable attention should be devoted to trying to explore the most likely nodes first. This can be done, for example, by applying the evaluation function at each level as the tree is generated and rearranging the nodes before proceeding deeper, so that the moves with the highest values will be examined first.

THE USE OF KNOWLEDGE IN GAMES

The minimax procedure and related game-tree-search methods are mathematically interesting and occasionally extremely powerful devices. At one time some scientists thought that these techniques, with some minor future development, were all that would be needed to enable a computer to achieve top-level performance at almost any game. We have now resigned ourselves to the fact that such formal search methods solve only a small, though important, part of the game-playing problem. Most interesting games have many facets that simply cannot be incorporated into a single numeric evaluation function. Success in chess, for example, requires an awareness of offensive and defensive maneuvers, forks and pins, long-range plans that need to be carried out or abandoned, standard openings and end games, and so on. One way of using such knowledge might be to supervise the ordering of look-ahead positions in order to assist the tree-pruning methods. However, it is more likely that the basic structure of a game-playing program must be determined by special properties of the game, as we learn how to build knowledge about such properties into programs; and the widely known game-tree-analysis methods presented above will be used only as a subroutine—a useful member of our bag of tools, but by no means capable of a major success on its own.

Most of the major game-playing programs in use at this time (1975) are based upon look-ahead and minimax techniques, with minor amounts of additional knowledge of the specific game tacked in. As might be expected, such programs have been most successful in games that have challenged the memory and bookkeeping ability of human players, and least successful in games about which there is considerable knowledge and literature. For example, there is a family of games reputedly from Africa and the Pacific Islands called either Kalah or Whari. In these games, there are no more than six possible moves from each position, each of which might cause complex changes in the situation. Short-range tactics and precision are extremely important, but there is very little long-range strategy. Computer programs at MIT and Stanford have probably been world's champions at this game for close to ten years. We cannot be sure, because skilled human players have been hard to locate.

Checkers is a game with somewhat more strategic interest and complexity. Still, most games between human experts are draws. In a non-draw game, it is generally not possible to identify the "winning" line of play; instead, one can usually find the "mistake" that the loser made. Dr. Samuel's program, discussed in Chapter 2, has an evaluation function good enough to avoid most mistakes. (It also has an interesting learning ability, which will be described in Chapter 5.) For several years it has been a master-level player, able to hold its own—but not to win regularly—among championship-level human players.

Chess is a much more complex, strategically based game. Although it has had more programming effort than any other game, the results are mediocre. The best programs (those at MIT, Northeastern, and Carnegie-Mellon, and several others including a Russian program that won the 1974 International Computer Chess Tournament) can beat most casual chess players, but do not do very well in tournament competition with humans. Look-ahead and minimax strategies are useful, but not enough specialized chess knowledge has yet been captured by a machine.

We conclude this section, as we began it, with the ancient game of Go. Whereas chess or checkers typically have in the neighborhood of ten to twenty possible moves at each position, Go usually has more than a hundred. Moreover, the evaluation of a position can be an extremely complex, subtle operation. As a result minimax strategies applied to the entire game are hopelessly swamped. Although local look-ahead is undoubtedly useful in certain tactical situations, some better organizing principle is needed to govern the overall play. No particularly effective one has yet been found. The small effort that has so far been devoted to the discouraging task of developing a Go-playing program has produced only weak, novice-level players.

Summary

Search is an important part of most problem-solving processes. The key ingredients in effective search are these.
1. Choosing the proper search space.
2. Pursuing an efficient, systematic search through the space.

3. Using knowledge of the problem domain whenever possible to guide the search.

The search space for many problems that we would like to solve with computers may be represented by *graphs*. A graph is a collection of points called *nodes* and connections called *arcs* that go from one node to another. Arcs may be *directed* (one way) or *bidirectional* (two way). When we traverse an arc we go from the *predecessor* node to the *successor* node of the arc. Arcs sometimes have a number associated with them, which represents the *cost* of traversing the arc.

A *tree* is a special type of directed graph that has a unique *root* node, and for which every node has a unique predecessor. Trees are simpler to analyze and search than graphs, and therefore trees are a preferred form of representation for many problems. However, the more flexible structure of graphs makes them much more natural representations for certain problems.

Trees and graphs may be used to represent real problems in a variety of ways. For example, in a *state description* formulation each node represents a stage in some process, and each arc represents an action that moves the processor from one stage to another. In a *problem reduction* formulation, each node represents a complete subproblem or subtask, and the arcs tell how the subproblem solutions must be combined in order to solve the complete problem.

The nodes and arcs of graphs may represent physical objects or states of the world, conceptual or mathematical objects such as equations, or simply an accumulation of facts or hypotheses. Once a problem has been represented by a tree or graph structure, the remaining task usually requires finding a complete path that traverses the structure from the root, or some other designated starting node, to a node with some special characteristics that identify it as a *goal* node.

Trees and graphs may be defined implicitly as well as explicitly. If defined implicitly, they may have an infinite number of nodes—even though each node must have only a finite number of successors. Procedures for finding paths in graphs may be compared and evaluated according to how effective they are at finding solution paths, how good the paths they find are (the "best" path is one which costs the least to traverse), and how much time and effort the procedure must expend to find good paths.

Typical search procedures include *breadth first*, which tries to look for solution paths in all directions at once; *depth first*, which tries to follow each path it discovers as far as possible before considering any others; and *progressive deepening*, which is a simple compromise between breadth first and depth first. A more effective compromise strategy, called A^T, is essentially a *cost-first* strategy; at every opportunity it extends whichever known path is least costly at the moment, and thus is guaranteed always to find the best (minimum cost) solution path.

Sometimes we have useful knowledge about a problem that is not captured in its tree or graph representation. It may still be possible to use this extra knowledge in order to help the search procedure. In particular, if we have some way of calculating an estimate of the cost of getting from a particular node to a goal node, then the algorithm called A* provides an optimum way of using this calculation to improve the efficiency of the search procedure.

A special kind of tree representation has been developed for the computer analysis of two-person games. In these game trees, a node represents a position in the game and arcs represent alternative move possibilities. Since alternate moves are made by opposing players, an impartial procedure that analyzes such game trees must reverse its view-point at each depth level. The *minimax* procedure is a rule for calculating the best move, assuming the information in the tree is accurate and neither player makes a blunder. Many "tree pruning" methods have been developed to improve the efficiency of the basic minimax method, and the resulting computer programs do quite well when playing simple games. For complex games such as chess and Go, however, game trees, even with the help of today's most powerful computers, cannot represent a large enough portion of the game to play a critical role in choosing the best move. Much more specialized knowledge of particular properties of each game must be built into the programs before computers can become masters of such intellectual games.

SUGGESTED READINGS

Doran, J. E., "New Developments of the Graph Traverser." In *Machine Intelligence,* Vol. 2, E. Dale and D. Michie (eds.), Oliver and Boyd, Edinburgh, 1968.

Hart, P. E., N. J. Nilsson, and B. Raphael, "A Formal Basis for the Heuristic Determination of Minimum Cost Paths." *Institute of Electrical and Electronic Engineers, Transactions on Systems Science and Cybernetics,* Vol. 4, no. 2, pp. 100–107, 1968.

Newborn, M. *Computer Chess.* Academic Press, New York, 1974.

Pohl, I., "Heuristic Search Viewed as Path Finding in a Graph." *Artificial Intelligence,* Vol. 1, no. 3, pp. 193–204, 1970.

4 Problem Solving Methods: Background and Formal Approaches

Recognition and derivation

When my college roommate and I worked together on mathematics problems, a striking difference in our approaches was apparent. He would often look at a complex problem, quickly write down an answer (almost always the correct one), and then attempt to justify it. He often had no idea how the answer had occurred to him, and had difficulty generating a complete, step-by-step proof—why bother with a proof; he already knew the answer. I, on the other hand, rarely had such flashes of inspiration. Instead, I had a knack for constructing systematic derivations and would plod along from the problem statement towards a logically proven answer. Of course, it was helpful for me to know in advance what the answer was likely to be, so we made a great team.

Our approaches illustrate two complementary ways of viewing any problem-solving task. His approach was based upon *recognition:* hunt through some search space—where the space may even be defined only subconsciously—and select something that seems to shout, "I'm the answer!" Then the solution path through the search space must be constructed, or some other argument generated, to justify the selection. My approach was more one of *derivation:* having no advance idea of what the answer would be like, I would use the information in the problem statement to focus in toward the solution by stripping away alternative possibilities until only the right answer remained.

Of course, one might say that there is no fundamental difference between the recognition approach and the derivation approach. An answer can be "recognized" only by the use of some recognition criteria, and the explicit statement and systematic application of such criteria might be called a derivational process. Similarly, a derivation might well be viewed as a search through some formally defined space for an object that is recognized as a valid solution or proof. Still, the flavors of the two kinds of approach are different. A recognition approach emphasizes a separation between the process of searching for the answer, and the recognition of the answer when it occurs. The search principles could be quite general: i.e., applicable to many different kinds of problems. Such search principles were the subject of the previous chapter. The generate and test processes of Chapter 2, (pp. 50–51) show how search (generate) can be completely separated from recognition (test).

Derivation approaches emphasize particular methods for proceeding directly and systematically from a problem statement toward a solution. Such methods, which blend answer recognition right into the search process (as its final action), have usually been developed initially to be useful for some very specialized class of problems—for example, the derivation of the solution to a first-order differential equation, or the derivation of the composition of a chemical compound. A derivational problem-solving method is highly structured to work from a particular representation of the problem towards a particular form of solution, and therefore cannot be transferred easily to other kinds of problems. However, attempts are often made, sometimes with considerable success, to apply such specialized methods more widely than they were originally intended to be.

Examples of both recognitional and derivational approaches have been programmed for computers, and each type of approach plays an important role in giving computers certain problem-solving abilities. The recognition approach is best known for its use in the field called *pattern recognition.* This subfield of computer science aims at developing the ability of computers to "recognize" patterns of data, such as the appearances of printed characters or the sounds of spoken words. Recognition here usually consists of classifying the data into one of a number of predetermined categories: i.e., the system would recognize that a printed character is the letter Q, or that a spoken word is "watermelon."

Computer study of the derivational approach has focused upon the derivation of formal proof methods for mathematical logic. Such logical proof methods are of special interest because they give the machine a basis for logical reasoning. The computer can then apply its reasoning techniques to a wide variety of subject domains, from mathematics to science to everyday common-sense problems.

The next section of this chapter will outline some of the main ideas of how computers do pattern recognition or, as it is more precisely called, pattern classification. Then, in the remainder of the chapter, we shall see how to computerize formal logical reasoning. The following chapter will consider how a computer might perform informal "common-sense" reasoning, and how formal and informal deductive methods can be combined into powerful automatic problem-solving systems.

Classification

Here is one way of viewing many problem-solving tasks. We know several possible answers, one of which is almost certain to apply to each problem. Whenever a new problem comes along, our task is to select the most appropriate answer. Call the answers *categories,* and the questions, *samples.* The task we have just mentioned can best be described as *classification:* take a brand-new sample, and classify it by naming the category or categories to which it belongs.

Classification is one of the most common and most basic operations in science and technology. Botanists classify plants. Librarians classify books. Mathematicians classify numbers. Physicists classify particles. Astronomers (and Hollywood producers) classify heavenly bodies. In almost every case, we know in advance the names and significant characteristics of perhaps a few dozen, or even a few hundred, categories, and must tell where the new sample lies in the established system.

Categories can be established in a variety of ways. They may be defined by some clear objective characteristics: "A rational number may be written as the ratio of two integers," or "A mammal is an animal form in which mothers nurse their young." Categories may be established by example: "Red Giants are stars that are more like Antares and Betelgeuse than any other category of stars." Categories may have many known members, or none at all: "A tachyon is a fundamental particle that always travels faster than the speed of light."

Occasionally a sample comes along that does not seem to fit any of the established categories: a duck-billed platypus, or a quasi-stellar object. On such occasions the scientist must decide whether to force the sample into the system (i.e., pick the closest known category as the answer) or change the system (i.e., create a new category). If he is too willing to add new categories, then the system will become splintered and lose much of its descriptive value; if he is too conservative and refuses ever to change the system, then the rigidity of the structure will prevent the categories from being "good" answers: i.e., precise classifications of the samples. The question of whether to modify a classification system constantly challenges the judgment of the scientists who most use the system. Another complication is that any basic change to the system may have complex ramifications throughout the system; for example, when a new category is added, many samples previously placed in other categories might need to be transferred to the new one.

Computer scientists became deeply interested in the techniques of classification in the late 1950's. This interest resulted largely from the simultaneous developments of a specific need for automatic classification methods, and a technical approach for achieving such methods. The need was for a method by which a computer could recognize printed characters; although computer data had normally been restricted to punched cards or magnetic signals, many new applications held promise of becoming feasible if computers could directly sense and understand optical images. Although the problem of identifying hand-printed characters is a clear problem of classification ("which of the 26 letter categories or 10 numeral categories does a given sample belong to?") this problem was initially thought of in terms of the perceptual recognition of visual patterns, and therefore was called a pattern-recognition task.

The original techniques proposed for automatic pattern classification were based upon studies of neurophysiology. In the 1950's scientists studying how nerve cells operate, and how groups of nerve cells are interconnected in living animals, began constructing theories that explained the elementary perceptual behavior of animals such as frogs and cats. Simplified versions of the organizational structures defined in these theories could be built, and the resulting devices were capable of performing elementary tasks of classification. The first such devices were specially designed combinations of electronic components, but by the early 1960's comparable performance could be obtained by appropriate programs for general-purpose digital computers. The interests of the physiologists, who wanted to understand natural biological systems, soon diverged from those of the computer scientists, who wanted to achieve improved problem-solving performance with their computer programs. Current pattern recognition algorithms bear little resemblance to current concepts of the behavior of brains. Instead, pattern recognition has developed into a major subfield of computer science, with its own terminology, professional associations, and publications. Within it a vast literature has developed, containing many esoteric mathematical results as well as practical recipes concerning automatic systems that not only can perform effective classification, but also can create and improve their own classification systems. It would take too much space and mathematical sophistication to discuss in depth the leading pattern-recognition techniques that have been developed. However, I think it is worthwhile to devote the rest of this section to a brief and admittedly oversimplified summary of the principal ideas.

Like almost all problem-solving methods, classification requires that the sample data first be represented in a certain way. In particular, the description of a sample to be classified must consist of a list of numbers. The number of numbers in the list, and the interpretation of each number, must be decided in advance by the designer of the system. The representational problem of creating the list of numbers to represent a real object—such as a newly discovered lizard or a newly composed symphony—has all the difficulties of other representation problems, as discussed in Chapter 2. The representation process may also omit key features of the sample, especially qualities that cannot easily be captured by numbers. Any such omission naturally reduces the effectiveness of the eventual classification. These problems of creating the representation are discussed in pattern-recognition literature under such headings as *pre-processing* and *feature extraction.* No widely useful general principles seem possible, since each type of object has unique characteristics that must be represented. Therefore most attention has been focused on the task of classifying samples once they have been represented.

The simplest classification problem is the *one-dimensional* problem, in which each sample is represented by a single number. For concreteness, let us suppose that we wish to classify the male population of San Francisco, and we represent each male by a number which is his age expressed in years. Each category will define an age group: i.e., it will contain males who are near each other in age. One way of specifying the categories is to divide the row of numbers into labeled regions; then each sample will simply be placed in the category named by the region containing the number of the sample. (See Figure 4.1.) For each new sample (male), we take his age, determine its place in the row, and see what category he falls into. This system assumes that we can firmly specify the boundaries between the categories before the classification process begins.

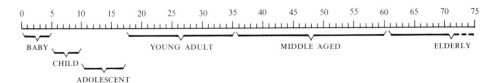

Figure 4.1   Categories by age.

A common alternative approach is to specify one typical member as a *prototype* of each class, rather than to specify the boundaries between classes. (Figure 4.2) This approach requires a little more work, but gives us a little more flexibility, during the classification process.
Given a new sample, say an 18-year old, how can we decide which category to place him in? We could take the label of the *closest* prototype, and

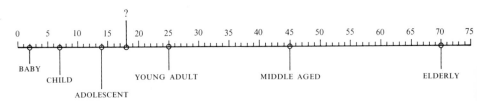

Figure 4.2   Age prototypes.

call him ADOLESCENT; or we could say that since the YOUNG ADULT prototype is farther from its neighbors than the earlier prototypes, it should
"control" a larger portion of the line, and therefore the YOUNG ADULT
classification is more appropriate for an 18-year-old. We might let ourselves be influenced by the previously observed individuals in the population from which our sample was drawn. For example, Figure 4.3,*a*
shows some samples drawn from a hypothetical group of high school
students and their teachers; Figure 4.3,*b* shows some ages of members of
a newspaper dealers' and newsboys' association. In which category would
you put the 18-year-old in each case?

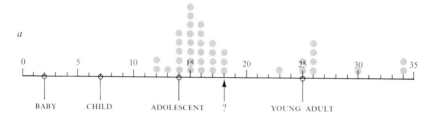

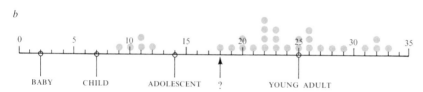

Figure 4.3 Distributions of ages. (*a*) High school students and teachers.
(*b*) Newspaper dealers and newsboys.

Perhaps you feel that the labels ADOLESCENT and YOUNG ADULT,
with corresponding prototypes of 14 and 25, are not appropriate for these
problems. Then your pattern classification method should—and most do—
permit the creation of new pattern prototypes and modification of old
ones. One commonly used procedure is to collect some samples from the
subject population, study them for a while, decide on that basis how
many prototypes or regions should be created, where they should be
placed, and how they should be used to help classify future samples,
and then proceed with the classification. From the data of Figure 4.3,*a*,
for example, we might decide that the category STUDENT should cover
the range from 11 to 19, and everything above that should be labeled
TEACHER.

One-dimensional representations are rather restrictive and uninteresting. Suppose we wish to categorize people as being either skinny,
normal, or fat; then we need at least two numbers for each sample
person: height and weight. We can plot these on a two-dimensional
graph, where the horizontal coordinate is height, and the vertical co-

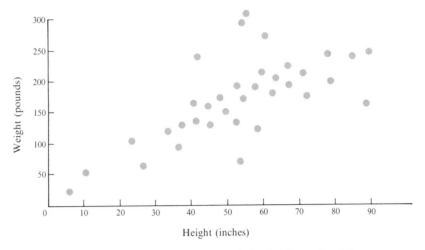

Figure 4.4 A distribution of people by height and weight.

ordinate is weight. Figure 4.4 plots a typical group of people. If we use a *region* approach, the simplest way to divide up the plane is with a couple of straight lines to define FAT, NORMAL, and SKINNY regions (Figure 4.5,*a*); but this division oversimplifies the situation—e.g., by calling all babies normal. If we want more precision and flexibility, we might use broken line segments (Figure 4.5,*b*), second-degree curves such as ellipses and parabolas (Figure 4.5,*c*), or more complex curves (Figure 4.5,*d*). Of course, these latter region boundaries are quite complex to describe and calculate analytically, so they are not often used.

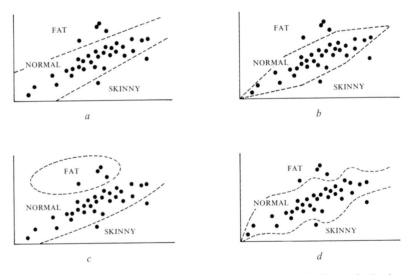

Figure 4.5. Some types of region boundaries. (*a*) Straight lines. (*b*) Broken line. (*c*) Second-degree curves. (*d*) Arbitrary curves.

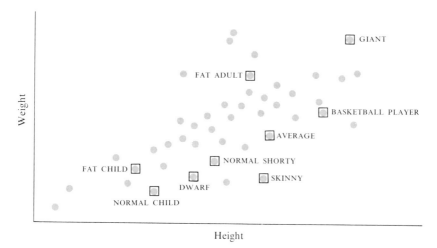

Figure 4.6 Some height-and-weight prototypes.

The prototype (rather than the region) approach is not very useful for large, diffuse categories such as these. It is more helpful if we are interested in many more-finely discriminated classifications, such as those of Figure 4.6. Here each prototype may be viewed as a precise definition or *template* against which other samples may be measured.

The idea of prototypes as templates might be clearer if we look at Figure 4.7, which classifies some upper-case letters of the alphabet from a common print font. The two features we measured here are width and number of straight line strokes. (Curved lines were ignored in the stroke count.)

We see that some letters—e.g., E and I—are well separated in this two-dimensional "feature space," so that samples selected from any printed page are likely to be represented by points that are very close to unique prototypes and therefore will be easy to categorize. Some parts of the space, however, are quite crowded, with prototypes of many different letters—e.g., Z, H, and A—almost coinciding, so samples of these letters will be impossible to distinguish from each other. The reason the system can confuse such obviously different letters is that the features we have measured to produce our pairs of numbers—our *representation*—did not include the important distinguishing features within these letter groups.

For good letter classification, we need a representation that is almost like a template or stencil of each letter; it has to capture all the important features of the shape. Unfortunately, the shapes of the letters of the alphabet are too complex to describe thoroughly with only two numbers. We need perhaps as many as ten or more numbers, representing such measurements as width, number of straight lines, number of curved lines, number of line junctions, number of enclosed areas, number of openings as seen from the right side, and so on. Similarly, in order

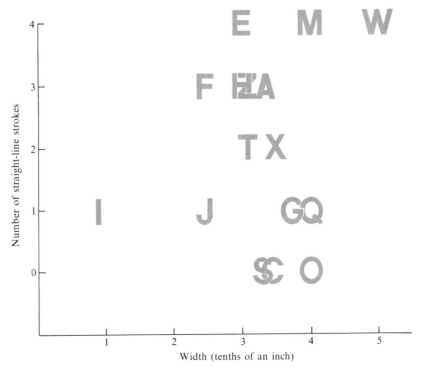

Figure 4.7 Classification of letters by strokes and width.

to classify people properly—e.g., for a computer dating service—we need numbers representing not only height and weight, but also age, sex, and perhaps body type, racial background, political beliefs, hair length, sexual habits, and so on.

A single number can be thought of as a point on a line, and a pair of numbers as a point in a plane. What can we do with these lists of five, ten, or fifty numbers? Luckily mathematicians are satisfied to deal in terms of five, ten, or fifty dimensional abstract "spaces," and are not at all bothered by the fact that such spaces cannot be constructed physically. Pattern-recognition literature is filled with the mathematics necessary to find clusters of "points" in high-dimensional spaces, to adjust the "positions" of prototypes, and to separate regions—e.g., in a 50-dimensional "space," by 49-dimensional "surfaces."

When pattern-classification techniques were first invented, the mathematical elegance of the basic ideas, to represent samples by lists of numbers and classify them according to their locations in high-dimensional space, was so attractive that some of the early workers were overly ambitious and optimistic about the general usefulness of the techniques. They tried to make every problem into a classification problem, and to solve every classification problem with the same basic recognition approach. Such ambition is neither unhealthy nor unusual, in computer science or in science in general. Every tool or technique, from calculus to quantum mechanics, has a certain domain of problems for which it is useful. The full utility of a tool cannot be appreciated until the limits of its domain are fully explored, so that we know when it will be helpful and when it will not. Unfortunately, some of the original ambitious hopes for the usefulness of pattern-classification methods were widely advertised and interpreted as claims, so that the subsequent failure to achieve those hoped-for levels of performance was especially disappointing.

We now understand the usefulness and the limits of pattern classification. This decision-making method has been found to be most effective in two types of problems.

> 1. Recognition of simple shapes—e.g., letters of the alphabet. There now exist many commercially available automatic systems that can read printing from several different type fonts or even hand printing. Pattern-classification methods provided the initial feasibility demonstrations for these systems, although some of these systems now use rather different engineering approaches.

> 2. Classification of complex signals—e.g., sonar echoes or brain waves. If the proper features are measured and the number of dimensions kept small (say, less than ten), such systems can be quicker and more consistent than human operators at recognizing such sound patterns as those generated under water by a particular type of ship. Such abilities can be used in automatic control systems: e.g., to recognize from various wind, force, and direction measurements that the automatic pilot of an airplane is drifting off course and needs some corrective action.

TﾑE CﾑT

Figure 4.8 The role of context in pattern classification.

Pattern-classification methods alone are virtually useless, however, in situations which require awareness of context or the use of knowledge. Because the middle letters of the two words in Figure 4.8 are identical, a pattern-classification system could not tell them apart, but any literate English-speaking person can recognize them as different, and might not even notice that they are badly formed. The objects in Figure 4.9 are all chairs; people can easily recognize them, although some of the chairs may have unfamiliar designs. The recognition criteria must include many things beside two-dimensional shapes. Any attempt to extract the knowl-

Figure 4.9 Chairs. What do they have in common?

edge necessary to distinguish chairs from other types of furniture by pattern-classification methods seems to require that the chairs first be recognized: i.e., the problem must be solved by other means.

In such situations, the recognition task cannot be accomplished purely by classification. Some sort of systematic derivational reasoning must also be used. In Chapter 7 we shall return to the problem of enabling computers to understand complex perceptual situations. First, however, we must see how a computer can perform basic reasoning functions.

Deduction. Basic concepts

Our visitor bore every mark of being an average commonplace British tradesman, obese, pompous, and slow. He wore rather baggy gray shepherd's check trousers, a not overclean black frock coat, unbuttoned in the front, and a drab waistcoat with a heavy brassy Albert chain, and a square pierced bit of metal dangling down as an ornament. A frayed top hat and a faded brown overcoat with a wrinkled velvet collar lay upon a chair beside him. Altogether, look as I would, there was nothing remarkable about the man save his blazing red head, and the expression of extreme chagrin and discontent upon his features.

Sherlock Holmes's quick eye took in my occupation, and he shook his head with a smile as he noticed my questioning glances. "Beyond the obvious facts that he has at some time done manual labor, that he takes snuff, that he has been in China, and that he has done a considerable amount of writing lately, I can deduce nothing else."

Mr. Jabez Wilson started up in his chair, with his forefinger upon the paper, but his eyes upon my companion.

"How, in the name of good fortune, did you know all that, Mr. Holmes?" he asked. "How did you know, for example, that I did manual labor? It's as true as gospel, for I began as a ship's carpenter."

"Your hands, my dear sir. Your right hand is quite a size larger than your left. You have worked with it, and the muscles are more developed."

"Well, the snuff, then?"

"I won't insult your intelligence by telling you how I read that."

"Ah. But the writing?"

"What else can be indicated by that right cuff so very shiny for five inches, and the left one with the smooth patch near the elbow where you rest it upon the desk?"

"Well, but China?"

"The fish that you have tattooed immediately above your right wrist could only have been done in China. I have made a small study of tattoo marks and have even contributed to the literature of the subject. That trick of staining the fishes' scales of a delicate pink is quite peculiar to China. When, in addition, I see a Chinese coin hanging from your watch chain, the matter becomes even more simple."

Mr. Jabez Wilson laughed heavily. "Well, I never!" said he. "I thought at first that you had done something clever, but I see that there was nothing in it, after all."

"I begin to think, Watson," said Holmes, "that I make a mistake in explaining. *'Omne ignotum pro magnifico,'* you know, and my poor little reputation, such as it is, will suffer shipwreck if I am so candid."

A. Conan Doyle
"The Red-Headed League"

Deduction means obtaining solutions to problems by using some systematic reasoning procedure. Although the results of deduction may be impressive, perhaps even startling, to the uninitiated, every step along the way can always be explained. Once all the steps have been spelled out and the complete proof presented, the results take on a straightforward, perhaps even obvious, appearance.

We sometimes refer to deductive procedures as *formal inference* and use special symbols and procedures called *mathematical logic.* I hope these references to formal mathematical methods will not frighten away those of you who do not consider yourselves mathematically inclined. The purpose of the mathematical notations that I shall shortly introduce is to make every reasoning step precise and thus prevent unintentional fuzzy thinking. Remember that unlike the governing principles of such natural sciences as physics and biology, which are determined by nature and must be discovered, the principles of mathematics are invented by man to serve his purposes. If a system of mathematical logic does not enable us to make the deductions we know are right, we may then define the system to be wrong, and we can change it. (Wouldn't it be nice if we could change at will the law of gravity or the laws of thermodynamics.)

In order to be as clever as Sherlock Holmes, we need to be able to do two things: (1) observe and identify relevant data, and (2) draw appropriate conclusions from the data. The first of these capabilities is the more difficult. Nobody yet fully understands how to separate the relevant from the irrelevant. (We shall discuss some approaches to this problem in Chapters 6 and 7.) The second capability, that of drawing conclusions from relevant data, is something most people can learn to do. By formalizing this process and studying the properties of the resulting formal systems, we can better ensure our accuracy and consistency in carrying out such reasoning tasks. We can also discover how to give a computer similar reasoning ability. The remainder of this section discusses such formal reasoning systems. Of course, in only a part of one chapter we cannot hope to get very deeply into the subject of formal logic; many specialized books are available for the interested reader. We shall attempt, however, to skim over enough of the concepts to understand the main ideas of recent exciting progress in the computer automation of logical reasoning.

Once again, the first step in problem solving is representation. In order to use a formal deductive system to help us draw conclusions, we must first represent the knowledge we bring to the problem—the premises—in the language of the logical system. This language consists of strings of symbols that are composed according to certain grammatical rules and that are called the *well-formed formulas*, or *wff's*, of the logic. In general, some of the wff's represent *propositions*, i.e., assertions that must be either TRUE or FALSE; we call this special class of wff's *sentences* of the logical system. For example, a wff representing the concept, "The color of the apple," is not a sentence, whereas a wff representing the concept, "The apple is green," is a sentence, although we do not know whether its *truth value* is TRUE or FALSE.

A typical task posed for a logical system is the following. Given some logical sentences representing premises, and a sentence called a *theorem*, which represents some assertion whose truth we wish to determine, demonstrate whether the theorem is guaranteed to be true provided only that the premises are true. If such a demonstration can be obtained, it is called a *proof* of the theorem from the given premises, and we say that the premises *imply* the theorem.

Some theorems can be proved to represent facts that are always true, without requiring any premises. Such theorems are called *tautologies*. For example, the theorem, "You are now reading this book," might be proved to be either true or false, depending upon premises about the position of the book and the current behavior of your eyes and brain; but the theorem, "You are now either reading this book or not reading this book," is a tautology. In fact, it is a tautology that has nothing to do with books, because I could just as well assert, correctly, that "you are now either gnarmpfsking or not gnarmpfsking," no matter what "to gnarmpfsk" might mean.

There are two approaches to attempting to construct proofs. One, called the *semantic* approach, depends heavily upon the meanings of the symbls in the wff's. In a sense, when we use a semantic proof, we reason primarily by considering all the possible interpretations of the wff's to be proved. In the other approach, called *syntactic*, we totally ignore the meanings of the symbols; instead, we use formal symbol-manipulation rules of the logical system to construct new wff's out of old ones. The syntactic approach is frequently easier to use, especially for a computer, because one can apply rules in a mechanical way without having to think about what they mean. Of course, the rules need to have been carefully designed so that they work reliably: i.e., so that they permit exactly the same theorems to be proved as can be proved by semantic methods.

A *logical system* consists of both a specification for the structure of the wff's of the system, and a set of rules, called the *rules of inference* of the system, for constructing proofs. Many different logical systems have been invented; in fact, each mathematician is free to invent his own as he sees fit. However, certain systems are so widely known and used that they are the ones that usually come to mind when we say we are going to use formal logic. When we want to apply formal logic to some problem, we usually pick one of these well-known systems whose rules of inference are known to be reliable, and then decide how to represent our premises in terms of the wff's of the chosen system. We shall now examine the two principal logical systems: propositional calculus and predicate calculus.

Deduction. Proposition calculus

In this most basic system of logic, every wff is a sentence. The most elementary kind of wff is a single *propositional variable*, usually denoted by a small letter near the center of the alphabet. The wff

$$p$$

for example, represents any proposition.

Complex wff's are built out of simple ones, and have truth values that depend upon the truth values of their components. The "glue" for constructing complex wff's in propositional calculus consists of a set of symbols called *propositional connectives*. We shall restrict ourselves here to three basic connectives. Although more are commonly used, these three are simple and sufficient to express any concept of propositional logic. They are the symbols $\sim$, $\wedge$, and $\vee$, which represent the concepts *Not, And,* and *Or,* respectively, That is, the wff

$$\sim p,$$

which is read "not p", is true whenever p represents a false proposition, and is false whenever p represents a true proposition;

$$p \wedge q,$$

read "p and q", is true if both p and q represent true propositions, and false otherwise;

$$p \vee q,$$

read "*p* or *q*", is true if either *p* or *q* is true, or if both are true, but false whenever they are both false.

Arbitrarily complex wff's may be constructed with these connectives and propositional variables. For example, the wff

$$p \wedge (\sim q \vee (r \wedge s))$$

is true whenever *p* is true and either *q* is false or both *r* and *s* are true. (Parentheses are used whenever necessary to avoid ambiguity.)

Now that we know the language of propositional calculus, we can look at examples of how to represent knowledge and how to carry out deductions in this language. One awkward problem of representation in logic is how to represent the concept of implication. Consider the statement, "If the temperature is less than 65°F, then I feel cold." Suppose we let *p* stand for the proposition, "The temperature is below 65°F," and *q* stand for the proposition, "I feel cold." How should we represent the compound proposition, "If *p* then *q*"?

We usually represent implication in propositional calculus by a horseshoe-shaped symbol—e.g., $p \supset q$—but this notational device does not tell us what such a relationship means in terms of the more-basic connectives, $\sim$, $\wedge$, and $\vee$. In normal English, an if–then statement usually carries the connotation of causality. One might assume that what I really meant by the above statement was that, when the temperature is below 65°F, I feel cold *because* the temperature is below 65°F. However, we also consider to be acceptable sentences such as "If the phone rings, then I am invariably in the shower," which does not depend upon causality, but rather merely talks about whether two facts may be true simultaneously; I may be in the shower without the phone ringing, but the phone does not ring unless I am in the shower. Semanticists and logicians have argued for hundreds of years over how implication is related to causality. Since causality is difficult to represent in logic anyway, we shall evade the problem and define the if–then relation purely in terms of simultaneous truth: we shall consider $p \supset q$ to be purely an abbreviation for the propositional calculus wff

$$\sim p \vee q.$$

To see whether this makes any sense at all, consider the four possible cases:

1. *p* true, *q* true.
2. *p* true, *q* false.
3. *p* false, *q* true.
4. *p* false, *q* false.

In cases 3 and 4, the phone is not ringing, so it doesn't matter whether I am in the shower or not; according to such evidence we may as well believe the implication $p \supset q$ is true. Case 1 is certainly direct evidence for the truth of the implication; the phone is ringing while I am in the shower. Only case 2—a ringing phone while I am in the kitchen—can prove the implication to be false; and this is the only case in which the wff, $\sim p \lor q$, is false. As another example, return to the earlier statement; the implication is said to be true if either the temperature is not below 65°F, (in which case it doesn't matter whether I feel cold or not because the implication doesn't really apply), or I feel cold (in which case it doesn't matter what the temperature is); but if at any time the temperature is below 65°F (p true) and simultaneously I do not feel cold (q false), then that situation would demonstrate that the asserted implication $p \supset q$ is false.

Now we are ready to look at typical theorem-proving tasks in propositional logic. We take the classical logical form called the *syllogism* as the first example. Here is a typical syllogism.

> *Premise 1:* If I read a boring book, I get sleepy.
> *Premise 2:* This book I am now reading is boring.
> THEOREM: I am getting sleepy.

Let us see if we can prove this theorem (in some way other than by falling asleep). First, we must represent the elementary propositions by propositional variables.

> Let p = I am reading a boring book,
> and q = I am getting sleepy.

Then the representation of the premises are

> *Premise 1:* $p \supset q$, (or equivalently, $\sim p \lor q$)
> *Premise 2:* p

And the theorem to be proved is simply
> THEOREM: q.

The best-known method for proving theorems in propositional calculus is called the method of *truth tables*. This is a semantic method, in which we examine all the possible combinations of interpretations for the propositional variables. These form the first columns of a table of truth values. From these we figure out the truth value of each premise, and then for each line of the table for which all the premises are true, we figure out the truth value of the theorem. The resulting table demonstrates whether the theorem is true whenever all the premises are, and therefore whether the theorem is proved. Table 4.1 is the truth table that proves syllogisms.

The task of constructing a truth table can certainly be programmed for a computer, and the truth-table method will work to prove or disprove any theorem of propositional calculus. However, this method is not entirely satisfactory, because it can be extremely inefficient. If n different propositional variables occur in the premises and the theorem, then a table with 2^n rows must be filled out; a problem with ten variables requires more than a thousand lines. Usually logicians can recognize rela-

Table 4.1 Syllogism Truth Table

Variables		Subexpression	Premise 1	Premise 2	Theorem
p	q	$\sim p$	$\sim p \vee q$	p	q
T	T	F	T	T	T
F	T	T	T	F	$-^a$
T	F	F	F	T	$-^a$
F	F	T	T	F	$-^a$

^{a}Since the premises are not all true, these lines are ignored.

tionships among the wff's of any particular problem that permit them to take major short-cuts. Unfortunately, for many years these shortcuts were not defined precisely enough to program for a computer—or even to be used by a logic student without occasional errors. About 1960 Hao Wang at Harvard University developed a syntactic method that is about as efficient as any general method for propositional calculus can be. It produces exactly the same results as truth tables, usually requires much less computational effort, and is so easy to program that it is frequently used now as an exercise in the use of symbol-manipulation programming methods.

Wang's Algorithm consists of writing down a series of lines, each simpler than the previous one, until a proof is completed—or shown to be impossible. Each line consists of any number of wff's, separated by commas, on each side of an arrow. A proof proceeds as follows.

Wang's Algorithm

1. As the first line, write the premises to the left of the arrow and the theorem to the right of the arrow:

$$\text{premise 1, premise 2, premise 3} \rightarrow \text{theorem}$$

2. If the principal connective of a wff is a negation, drop the negation sign and move the wff to the other side of the arrow; for example,

$$p \vee q, \ \sim(r \wedge s), \ \sim q, \ p \vee r \rightarrow s, \ \sim p$$

is changed into

$$p \vee q, p \vee r, p \rightarrow s, r \wedge s, q.$$

3. If the principal connective of a wff on the left of the arrow is $\wedge$ or on the right of the arrow is $\vee$, replace the connective by a comma; for example,

$$p \wedge q, \ r \wedge (\sim p \vee s) \rightarrow \sim q \vee \sim r$$

is changed into

$$p, q, r, \ \sim p \vee s \rightarrow \sim q, \ \sim r.$$

4. If the principal connective of a wff on the left of the arrow is $\vee$ or that on the right of the arrow is $\wedge$, then produce two new lines, each with one of the two sub-wff's replacing the wff; for example,

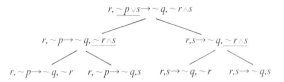

All the resulting lines must be proved in order to prove the original theorem.

    5.   If the same wff occurs on both sides of an arrow, the line is proven.

    6.   If no connectives remain in a line and no propositional variable occurs on both sides of the arrow, the line is not provable. In fact, assigning all the variables on the left to be TRUE and all the variables on the right to be FALSE will provide an example of the falsity of the theorem.

      Like most syntactic procedures, Wang's Algorithm may seem rather mysterious. But it is guaranteed to work, as the clever reader can convince himself by figuring out the significance of each of the six rules.

      Whenever rule 4 is used, the attempted proof is split into two sub-proofs, so that this algorithm produces a binary tree of groups of lines. If m is the number of occurrences of connectives in the premises and theorem, Wang's Algorithm requires somewhere between m and 2^m lines to be produced. Since we are usually not so unlucky as to need rule 4 for every connective, many fewer than 2^m are usually needed; and if we notice the condition of rule 5 early enough, even fewer than m lines are possible. Figure 4.10 shows Wang's Algorithm applied to the basic syllogism.

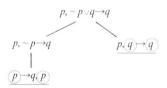

Figure 4.10   Wang's Algorithm for a syllogism.

      The simplest computer implementation of Wang's Algorithm would systematically eliminate connectives from successive lines, say from left to right, and perhaps go down the tree in depth-first manner, which is safe because we know that every branch must end and must be explored. However, if we keep in mind that we are trying to satisfy rule 5 as soon as possible, we can usually find a proof sooner. There is therefore still room for the programmer to use his ingenuity and try to build into the algorithm some of his extra knowledge—about the rule 5 terminating condition—to make the search through the space of lines more efficient.

THE PROBLEM

The facts:
The maid said that she saw the butler in the living room. The living room adjoins the kitchen. The shot was fired in the kitchen, and could be heard in all nearby rooms. The butler, who has good hearing, said he did not hear the shot.
To prove:
If the maid told the truth, the butler lied.

THE REPRESENTATION

---

p = The maid told the truth
q = The butler was in the living room·
r = The butler was near the kitchen
s = The butler heard the shot
u = The butler told the truth

Original Statement	Equivalent Form	Meaning
		Premises
$p \supset q$	$\sim p \lor q$	(If the maid told the truth, the butler was in the living room.)
$q \supset r$	$\sim q \lor r$	(If the butler was in the living room, he was near the kitchen.)
$r \supset s$	$\sim r \lor s$	(If he was near the kitchen, he heard the shot.)
$u \supset \sim s$	$\sim u \lor \sim s$	(If he told the truth, he did not hear the shot.)
		Theorem
$p \supset \sim u$	$\sim p \lor \sim u$	(If the maid told the truth, the butler did not.)

Figure 4.11 A mystery solved by propositional calculus. (*a*) The problem and its representation.

Figure 4.11,*a*, *b*, and *c*, shows a more complex exercise in propositional calculus, with both truth table and Wang's Algorithm proofs.

Before leaving propositional calculus, I would like to present one more method of proof, called *propositional resolution*. It is similar in efficiency to Wang's Algorithm, although it is based upon a rather different approach. Our main reason for being interested in propositional resolution is that it is a special case of *resolution*, a proof procedure for predicate calculus, to be discussed below.

First, we must understand something about equivalence of logical sentences. Two sentences are said to be *equivalent* if, whenever their corresponding variables are given the same values, the sentences have the same truth values. For example, the following two sentences

$$s_1 = \sim(p \lor q)$$
$$s_2 = \sim p \land \sim q$$

Variables					Subexpressions					Premises				Theorem
p	q	r	s	u	$\sim p$	$\sim q$	$\sim r$	$\sim s$	$\sim u$	$\sim p \vee q$	$\sim q \vee r$	$\sim r \vee s$	$\sim u \vee \sim s$	$\sim p \vee \sim u$
T	T	T	T	T	F	F	F	F	F	T	T	T	F	—
F	T	T	T	T	T	F	F	F	F	T	T	T	F	—
T	F	T	T	T	F	T	F	F	F	F	T	T	F	—
F	F	T	T	T	T	T	F	F	F	T	T	T	F	—
T	T	F	T	T	F	F	T	F	F	T	F	T	F	—
F	T	F	T	T	T	F	T	F	F	T	F	T	F	—
T	F	F	T	T	F	T	T	F	F	F	T	T	F	—
F	F	F	T	T	T	T	T	F	F	T	T	T	F	—
T	T	T	F	T	F	F	F	T	F	T	T	F	T	—
F	T	T	F	T	T	F	F	T	F	T	T	F	T	—
T	F	T	F	T	F	T	F	T	F	F	T	F	T	—
F	F	T	F	T	T	T	F	T	F	T	T	F	T	—
T	T	F	F	T	F	F	T	T	F	T	F	T	T	—
F	T	F	F	T	T	F	T	T	F	T	F	T	T	—
T	F	F	F	T	F	T	T	T	F	F	T	T	T	—
F	F	F	F	T	T	T	T	T	F	T	T	T	T	T
T	T	T	T	F	F	F	F	F	T	T	T	T	T	T
F	T	T	T	F	T	F	F	F	T	T	T	T	T	T
T	F	T	T	F	F	T	F	F	T	F	T	T	T	—
F	F	T	T	F	T	T	F	F	T	T	T	T	T	T
T	T	F	T	F	F	F	T	F	T	T	F	T	T	—
F	T	F	T	F	T	F	T	F	T	T	F	T	T	—
T	F	F	T	F	F	T	T	F	T	F	T	T	T	—
F	F	F	T	F	T	T	T	F	T	T	T	T	T	T
T	T	T	F	F	F	F	F	T	T	T	T	F	T	—
F	T	T	F	F	T	F	F	T	T	T	T	F	T	—
T	F	T	F	F	F	T	F	T	T	F	T	F	T	—
F	F	T	F	F	T	T	F	T	T	T	T	F	T	—
T	T	F	F	F	F	F	T	T	T	T	F	T	T	—
F	T	F	F	F	T	F	T	T	T	T	F	T	T	—
T	F	F	F	F	F	T	T	T	T	F	T	T	T	—
F	F	F	F	F	T	T	T	T	T	T	T	T	T	T

Figure 4.11 A mystery solved. (*b*) Proof by truth table.

are equivalent, as can be seen from the following truth table:

Variables		Subexpressions			s_1	s_2
p	q	$\sim p$	$\sim q$	$p \vee q$	$\sim(p \vee q)$	$\sim p \wedge \sim q$
T	T	F	F	T	F	F
F	T	T	F	T	F	F
T	F	F	T	T	F	F
F	F	T	T	F	T	T

Second, we must understand *conjunctive form*. A sentence is said to be in

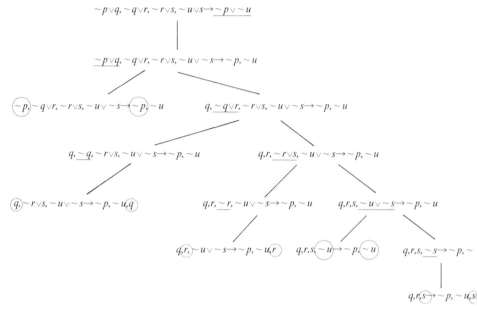

Figure 4.11 A mystery solved. (c) Proof by Wang's Algorithm.

conjunctive form if (1) *negation* symbols ($\sim$) apply only to variables, never to parenthesized expressions; and (2) *or* symbols ($\vee$) connect only variables or negated variables, never parenthesized expressions containing *and* symbols ($\wedge$). For example, s_1 above is not in conjunctive form, but s_2 and the following expression are:

$$(p \vee q \vee \sim r) \wedge s \wedge (\sim p \vee s).$$

Each of the wffs that are *and*ed together are called *clauses*. The example immediately above contains three clauses:

$$p \vee q \vee \sim r, \quad s, \quad \text{and} \quad \sim p \vee s.$$

A resolution proof is usually posed in the following way. Assume that the theorem is false, and therefore that its negation is true. Then show that this assumption, taken together with the premises, leads to an impossible situation; therefore the theorem cannot be false, so it must be true. The impossible situation, called a *contradiction*, is that, if the assumptions hold, some variable and its negation must both be true. (We denote the discovery of such a contradiction by the symbol $\square$.)

The resolution proof procedure consists of first replacing all the premises, and the negation of the theorem, by equivalent sentences that are in conjunctive form (a systematic procedure for finding a conjunctive-form equivalent for any sentence is well known). Then all these clauses are placed in one group. Two clauses are selected: one that contains some variable v and another that contains its negation $\sim v$. A new clause is generated, containing all the *or*ed elements of the two selected clauses except for v and $\sim v$. We say that this new clause has been *deduced* from the two selected clauses by resolution. (You can verify by truth tables, for example, that from the premises $p \vee q \vee \sim r$ and $\sim p \vee s$, the theorem $q \vee \sim r \vee s$ can be proved.) The newly generated clause is added to the group of clauses and the process continues, until either (1) a contradiction is deduced, proving the desired theorem, or (2) no more new clauses can be generated, and the theorem is false. For a simple syllogism, a resolution proof looks like this:

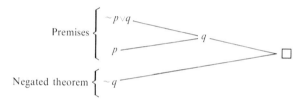

A proof of our example of Figure 4.11,*a* is given by resolution in Figure 4.11,*d*.

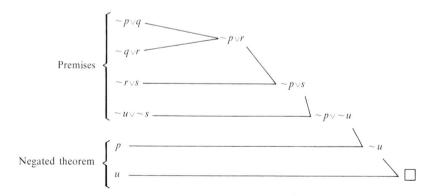

Note: $\sim(\sim p \vee \sim u)$ is equivalent to $p \wedge u$

Figure 4.11 A mystery solved. (*d*) Proof by propositional resolution.

Deduction. Predicate calculus

Propositional calculus is of limited interest primarily because its most elementary units, the propositional variables, are already sentences; there is no way to get "inside" an elementary proposition to see why it is true or false, or to see if it is related to other propositions in any way besides their truth values. I can represent a fact such as "John's father is a Mason" by propositional variables, but I have no way of representing "John's father" or even "John."

Predicate calculus remedies this defect. Its most elementary symbols are *individual variables* (x, y, z), that represent individual entities: apples, people, numbers, or simply things. It also contains *function* symbols (f, g, h) that tell how to change one individual into another. For example, if our individual variables stand for people and f is the "father" function, then the symbol

$$f(x)$$

represents the man who is the father of whoever is represented by x. Since we can also use *constants,* represented by capital letters, to name particular individuals, we can represent John's paternal grandfather (whose name we may not know) by

$$f(f(\text{JOHN})).$$

A *predicate* is a function whose value is a truth value, TRUE or FALSE, depending upon which individual it is applied to. If M is the predicate that specifies membership in the Masons, then $M(x)$ is TRUE whenever x represents a member of the Masons and FALSE otherwise. We represent the fact that John's father is a Mason by asserting

$$M(f(\text{JOHN}))$$

to be true, provided we have also adequately defined f to be the father function and M to be the Mason-membership predicate.

Some predicates (and also functions) may be applied to more than one object (called "arguments"); for example, the arithmetic relation

$$x > y$$

might be represented in predicate calculus by

$$GREATER(x,y),$$

where the predicate *GREATER* has the value TRUE whenever its first argument represents a number larger than its second argument, and FALSE otherwise. Thus

$$GREATER(squareroot(16),z)$$

has the value TRUE whenever z is a number less than 4 (if the *squareroot* function has its usual mathematical meaning).

Formulas consisting of a predicate symbol applied to appropriate arguments—e.g.,

$$GREATER(squareroot(16),z), \quad \text{and} \quad M(f(y)),$$

are called *atomic formulas,* and play approximately the same role in predicate calculus that propositional variables do in propositional calculus. Atomic formulas are wff's of predicate calculus, and so are atomic formulas connected by the propositional connectives $\sim$, $\wedge$, and $\vee$: the following is a wff,

(4.1) $$\sim P(x) \wedge (Q(g(y)) \vee R(y,x)).$$

However, we do not yet call such wff's "sentences." The truth values of such wff's depend upon the arbitrary assignments of particular individuals to the individual variables x and y. A sentence must have a truth value that is not so easily affected. Therefore we shall make the following rather stringent limitation on our wff's: if an individual variable occurs in a wff, we shall require the variable to have one of the following two interpretations.

1. The wff is asserted to be true for at least one value of that variable, although we do not know which. In this case we put the "exists" symbol ($\exists$ *variable*) in front of the wff for each such variable.

2. The wff is asserted to be true for every possible assignment of particular individuals. In this case we put the "for all" symbol ($\forall$ *variable*) in front of the wff for each such variable.

For example, if a_1, a_2, a_3, and so on, are names of individuals in our domain of interest (numbers, people, or whatever), then one sentence based upon the above wff (4.1) would be written

$$(\forall x)(\forall y)[\sim P(x) \wedge (Q(g(y)) \vee R(y,x))],$$

which may be viewed as an abbreviation for all the following:

x	y	
a_1	a_1	$[\sim P(a_1) \wedge (Q(g(a_1)) \vee R(a_1,a_1))]\wedge$
a_1	a_2	$[\sim P(a_1) \wedge (Q(g(a_2)) \vee R(a_2,a_1))]\wedge$
a_2	a_1	$[\sim P(a_2) \wedge (Q)g(a_1)) \vee R(a_1,a_2))]\wedge$
a_2	a_2	$[\sim P(a_2) \wedge (Q(g(a_2)) \vee R(a_2,a_2))]\wedge$
a_3	a_1	$[\sim P(a_3) \wedge (Q(g(a_1)) \vee R(a_1,a_3))]\wedge$

and so on.

A wff in which every individual variable is governed by one of the so-called "quantifier" symbols, $\exists$ and $\forall$, is called a *sentence* of predicate calculus.

This completes our presentation of the *language* of predicate calculus: sentences formed from individual variables and constants, function symbols, predicate symbols, propositional connectives, and quantifiers. Before going on to a study of how this language is used, there are three things you should know about predicate calculus that I shall have to ask you to accept on faith, since their proofs are mathematically complex and would take much more space than we can devote to them here.

1.   Predicate calculus is an adequate language for expressing almost any mathematical concept or computational principle.

2.   If the domain of individuals is permitted to have an infinite number of objects (e.g., the integers) then there exist theorems of predicate calculus that are always true and yet cannot be proved to be true by any systematic procedure (such as Truth Tables or Wang's Algorithm for propositional calculus). This unfortunate property, called *undecidability*, applies not only to predicate calculus but also to any other formal system of comparable expressive power.

3.   There do exist *proof procedures* for predicate calculus. A proof procedure is a systematic procedure that is guaranteed to produce the proof of any provable theorem, and to demonstrate the falsity of any nontheorem. For the true but unprovable theorems, a proof procedure simply would keep running forever. Unfortunately, after a proof procedure has been working on a theorem for some seconds—or hours, or weeks—we can never be sure whether it will produce a definitive answer in the next few moments, or whether it is working on an unprovable theorem. (Recall the discussion of "Fermat's last theorem" in the previous chapter.)

Now that I have stated that one of the properties of predicate calculus (and any similar formal system) is undecidability, I must hasten to point out that this is much less important than some people seem to believe. The undecidability principle is an annoyance to logicians, but one they can easily live with once they understand it—somewhat like the Heisenberg uncertainty principle in physics. That understanding begins with the realization that two widely quoted statements are false and misleading.

False conclusion 1. The undecidability principle proves that formal systems, and therefore computers, cannot do logical reasoning as well as human beings can.

In order to draw this conclusion, one must assume that human beings have some way of reasoning logically that does not make use of a formal system, and hence is not itself governed by the undecidability principle. What might this way be? Surely not some kind of abstract intuition or inspiration, or any human would have trouble convincing other humans of the correctness of the results of his reasoning. (One mathematician is said to have claimed that he derives his results about the infinite set of integer numbers by considering them all; he thinks about "one, two, three—and just sort of runs through them!" I don't know what he means by "runs through," but I'm sure he does not consider every number in turn, ". . . . 1,827,352–1,827,353–1,827,354 . . . .") Perhaps the difference between human and machine behavior is explained by the ability of the human to use his extensive knowledge of the subject matter to guide him in changing representations in order to get to a better search space, perhaps a different, higher-level formal system, in which to look for a solution. The reason computers cannot perform similarly is that we have not yet learned how to program them so that they can acquire, store, and use knowledge in such ways; but this has nothing to do with the undecidability question.

False conclusion 2. The undecidability principle has a major impact upon the development of automatic theorem-proving methods.

In truth, the undecidability principle is an abstract theoretical result that has essentially no impact upon the development of automatic theorem-proving methods. Consider three groups of theorems: Group A contains theorems that we know how to prove using less than, say, thirty minutes of computer time; Group B contains theorems that would take between a year and a million years of computer time to prove by presently known methods; and Group C contains theorems that would take forever to prove—i.e., they are undecidable. Now there is certainly an interesting and theoretically sharp distinction between Groups B and C; the theorems of one are said to be provable, those of the other are not. But in practical theorem-proving this distinction vanishes. What use is it to know that the theorems of Group B have proofs, if we can never wait long enough to construct one? Even if we were told that a particular theorem was in Group B, that knowledge would not help us prove it; any more than the knowledge that all possible chess games have a finite but ridiculously large (about 10^{120}) number of positions helps us find the best opening move. Therefore current research on theorem-proving methods is aimed at developing techniques that will move some of the Group B theorems into Group A. Since Group B seems to contain a large number of interesting theorems the fact that some theorems must remain forever out of reach in Group C does not especially concern us. In fact, since 1965 giant steps have been taken to improve the efficiency of automatic theorem-proving methods, and many theorems have been transferred from Group B to Group A. The techniques that have accomplished this are the subject of the next section.

Predicate calculus proof by resolution

The principal method of theorem-proving in predicate calculus is a method of proof by contradiction, similar to the propositional-resolution method discussed earlier. We assume that the negation of the theorem to be proved is true, and attempt to deduce a contradiction from that negation and the original premises. As in the propositional case, we begin the proof by placing the premises and the negated theorem into conjunctive form. Moreover, this conjunctive form has separate ∀ quantifiers for the variables in each clause, and no ∃ quantifiers. Since all variables are therefore known to be governed by ∀ quantifiers, we do not need to write down the quantifier symbols, and the resulting expressions are called the *quantifier-free* form of predicate-calculus language. There is a well-known, systematic procedure for taking any sentence of predicate calculus and producing a corresponding sentence—i.e., group of clauses— in a quantifier-free form with the property that the quantifier-free expression is a provable theorem· if and only if the original sentence is provable. Since the quantifier-free form often resembles the original form fairly closely, we can look at an example without bothering to go into the details of the transformation procedure.

We shall use a simple reasoning problem to show how predicate-calculus theorem-proving methods can be applied. Although most of the research on theorem-proving methods has been aimed at using them for doing abstract mathematics, examples of such uses are difficult for the nonmathematician to understand. Also, since the general goal of this book is to show how new computer techniques can be applied to many different subjects, it will be useful for us to explore the convenience— and difficulties—of applying theorem-proving techniques to nonmathematical areas. Therefore let us turn to the problem of Mrs. Coleman. She wishes to telephone her husband, who is a physician, but does not know the phone number at which he can be reached. She calls his answering service, and is told that

> Dr. Coleman is visiting with Dr. Gordon

and that

> Dr. Gordon is at patient Wagner's residence.

She can now solve her problem by reaching for the phone book to look up Wagner's number, and confidently expect to be able to talk to her husband at that number.

Now let us change the setting to the year 1990. The answering service is now a computer that uses predicate calculus. How shall it reply to Mrs. Coleman when she asks, "Is there a telephone number where I can reach Dr. Coleman?" In order to represent this situation in predicate calculus, we need to define some predicate and function symbols.[1]

Let $AT(x,y)$ represent the assertion that person x is at place y; i.e.,

---

[1] The definitions of the meanings of these symbols are purely for our convenience in writing and thinking about logical expressions. These definitions are never read or understood by the computer. We forget too easily that the word *VISITS*, for example, has no more meaning to the computer than the word *BASINGSTOKE;* its meaning must be specified in the predicate calculus by relationships given in the form of logical premises.

if x is at y, then $AT(x,y)$ will have truth-value TRUE, and otherwise it will be FALSE.

Similarly, $NUMBER(x,y)$ means that person x can be reached by calling phone number y.

$VISITS(x,y)$ means person x is visiting person y.

The function *look-up*(x) corresponds to the operation of looking something up in a phone book; it takes a place x as an input and produces a telephone number as its value.

Now we can write down the premises needed to solve Mrs. Coleman's problem. First, we certainly need the specific facts.

Premise 1: Coleman is visiting Gordon:

$$VISITS(\text{COLEMAN,GORDON}).$$

Premise 2: Gordon is at Wagner's residence:

$$AT(\text{GORDON,WAGNERS}).$$

Next, we need some general knowledge about the relationship between the meanings of AT and $VISITS$: namely, if x visits y while y is at place z then x is at the place z also, and this relationship holds for all people and places.

Premise 3: $(\forall x)\,(\forall y)\,(\forall z)\,[(VISITS(x,y) \wedge AT(y,z)) \supset AT(x,z)]$

Finally, the predicate-calculus explanation of the predicate $NUMBER$: if a person u is at a place v then he can be reached at the number found by looking up (with the function *look-up*) the place v.

Premise 4: $(\forall u)\,(\forall v)\,[AT(u,v) \supset NUMBER(u,look\text{-}up(v))]$

The question Mrs. Coleman poses might be phrased, "Does there exist a number at which Dr. Coleman can be reached?" or in predicate calculus,

THEOREM: $(\exists n)\,NUMBER(\text{COLEMAN},n)$

It can be shown that the negation of this theorem is equivalent to the assertion, "For every number n, it is not true that COLEMAN can be reached by dialing n."

NEGATED THEOREM: $(\forall n)\, \sim NUMBER(\text{COLEMAN},n)$

In order to answer the question our automatic answering service must be able to prove that the quantifier-free representation of the four premises and the negated theorem lead to a contradiction. All these clauses are shown in Table 4.2.

Before trying to derive a contradiction from this set of clauses, we must understand a little more deeply what each type of clause means. Consider first an atomic formula that contains no variables, e.g., the first clause $VISITS(\text{COLEMAN,GORDON})$. This formula represents an elementary fact—a *proposition*—whose truth-value is either TRUE or FALSE: either Coleman is really visiting Gordon, or he is not. Thus an

Table 4.2 Quantifier-Free Form of Mrs. Coleman's Problem. All variables are assumed to be ∀-quantified.

1. *VISITS*(COLEMAN,GORDON)
2. *AT*(GORDON,WAGNERS)
3. ~ *VISITS*(x,y) ∨ ~*AT*(y,z) ∨ *AT*(x,z)
4. ~*AT*(u,v) ∨ *NUMBER*(u,look-up(v))
5. ~*NUMBER*(COLEMAN,n)

atomic formula that contains no variables plays exactly the same role in predicate calculus that a propositional variable plays in propositional calculus. For example, consider the following simplified version of the premises for Mrs. Coleman's problem.

1. Dr. Coleman is visiting with Dr. Gordon
2. Dr. Gordon is at the Wagners' residence
3'. If Coleman visits with Gordon and if Gordon is at the Wagners' then Coleman will also be at the Wagners'.

The clauses representing the premises are:

1. *VISITS*(COLEMAN,GORDON)
2. *AT*(GORDON,WAGNERS)
3'. ~ *VISITS*(COLEMAN,GORDON) ∨ ~*AT*(GORDON,WAGNERS) ∨ *AT*(COLEMAN,WAGNERS)

Now let us ask, "Is Coleman at Wagners?"

THEOREM: *AT*(COLEMAN,WAGNERS)

NEGATED THEOREM: ~*AT*(COLEMAN,WAGNERS)

If we treat each of the three atomic formulas occurring in this set of clauses exactly like a propositional variable, the proof of this theorem from these premises (i.e., the justification for a "Yes!" answer) can be done by propositional resolution, and is shown in Figure 4.12.

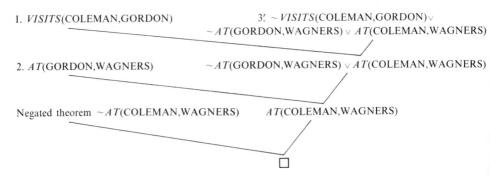

Figure 4.12 Predicate-calculus proof by propositional resolution.

Now, what is the relationship between clause 3(Table 4.2) and clause 3'? If in clause 3 we let

$$x = \text{COLEMAN}, \ y = \text{GORDON}, \text{ and } z = \text{WAGNERS},$$

we get precisely clause 3'. We call 3' an *instance* of 3, because it can be obtained from 3 by choosing appropriate values for variables. Since the variables of clauses are assumed to be $\forall$-quantified (3 is asserted to be true for all values of x, y, and z) then whenever 3 is true 3' is certainly true. In fact, a clause containing variables may be thought of as an abbreviation for the infinite set of all the possible instances of the clause. Thus clause 3 can be viewed as a shorthand way of saying,

"If Smith visits Jones and Jones is at Brown's house then Smith will be at Brown's house,"

and

"If Gordon visits Coleman and Coleman is at Wagner's house then Gordon will be at Wagner's house,"

and

"If Coleman visits Gordon and Gordon is at Wagner's house then Coleman will be at Wagner's house,"

and

"If Coleman visits Coleman and Coleman is at Coleman's house then Coleman will be at Coleman's house,"

and a lot of other sillier things like

"If Kelly's house visits 571,210 and 571,210 is at Rosen then Kelly's house will be at Rosen,"

and so on; because x, y, and z may each take on as values any of the objects in our world of interest, which includes all possible people, places, and telephone numbers.

In the early 1930's Herbrand proved that if a set of clauses that have variables is in fact contradictory then there must exist some finite set of variable-free instances of those clauses that can be shown to be contradictory by propositional methods. In the early 1960's several logicians tried to use this method to prove theorems with computers. The computers were programmed to systematically generate a set of instances and test whether those instances led to a contradiction, using some propositional method such as a form of Wang's Algorithm. If no contradiction could be deduced, more instances were generated and added to the set produced previously, and the enlarged set was tested, and so on. Since most of the instances produced in this way were silly and even most of the meaningful ones were irrelevant, such methods did not work very well.

Then, in 1964, J. A. Robinson developed the *resolution principle*, a method for generating only instances that are likely to be relevant.

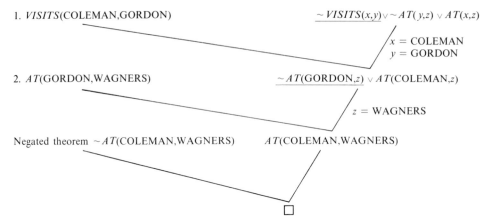

Figure 4.13 A resolution proof requiring a substitution instance.

Basically, we attempt to make inferences by propositional resolution: i.e., find an atomic formula in one clause and its precise negation in another, so as to deduce a new resolvent clause. If the atomic formula and its negation are not quite identical but contain variables and thus have instances that would be identical, then the resolution principle says to choose those instances only and immediately perform the inference step; the complete instance clauses need never be written down. Figure 4.13 shows the proof that Coleman is at the Wagners', by resolution, where premise 3′ of Figure 4.12 has been replaced by the more general form, premise 3 of Table 4.2.

Note that the clause produced in the first step of Figure 4.13, $\sim AT(\text{GORDON},z) \vee AT(\text{COLEMAN},z)$, contains both constants and a variable. Thus it is itself an abbreviation for an infinite set of possible clauses—depending upon the value of z chosen. One of the strengths of the resolution method is that it does not require instances to contain only constants. Instead, it produces the most general instances that still permit the propositional resolution step to take place: i.e., the instances chosen contain the most general possible arrangement of variables that may be used as the basis for subsequent resolution steps. A key result that makes resolution such a practical method is that, if there exist any identical instances of two different atomic formulas, then even though an infinite number of such instances may exist it is sufficient to choose only one. That one can be so chosen that all others will be instances of it; that one instance will summarize all possible useful substitutions. Moreover, a straightforward algorithm exists for finding this most general instance for any pair of atomic formulas.

Figure 4.14 shows the full solution to Mrs. Coleman's problem.

The above discussion has presented only the skeleton of the resolution approach to predicate-calculus theorem proving. Much more is needed before the theorem-proving method can be considered completely defined. In particular, we have said nothing about how we decide which

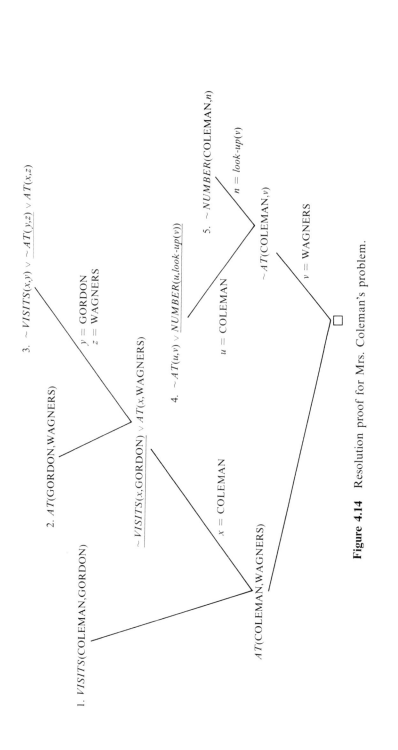

Figure 4.14 Resolution proof for Mrs. Coleman's problem.

two clauses to try to resolve together, and which atomic formulas to select in those clauses. It is known that, if a proof exists, then certain systematic searches are guaranteed to find one. For example, suppose we consider the initial set of clauses to be the top node of a tree; each possible resolution that can be performed between two clauses in the set produces a different successor node that consists of all the original clauses plus the newly produced resolvent clause. Then a contradiction is certain to occur at some finite depth in this tree, so that a breadth-first search is sure to find it. However, such a search will pursue many paths that are not the route to any proof; equivalent nodes will be regenerated in many different places in the tree; and parts of many different proofs will be obtained. Figure 4.15 shows part of this tree for Mrs. Coleman's problem. Clearly, more-efficient methods are needed to search for resolution proofs, and considerable effort has been devoted to developing such "refinements" of resolution. The most effective of these refinements include the *set of support* strategy, which specifies that we require every proof to begin by using a clause from the negation of the theorem because the negation of the theorem is the source of the eventual contradiction and therefore will have to be included in the proof at some stage anyway; the *linear format* strategy, which tries to keep us on the track towards a single proof by always making immediate use of the results of the previous resolution step; and the *unit preference* strategy, which observes that we get closer to the desired contradiction only when we resolve with a clause containing a single atomic formula, so that we should always try to resolve with such clauses first. By combining these three strategies, we reduce the search tree of Figure 4.15 to the one of Figure 4.16, which leads directly to two proofs.

For more-complicated mathematical problems these strategies, although helpful, are not nearly so overwhelmingly effective. Many more-complex and more-subtle strategies have been proposed; the theory of computer proofs by resolution is under continuing active study, and in fact lies at the center of a new research field called "computational logic." This field is primarily concerned with how to enable computers to help solve difficult mathematical problems. Although we are delighted to use whatever results come out of such studies, those of us who are interested in how to apply computers to a broad spectrum of new problem areas should not be distracted into pursuing resolution theory in depth. We have more pressing problems to consider: those concerning such issues as the usefulness of predicate-calculus methods for answering questions and for representing general knowledge.

With respect to question answering, let us return once more to Mrs. Coleman's problem. She wants to telephone her husband; so she calls his automatic answering service and asks, "Is there a number at which Dr. Coleman can be reached?" The computer thinks it understands her question, translates it to predicate calculus, negates it, adds its clause form to that of several relevant facts in its memory, generates a

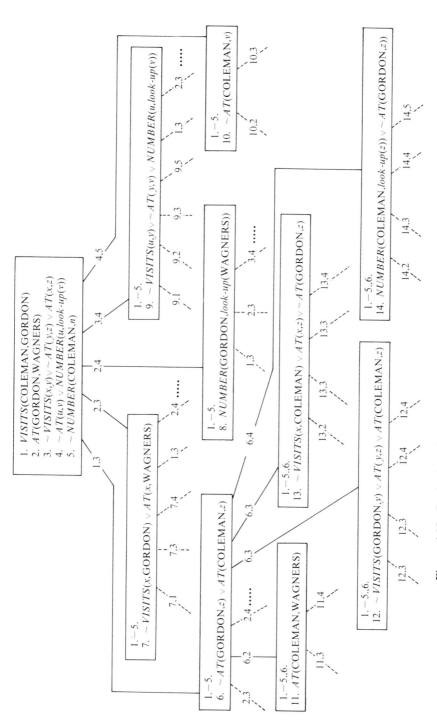

Figure 4.15 Beginning of complete resolution search tree for Mrs. Coleman's problem. Numbers on branches identify the clauses that have been selected for resolving.

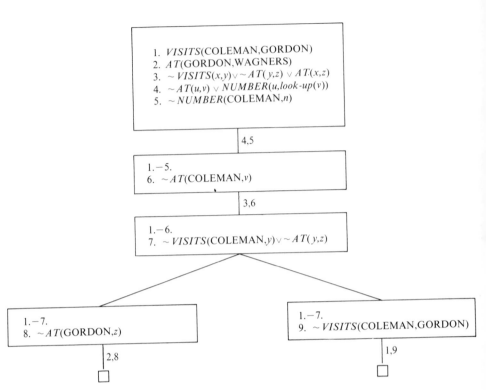

Figure 4.16 Resolution search tree for Mrs. Coleman's problem using refinement strategies.

resolution-proof tree using set-of-support, linear-format, and unit-preference strategies, deduces a contradiction, and, within a few seconds, smugly replies "Yes!" This response is likely to cause Mrs. Coleman to curse the day the answering-service operator was replaced by a computer. She is now frustrated because she knows that there definitely is a number at which he can be reached, but still has no idea what the number is. Suppose she shouts back at the computer, "Well, what *is* the number, stupid?" Need this leave the computer hopelessly and helplessly embarrassed? Not if it knows the "answer extraction" trick developed in the late 1960's just for such purposes.

In order to deduce a contradiction, a resolution type of theorem prover must generally discover for itself some useful specific facts relevant to the problem at hand. However, these facts are generally buried in the proof; they are not of interest in mathematical theorem-proving applications, where the only question of interest to mathematicians is whether or not a particular formal statement is a theorem. To answer questions, we can obtain more data from a proof by first constructing an ordinary resolution proof—e.g., the proof of Figure 4.14. In such a proof, every resolvent is a logical consequence of its ancestors; an obvious con-

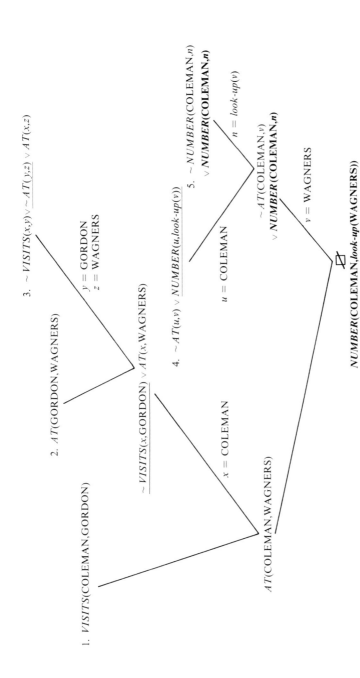

Figure 4.17 Answer construction for a resolution proof.

tradiction has been deduced because the negated theorem contradicts the premises. After completing the proof, we go back and replace the negated theorem by a clause that asserts, "Either the theorem is false or it is true." Since this statement is a tautology, it adds no information to the existing clauses—the premises. It does not restrict or contradict them in any way. Now if we attempt to reconstruct precisely the same proof as before, we will be able to deduce only true consequences of the premises. In particular, at the point where we previously deduced a contradiction, we must now deduce the specific consequence of the premises that was contradicted by the negation of the theorem; this consequence turns out to be the most precise answer to the question that the system can construct. Figure 4.17 shows the modified version of the proof of Figure 4.14. The answer produced is *NUMBER*(COLEMAN,*look-up*(WAGNERS)), which might be paraphrased, "Coleman can be reached at the number found by looking up Wagner's residence in the phone book." Since an automatic answering service presumably will be equipped with an automatic telephone directory, the look-up operation can also be performed so that Mrs. Coleman can be told, e.g., "The answer is 444-3460."

Other formal systems

Before leaving the subject of formal deductive systems, we should consider at least briefly some systems beyond propositional calculus and predicate calculus. Propositional calculus is the basic system for dealing with elementary propositions, and therefore is included as part of most other systems. By adding individual variables, functions, and quantifiers, the predicate calculus makes a great leap in expressive power beyond propositional calculus. The form of predicate calculus we have discussed, which strictly speaking should be called *first-order* predicate calculus, is sufficiently general to use for representing most mathematical concepts, yet sufficiently constrained to allow the development of relatively efficient proof procedures such as resolution. Still, first-order predicate calculus can be an inconvenient system in which to express many types of knowledge that arise in normal reasoning situations. Although we can usually figure out some way to represent almost any fact by an assertion in this calculus, the resulting encoding may be so awkward that we have trouble figuring out the meanings of the logical statements, and so complicated that resolution-proof methods are no longer practical. Representing certain complex concepts such as time, belief, or causality in first-order predicate calculus is somewhat analogous to coding a complex symbol-manipulation task such as solving calculus problems in an algebraic programming language such as FORTRAN; although theoretically possible, the encoding may be so complicated that its accurate completion is not feasible, and we are forced to try to develop more-natural, special-purpose systems. At least three alternative forms of logical systems more general than first-order predicate calculus have been proposed.

Higher-order logics. In first-order predicate calculus, functions, predicates, and quantifiers may only be applied to individuals. Functions such as *look-up* or *father* tell how to replace one individual, such as a place or a person, by another individual, such as a number or another person; predicates such as *AT* assert the truth of a relation between individuals, in this case a person and a place; and quantifiers assert that "there exists an individual" such that a certain statement is true, or that "for all individuals" that are related by certain predicates and functions a certain statement is true. First-order predicate calculus does not permit quantifiers to range over predicates or functions, or predicates or functions to be applied to other predicates or functions. Yet such use is sometimes very convenient. For example, suppose we wish to make up some premises that explain the meaning of the predicate *EQUAL*. One important property of equality is that, if two objects are equal, then the same result is achieved when an arbitrary function is applied to either one. That is, if $EQUAL(x,y)$ then

$$EQUAL(father(x), father(y)),$$
$$EQUAL(look\text{-}up(x), look\text{-}up(y)),$$
$$EQUAL(squareroot(x), squareroot(y)),$$

and so on. Higher-order predicate calculus would permit us to say all this with a single statement:

$$(\forall f) \, [EQUAL(x,y) \supset EQUAL(f(x),f(y))]$$

Similarly, a predicate of two arguments is said to be *symmetric* if the order of its arguments is not important; thus *EQUAL* and *TOUCHING* are symmetric relations, but *GREATER* and *ABOVE* are not. In higher-order logic we might let a predicate *SYMMETRIC* mean that its argument, another predicate, is symmetric. The crucial property of *SYMMETRIC* could be defined something like this:

$$(\forall P) \, [SYMMETRIC(P) \supset (\forall x)(\forall y) \, [P(x,y) \supset P(y,x)]]$$

Many attempts have been made recently to develop automatic proof methods, perhaps analogous to resolution, that will work in higher-order logic. Results have been disappointing; the only methods developed thus far are so much less efficient than methods of proof in first-order logic that they cannot yet be considered feasible for use in any practical decision-making problem.

Modal logics. In ordinary logic of the kind we have been discussing, we can have only one degree of knowledge about the truth of assertions: they are either known to be true, or not. In *modal* logics, we permit several degrees of knowledge about assertions. In one widely studied form of logic, assertions can be described as being either possibly true, true, or necessarily true. The basic task in such a system is to try to establish the degree of knowledge of truth of a theorem, given a set of premises containing facts that are variously labeled as necessary, true, or merely possible. An interesting generalization of modal logic is *probabilistic* logic, in which the degree of knowledge of the truth of an assertion is expressed by any number between zero and one: an assertion whose truth has a probability of 1 is certainly true, one whose probability is 0.75 is likely to be true only three times out of four, and so on. Given premises with associated probabilities, how can we establish the probability of truth of a theorem? This theory has received disappointingly little attention, considering its potential usefulness. Success in so much of real, every-day problem solving, from predicting the weather to diagnosing illnesses to managing corporations, depends upon effectively judging and logically combining probabilities. The time is now ripe for someone to combine probability theory and theorem proving to produce a new basis for automatic problem-solving systems. Perhaps by the time this book is published some bright computer-science graduate student will have produced an important thesis in this area.

Multivalued logics. Thus far we have discussed logical systems in which assertions must have one of two values: TRUE or FALSE. In an undecidable system, we may not be able to find out which value a particular sentence has, and in a modal system, we may have a certain degree of judgment about the truth of a sentence; but in each case the underlying value of the sentence itself is indeed either TRUE or FALSE. However, representation of some concepts might be more convenient in a logic in which the truth value of an assertion could take on more than two values. Such logics are called *multivalued.* In a multivalued logic the truth values could represent different degrees of truth (such as extremely, moderately, or slightly), or they might just represent different, noncomparable values: TRUE, FALSE, and ??. Here the ?? value does not mean that the sentence is either TRUE or FALSE but we do not know which; rather, it means that the sentence is known to be neither TRUE nor FALSE, and therefore is put into a third, "undefined" category. One use for such a system is in the study of computer programs. A program can be considered TRUE if it always produces correct answers; FALSE if it has an error in it that lets it sometimes produce wrong answers; and ?? if it gets into an infinite loop and never produces an answer.

A recent innovation in logic is the development of a theory of so-called *fuzzy* logic, in which an assertion can have an infinite number of degrees of truth, represented by numbers between zero and one. (It is necessary to distinguish between a probabilistic logic, in which we can know what chance a statement has of being absolutely true, and a fuzzy logic, in which we can know absolutely that a statement is true only to some degree.) Fuzzy logic is especially useful for relative concepts—e.g., "It is cold," or "He is tall." If we know that a man is 6 feet tall we might assign the assertion that he is a tall man a truth value of, say, 0.8, whereas the truth value of a statement that a man of 5'4" is tall might be considered less than 0.1. Clearly this is a more accurate representation of tallness than one obtained by picking an arbitrary threshold— e.g., 5'8"— and saying that anyone above that height is absolutely tall and anyone below it is not tall at all.

Fuzzy logic (and a corresponding fuzzy set theory) has been the subject of several research studies since about 1965. Although the theoretical properties of fuzziness are being explored, this theory has not yet been applied to any practical problem-solving areas or integrated with the theorem-proving research being conducted on ordinary predicate calculus. Fuzzy logic, like probabilistic logic, is a promising area for further exploration and application.

Summary

Recognition and *derivation* are two contrasting approaches to solving problems. In the recognition approach, characteristics of the problem situation rather directly determine the problem's solution. The theory of pattern classification is a prime example of the recognition approach to problem solving. The derivational approach emphasizes systematic deductive methods for proceeding from a problem statement to its solution. Theorem proving in mathematical logic is a typical derivational problem-solving method.

Classification is a basic operation in much of science. Since the late 1950's, computers have been used to classify automatically many types of patterns, such as printed characters, EEG traces, and sonar echoes. Pattern classification usually consists of two distinct phases: in the *feature-extraction* phase, key distinguishing features of the sample are measured, and the sample is then represented abstractly by a list of numbers; in the *classification* phase, the abstract pattern is located in a high-dimensional mathematical space and then identified with the category that governs the relevant region of the space. Effective pattern classification depends upon effectively extracting the important features of the data patterns, and appropriately defining the category regions. The usefulness of pattern-classification methods is therefore limited to situations that do not require broader knowledge of the characteristics of the problem domain.

Deductive inference, using the special symbols and procedures of mathematical logic, is a derivational approach that can be used in a wide range of problem-solving situations. Here a problem situation is represented by formal expressions that stand for some premises, and the particular problem is represented by a *theorem* to be proved from those premises. The proof method may be *semantic*, relying upon the possible meanings of the expressions, or *syntactic*, consisting of abstract symbol-manipulation rules. In either case, it relies upon some established logical system and its associated *rules of inference.*

Propositional calculus is the most basic widely used logical system. Its formulas are composed of propositional variables, and propositional *connectives* representing the concepts *not, and,* and *or.* Computers can prove theorems in propositional calculus by using the method of *truth tables,* a more efficient method called *Wang's Algorithm,* or a new method called *propositional resolution.* Resolution proves a theorem by establishing, in an efficient, stylized manner, that if the theorem were false then an impossible, contradictory situation would result.

Propositional calculus deals only with true or false sentences; it provides no way to reason about individual entities and their properties. *Predicate calculus* is a much more powerful logical system that deals with individuals, functions, and relations. Almost any interesting reasoning problem, about mathematics or about general common-sense knowledge, can be encoded into predicate calculus. The predicate-calculus version of resolution, with its recent refinements, is a reasonably efficient basis for enabling computers to do logical reasoning. The *answer-extraction* modification of resolution permits these computer systems not only to prove the truth of certain theorems, but also to construct definite answers to questions of the form, "What object has the following specified properties?"

Because predicate calculus still has major shortcomings in its expressive power and in the speed of its proof procedures, scientists are continuing to explore other formal systems that might help computers to reason. Higher-order logics, modal and probabilistic logics, multivalued and "fuzzy" logics are all candidates for future computer reasoning systems.

SUGGESTED READINGS

Chang, C., and R. C. Lee. *Symbolic Logic and Mechanical Theorem Proving.* Academic Press, New York, 1973.

Duda, R. O., and P. E. Hart. Pattern Classification and Scene Analysis. John Wiley & Sons, New York, 1973.

Luckham, D., and N. J. Nilsson. "Extracting Information from Resolution Proof Trees." *Artificial Intelligence,* Vol. 2, no. 1, pp. 27–54, 1971.

Mendelson, E. *Introduction to Mathematical Logic.* D. Van Nostrand Co., Princeton, N.J., 1964.

Minsky, M., and S. Pappert. *Perceptions: An Introduction to Computational Geometry.* MIT Press, Cambridge, Mass., 1969.

Pattern Recognition: The Journal of the Pattern Recognition Society (quarterly). Pergamon Press, New York. 1969–

Problem Solving 5
Methods:
Informal and
Combined Approaches

Informal problem-solving methods

How do most people solve common, everyday problems? Suppose Mr. Pollack is driving to a ski resort in his little foreign car. On the way he encounters a snow storm, and finds he must mount his brand new tire chains on the wheels of his car. This problem—how to mount the chains on the wheels—can be divided into many little subproblems. Do the chains go on the front or the rear wheels? Should they be wrapped around a wheel by jacking the wheel off the ground, by driving the car onto the chains, or by figuring out how to use the funny little "mounting tools" that come with the chains? Which side of the chains should be up? How does the peculiar linking mechanism work? And so on. Mr. Pollack must solve these problems as quickly as possible, so that he can accomplish the task without freezing his fingers and soaking his clothes, and so that he can still get to the ski area without missing too much of the day's activities. Well, exactly how is this kind of problem usually attacked? By encoding the known facts as predicate-calculus .axioms, and using theorem-proving methods? Not likely! Instead Mr. Pollack (and millions of others) use *informal* problem-solving methods.

(If this chapter were to end here, many of you might think you had learned how people solve problems—namely, by a technique called "informal problem solving." Actually, all you have learned so far is a name for the technique, that tells you nothing at all about how the technique works. If you ask a doctor, "What's wrong with me?" and he says, "Oh, you have supercallifragilisticexpialiditis," you might think, in the same way, that your question had been answered, when in fact you have been given only a name that upon reflection is meaningless to you. Scientists often like to make up complicated-sounding names and pass them off as answers instead of actually explaining things. Don't let them get away with it!)

Informal problem-solving methods are especially intriguing because of their extreme generality. Problem-solving methods that most scientists develop work only in highly specialized, highly technical areas: e.g., a method for solving second-order linear differential equations with constant coefficients, or a method for estimating the distances of stars less than twenty light years away. Informal problem-solving methods, in contrast, seem to be applicable to a wide variety of problems, most of which may be brand new to the person using the methods: even though Mr. Pollack may never have been called upon to mount tire chains before, he need not be at a total loss as to how to proceed.

There are at least three different kinds of scholars who might like to understand in some detail the nature of these informal methods.

Psychologists are interested in how the human mind works, and therefore would like to know about the problem-solving methods that human beings develop, discover, or learn without any special training. How computers can help in this area is discussed in Chapter 9.

Educators are interested in developing better problem-solving ability in students, and therefore need to know what abilities are likely to be present to begin with and how they differ from person to person. The role of computers in education is also discussed further in Chapter 9.

Computer scientists want to make computers more useful in a variety of applications, and therefore are interested in learning how to increase the generality and power of automatic problem-solving methods. If human informal problem-solving methods can be sufficiently understood, perhaps they can be transferred to machines and serve as a basis, or at least a component, for better machine problem-solving methods.

In this chapter we are interested primarily in this third viewpoint: how to use our understanding of human problem-solving behavior to help us build better automatic systems. We shall take as our point of departure some ideas that were initially motivated by the psychological viewpoint: What formal representation of information and knowledge would explain the way people attack problems? A computerized version of such an explanation, called the General Problem Solver system, is the subject of the next section. Later in the chapter we shall discuss how such informal methods have been combined with theorem-proving methods in an attempt to build better automatic problem-solving systems.

Note that, as we come to understand a process, its informality disappears. In fact, we might define *understanding* as the ability to re-express some concept in terms of concrete mathematical expressions or computer algorithms. Calling a method "informal" merely masks the fact that we do not really know how it works. We should not be disdainful, however, of methods that we do understand. Just as a magician's best effect is changed in our minds from mysterious magic to a simple trick when we learn its secret, even though its outward appearance is the same, so is the respect for human knowledge and problem-solving ability unfairly degraded in many people's minds when they learn that similar abilities have been demonstrated by computers. Instead, we should appreciate our growing understanding of certain human mental abilities, and our growing facility with computers that enables them to imitate some of those abilities. Such understanding and imitation in no way reduces the marvel of the existence of such abilities in the first place.

Formalizing informal reasoning

A high school student figures out how to do a geometry problem. Mr. Pollack figures out how to mount the new chains on his car's tires. Mr. Fischer figures out what move to make in a friendly neighborhood chess game. (Not Bobby Fischer, the chess champion: Herman Fischer, who works in a machine shop down the street.)

What, if anything, makes these diverse activities similar? Is there some common denominator, some standard way of viewing any task, that enables people to apply their reasoning abilities with flexibility to any problem that arises? Psychologists have developed various approaches to explaining such complex cognitive behavior, and one is particularly appealing from the point of view of this book. This approach has been embodied in a computer program, called the General Problem Solver (GPS), that demonstrates a way to redirect a single central mechanism to a variety of different tasks with a minimum of effort. Here is an overview of how it works.

We begin by attempting to describe any problem in terms of two basic concepts: *objects* and *operators*. The objects may be physical things like tires, abstract notions like geometric lines, or imaginary situations like positions arising in a hypothetical chess game; they are the quantities that the problem solver must somehow manipulate. The operators are the alternative actions, the rules, the transformations that are available; they are the mechanisms with which the problem solver may carry out his manipulative activities. Appropriate objects and operators can be defined to represent almost all problem situations, although such representations are sometimes rather awkward. Once a problem situation is so described, many interesting problems can be restated simply as the problem of finding the sequence of operators that will transform some particular object into some other particular object (or into an object that has some particular characteristics).

If we wish to change one object into another by applying operators, we need some way to recognize whether two objects are the same, or, if they are not the same, how they differ. We thus need to be able to describe the various ways in which objects may differ from each other, and we need to have some mental process (or computer program) that can compare two objects and identify the differences.

Finally, we wish to use the differences to guide our choice of operators; there is usually no point in applying an operator that will have the effect of creating additional differences between a current object and a desired object, instead of removing the existing differences. Therefore we need to know which differences each operator is most likely to affect.

Thus the GPS approach is to give every informal reasoning problem a framework containing the following elements:

1. A class of objects (possibly containing a very large or even infinite number of specific objects)—e.g., configurations of pieces on a chess board, or wff's of predicate calculus.
2. A list of operators (usually rather short, typically less than twenty)—e.g., the legal moves of chess, or the rules of inference of logic.
3. A process for identifying the major differences between two objects or groups of objects—in chess, programs that measure features such as piece advantage, mobility, or degree of center control; in logic, measures of the complexity of expressions or counts of the different symbols that appear in them.
4. A "table of connections" that tells which differences each operator can change (with luck, reduce)—e.g., the facts that captures change piece advantage, castling can reduce king danger; substitution changes certain symbols, resolution creates new clauses.

These four elements can define a family of similar problems—e.g., chess problems or geometry problems. To specify a particular problem within the family, we now need only add one more.

5. The specific object or group of objects that represent the initial configuration, and the specific object or group of objects that represent the desired outcome—in chess, an initial position and a goal, e.g., "White to move and mate in three;" in logic, the theorem to be proved. And the task to be done, implicitly, is to find a sequence of operators that accomplishes the desired transformation.

An important feature of this characterization of problem solving is that it separates task-dependent information, the specifications of items 1 through 5 above, from the common reasoning aspects of every task, the strategies for using such specifications to construct sequences of operators. Various strategies for finding an effective sequence of operators can be proposed, and the GPS computer program, developed at Carnegie-Mellon University, was a tool for comparing and experimenting with such proposals. The simplest strategy, perhaps, was the one used in an early version of GPS (around 1960). It consisted basically of two highly interconnected subroutines.

1. To *transform* object A into object B.
   a. Identify the principal difference between the objects. (If there is no difference, the transformation is complete.)
   b. Select the most relevant operator from the table of connections.
   c. Apply the operator to object A. Call the resulting object C.[1]
   d. Transform object C into object B.
2. To *apply* an operator to an object.
   a. Transform the object into one that the operator can be used upon.
   b. Carry out the operation, producing a new object.

The discovery of the importance of an *apply* type of goal was one of the early results of these studies. It seems to be almost universally true that, when we decide upon a course of action to accomplish some primary goal, some subsidiary problems immediately pop up that must be solved before the course of action can be carried out. If the chess king is in danger early in the game, the best action might be to castle—but in order to do that, we must first move a bishop out of the way. If the classroom is too cold, we should close the window—but in order to do that we must first find the window pole and carry it to a place from which the window can be reached. If we want to send a message to someone in another city, we can write him a letter—but first we must find a pen, and if the pen is out of ink we must refill it, and if we have no refills we must buy some, and to do that we must get some money, and on, and on, and on. Every time we think we have discovered a way to solve a problem, the process of trying to carry out the solution raises new and different problems. The original GPS system, which consisted of linked *transform* and *apply* subroutines, demonstrated one way to find your way through this thicket: simply proceed one step at a time, devoting all your reasoning powers to the biggest problem that you are currently aware of, until you either solve it or replace it with a more immediate "but first . . ." problem that draws all your attention instead. Of course, each time you turn to a new problem you must note where you were, so when (or if) you actually solve some sub-sub-sub-problem, you can "back up" and make use of that solution as you proceed towards the main goal.

The singlemindedness of this problem-solving approach has a critical flaw. Like any depth-first search process (see Chapter 3) it is forced

---

[1] We hope that C is more like B than A was. If we are lucky, C will be precisely B and we are through.

to keep pursuing a single approach, even though alternative approaches lurking around the corner may become relatively much more attractive. (In the message-sending example, at some point we should consider whether to use a pencil instead of a pen, or perhaps whether to telephone instead of write.) Therefore several years' effort went into experimenting with more sophisticated ways of structuring the general reasoning processes. Late versions of GPS (those developed in the mid 1960's) build tree structures of alternative operators and goals, and have mechanisms for deciding when to abandon one train of "thought" about a problem to move elsewhere in the tree; they maintain a sense of direction by requiring progress to be made in an overall sense, but permit occasional local increases in complexity to occur; and they watch for, and avoid, lines of attack that lead to repetitions of the problem solver's previous activities. The representations and meanings of such terms as objects, operators, differences, goals, table-of-connections, and so on, have been considerably refined and standardized. The resulting system is able to solve many different mathematical problems and puzzles, including, for example, simple theorem-proving tasks using resolution in predicate calculus, and the Tower of Hanoi puzzle with four discs.

GPS has a major advantage over the more formal tree-searching algorithms discussed in Chapter 3. It is not constrained to select operators in sequence from the first operator, which is to be applied to the initial state, to the last operator, which is to reach the goal. Instead, it looks at the initial object and the goal object, and goes to work on trying to reduce the most important difference between them. The operator that succeeds in reducing this difference might eventually have to be applied somewhere in the middle of the complete sequence of operators that solve the problem. By deciding upon this operator first, the problem solver overcomes a major hurdle and replaces the entire task by two simpler subtasks: getting from the initial state to one in which the chosen key operator can properly be used, and getting from the state that exists after that operator is used to a final solution.

Consider Mr. Pollack's chain-mounting problem again. A straightforward tree-searching procedure for putting on the chains would have to consider first the alternative actions that are immediately possible when he stops his car: wait for the snow to melt, or try to drive on without chains, or turn around and go back home, or get out of the car. If we assume he gets out of the car and is standing in the snow storm, his next choices might include: get back into the car, or open the trunk, or jump up and down to keep warm. If he opens the trunk, then he can get the chains out, or get the jack out, or get the suitcases out, or crawl in, and so on. Eventually, if he follows the most direct course of action, he will find himself lying in the slush under the car, with the chain wrapped around the wheel, and his fingers jammed up between the freezing axle housing and the hot exhaust pipe, trying to figure out how the newfangled linking mechanism works.

The GPS approach might begin by observing that a key difference between having no chains on the wheels and having chains that work correctly on the wheels is that each chain must be linked onto a wheel. Therefore an understanding of the linking mechanism may be singled out as the first problem that must be solved. This problem can be tackled by studying the manufacturer's directions or by experimenting with the actual chains, while seated in the warm dry car. Once the linking mechanism is understood, the next problem is how to get to a situation in which it is appropriate to close the links, so he might then focus attention on the wrap-the-chain-around-the-wheel problem. Thus the overall task is broken down into a sequence of progressively less crucial subproblems whose solutions each fill in a different portion of the overall solution.

In the above example I gave Mr. Pollack some frivolous alternatives: jump up and down, or crawl into the trunk. However, this is not pure silliness. Mr. Pollack really does have the option at any time of doing these or an infinite number of other irrelevant things. One of the difficulties of research on problem-solving methods is how to restrict the system's attention to only the relevant things, without "cheating" by restricting the system so narrowly that it cannot help but stumble over the right solution. The pure tree-searching problem solver must consider all the options of which it is aware. The GPS-like problem solver can be somewhat better focused if it has a good difference identifier and table of connections. In both the pure and the GPS methods, however, most of the focusing of attention should be taken care of at the problem-representation stage, when information about the particular problem domain is encoded into the terminology of the problem solver; the problem solver itself need never even be aware that frivolous options are available.

The representation stage is so important that we should give a little more attention to it here. The fact that the GPS program successfully solved problems from several different task domains is at least as much a tribute to the cleverness of the programmers who encoded those tasks into GPS's *object, operator,* and *difference* terminology, as it is a tribute to GPS's true generality.

For just a taste of the variety of encodings possible, we return one final time to the chain-mounting problem. What should we choose as the objects and operators so that GPS can plan a solution for us?

1. The most obvious set of objects are the physical objects involved in the problem: chains, tires, the car, the driver. However, unless we supply someone with a welding torch and a sledge hammer, these objects are not changed in the course of solving the problem. There is no physical object that we wish to create as the solution, and no convenient operators for transforming one object into another.

2. The objects could be facts about the condition of physical objects or relations between physical objects, e.g., the chain is unlinked, the tire is not touching the chain, the chain is lying on the ground with the

wrong side up, and the jack is disassembled. Here the natural physical operations—turn the chain over, drive onto the chain, and so on—can be used directly as GPS operators that have clearly understood effects upon the GPS objects. One minor difficulty is that the goal is not a single desired GPS object (fact), but a whole collection of them that must be true simultaneously: the chains wrapped around their respective tires, right side out, linked, adjusted, and so on.

    3.   One commonly used representation consists of treating the state of the world—everything that is true at a given instant of time—as a single formal object. (Of course, only those aspects of the world that are relevant to the problem are included in the state description; the place where the chains are located is certainly part of the state-object, but the price of butter is not, unless Mr. Pollack uses butter to put on his burns from the hot exhaust pipe.) Once again, physical actions are equivalent to formal operators; they transform objects (states) into other objects. Finally, the goal is to achieve (create) any single object that has all the desired characteristics: chains wrapped, linked, adjusted, and the car on its way.

    The third representation seems at first glance to be very powerful, but in practice it sometimes requires a considerable amount of inefficient bookkeeping. The source of this difficulty has been called the *frame problem*, which is the subject of the next section.

The frame problem in problem-solving systems

Problem-solving activity can usually be divided into two consecutive phases: *planning*, which consists of thinking about how the problem can be solved, and *execution*, which consists of carrying out the preconceived plan. During the execution phase, only one situation is important at any instant—namely, the one that exists at that instant—and each action that is executed according to plan has the effect of transforming the situation into the situation of the following instant. If the plan was constructed properly, with full attention to all relevant details of every situation, then execution will proceed exactly as the planner predicted and the execution phase is thus reduced to an uninteresting "clean up" activity. This is the case in task domains such as mathematics, games, and puzzles, where all the facts are given explicitly in the problem statement, so the interesting problem solving activity is almost pure planning. In task domains that interact with the real physical world, plans are rarely perfect, so the execution phase becomes a crucial part of the problem solving process. We shall return to this issue in Chapter 8, when we discuss robot systems.

    The planning phase can almost never be limited to a single situation. In fact, effective planning is usually based upon considering alternative courses of action and comparing a variety of hypothetical situations. Furthermore, a situation can rarely be fully defined by a single data structure; not only its explicit characteristics, but also the ways in which it was derived from or is related to other situations, can be important problem-solving considerations. The frame problem is the problem of maintaining an appropriate informational context, or frame of reference, at each stage during problem-solving processes.

We can illustrate some key aspects of the frame problem with a simple example. Suppose we wish to solve some problems that arise in a sparsely furnished room. The initial situation is described by the following facts (which could be expressed in a logical language or some other precise notation if we wished).

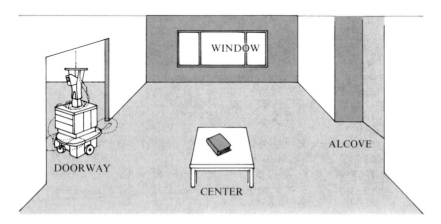

Figure 5.1 Initial room-problem situation: State S_0.

FACT F1.   A table is in the center of the room.

FACT F2.   A book is on the table.

FACT F3.   Sam is in the doorway. (Sam might be a child, a pet monkey, or a robot; it does not matter for this example.)

FACT F4.   In addition to the center and the doorway, places in the room that may interest us are a window and an alcove. (See Figure 5.1.)

Now suppose that Sam knows how to do only two things.

ACTION A1.   Go from one place to another.

ACTION A2.   Move the table from one place to another. (The possible places of interest are the locations within the room: center, door, window, and alcove.)

And these are, by definition, the only actions that can occur in the little world of our example. Consider the following possible problems whose solutions some problem solver must plan. (Sam will be responsible for carrying out the plans.)

GOAL 1.   *Sam should be in the alcove.*

This can be accomplished by directing Sam to perform an action of type A1: "Go from the doorway to the alcove." After this has been done, however, the problem solver must somehow know that Facts F1, F2, and F4 are still true, but that F3 must be replaced by a new fact.

FACT F3′.   Sam is in the alcove.

However, it also may be possible to solve the problem by directing Sam with an A2 action: "Move the table from the center to the alcove." In fact, this might be a better solution if the table is in the direct path and Sam finds it easier to push the table along with him than to figure out how to go around it. In this case, F1 would also have to be changed.

GOAL 2.   *The table should be in the alcove.*

This task removes the above ambiguity. The only reasonable way to get the table to the alcove is for Sam to push it there, changing both F1 and F3.

How can we decide which facts to change and which to leave intact? We can think of simple procedures for deciding, but they all seem to fail in certain cases. For example, suppose the procedure is:

Procedure a.   "Determine which facts change by comparing the goal statement with the known facts."

Since Goal 1 specifies a new location of Sam, then any location of Sam given in the initial situation is no longer valid. But this procedure fails if we achieve Goal 1 by the second method, in which Sam moved the table simply because it was in the way; this had little to do with the goal statement. Similarly, Goal 2 does not say anything direct about Sam's location, which must of course change if anything else is to move (since the only way for an object to move is for Sam to move it.)

A better procedure for deciding what facts are changed by actions is this:

Procedure b.   "Specify which facts are changed by each action operator."

Thus every time A1 is used, all knowledge of Sam's location must be updated; every time A2 is used, the locations of both Sam and the table must be corrected. This procedure is sufficient most of the time, but it has occasional serious difficulties. For example, suppose that before any moving around had taken place, someone had asked our problem solver to describe where in the room the book was located. Only a very simple deductive program is needed to figure out, from F1 and F2 and some understanding of the related concepts,[2]

FACT F5.   The book is in the center of the room.

---

[2] This understanding can take the form of an additional fact, namely a general rule that an object's location is the same as that of the object on which it is resting.

A prudent system might not only display F5 as the answer, but also store it away with the other facts for possible future use. Now, however, after Goal 2 has been achieved, F5 will no longer be true, even though F5 has no apparent relation to the *move* action A2.

Even more complex situations arise when sequences of actions are required. Consider:

GOAL 3. *Sam should be by the window while the table is in the alcove.*

The solution requires two actions, "Move the table from the center of the room to the alcove" and then "Go from the alcove to the window," in that order. An effective problem solver must have access to the full set of facts that apply to each situation, including derived consequences that will be true as a result of each possible action, in order to produce a correct sequence.

Note that the frame problem, like the traveling-salesman problem (Chapter 2), is a problem of finding a practical solution, not merely finding any theoretical solution. We wish to learn how to build computer programs capable of solving significant problems in complex domains; therefore they must be able to find the facts that apply to any given situation without wasting an inordinate amount of time or memory. Let us now look at some of the approaches that have been tried.

COMPLETE FRAME DESCRIPTIONS

A problem situation can sometimes be completely described by some data structure—e.g., a set of facts represented by statements in predicate calculus. If we think of each such data structure as an object, and each possible action as an operator that transforms one object into another, then we can use a GPS-like system to construct an object for which the desired goal conditions are true. Unfortunately, when the data base defining each situation reaches a nontrivial size, it becomes impractical to generate and store all the complete situation objects that need to be considered. In fact, GPS was indeed limited even in simple problems by the amount of memory space needed to hold all the objects under consideration. For more complex problems, it is not unreasonable to suppose that each situation needs to be represented by about a thousand elementary facts. If an average of six different actions is plausible in any situation, and if four successive actions may typically be needed to achieve a desired goal, then there are $6^4 = 1296$ possible intermediate and terminal situations to be considered. Storing a thousand facts to define each of more than a thousand situations would mean storing more than a million facts, which is not yet feasible in commonly available computers, at least not if all the facts must be kept immediately accessible in main memory.

If each of the thousand contemplated actions caused changes in, say, only about three of the thousand facts, then storing just the change information at each node in the problem-solving tree does seem feasible, provided appropriate bookkeeping is done to keep track of which of the original facts still holds after a series of actions. This bookkeeping seems to require considerable program structure in addition to (and quite separate from) the basic object, operator, and difference structure of a GPS-type system. The following approaches are concerned with this new bookkeeping problem.

STATE VARIABLES

One way to keep track of situations is to assign them names, called *state names*. In this formulation, actions are "state transition rules," that is, rules for transforming one state into another. Each rule usually summarizes a large number of similar but distinct possible changes in a situation—e.g., the changes that would result from any *move* action.

In 1969 Cordell Green described an approach of this kind in detail. The basic notation used is that of the predicate calculus. Each fact is labeled with the name of the state in which the fact is known to be true. Additional facts that are state-independent describe the transitional effects of actions. For example, if S_0 is the name of the initial state and *AT(object, position, state)* is a predicate asserting that object *object* is at position *position* in situation *state*, then the conditions of the previous example may be partly defined by the following axioms:

AXIOM 1.	$AT(\text{TABLE, CENTER, } S_0)$	(from F1)
AXIOM 2.	$ON(\text{BOOK, TABLE, } S_0)$	(from F2)
AXIOM 3.	$AT(\text{SAM, DOORWAY, } S_0)$	(from F3)
AXIOM 4.	$(\forall x, y, s) [AT(\text{SAM}, x, s) \supset$	
	$AT(\text{SAM}, y, go(x,y,s))]$	(from A1)

The first three axioms are straightforward predicate-calculus representations of facts F1, F2, and F3, where AT and ON are predicates and S_0 is a name given to the initial state. Axiom 4 describes the effect of the action A1, and the function *go* names the actual operation of going. More precisely, Axiom 4 says that if x and y are any place names, and s is any state name, and if Sam is at place x when the state is named s, then Sam will be at place y in the state obtained by applying the operator, "go from x to y," to the state s.

Each action, in this formalism, is viewed as a mathematical function. One argument of the function is always the state in which the action is applied, and the "value"—the result—of the function is the state achieved as a result of the action. Thus, for example, the value of $go(\text{DOORWAY, WINDOW, } S_0)$ is the name of the state achieved by Sam's going from the doorway to the window, starting from the initial state S_0.

The appeal of this approach is that, if we have a theorem-proving program, no special problem-solving mechanisms or bookkeeping procedures are necessary. Action operators may be fully described by ordinary axioms (such as Axiom 4 for the *go* operation) and the theorem-proving program, with its built-in bookkeeping, becomes the problem solver. For example, Goal 1 may be stated in the form, "Prove that there exists a state in which Sam is in the alcove," or, in predicate calculus, "Prove the theorem:

(5.1) $(\exists s)\, AT(SAM, ALCOVE, s)$."

From Axiom 3 and Axiom 4 we can prove by resolution that (5.1) is indeed a theorem, and by answer extraction (Chapter 4) the theorem prover can show that $s = go(DOORWAY, ALCOVE, S_0)$, which is the solution. (Figure 5.2)

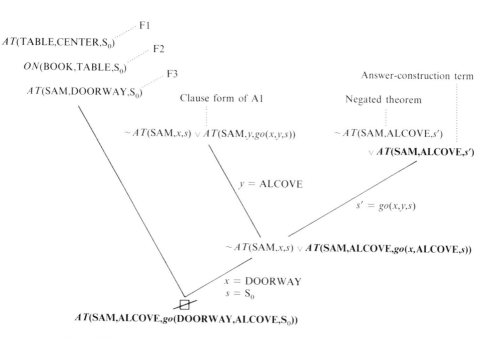

Figure 5.2   Deriving a plan by resolution and answer construction.

For more complex actions, however, the major problem with this approach emerges: *After each state change, the entire data base must be re-established.* We need additional axioms that tell not only what things change with each action, but also what things remain the same. For example, we know that the table is at the center in state S_0 (From Axiom 1), but if Sam happens to wander over to the window, the stage changes from S_0 to $S_1 = go(DOORWAY, WINDOW, S_0)$, and Axiom 1 no longer tells us anything about where the table is. In order to be able to figure out that the table did not walk away when Sam moved, we need another axiom, such as:

$$(\forall x,y,u,v,s) \; [(AT(x,y,s) \; \wedge \; x \neq \text{SAM}) \; \supset \; AT(x,y,go(u,v,s))]$$

which means that when Sam goes from u to v the object x remains where it is, at y. Thus a prodigious set of axioms is needed to define explicitly how every action affects every predicate, and a great deal of theorem-proving effort is needed to "drag along" unaffected facts through state transitions. Clearly this approach will not be practical for problems involving many facts.

THE WORLD PREDICATE

Instead of using a variety of independent facts to represent knowledge about a situation, let us now suppose that we take all the facts about a particular world and view the entire collection as a single entity, the model $\mathcal{M}$. We may then use a single predicate P, the *world predicate*, whose arguments are models and state names. $P(\mathcal{M},s)$ is to be interpreted as meaning that s is the name of the world that satisfies all the facts in $\mathcal{M}$. One possible structure for $\mathcal{M}$ is a set of formal statements, each of which represents some elementary relation; for example,

"$AT(\text{SAM,DOORWAY})$" and "$ON(\text{BOOK,TABLE})$"

could both be elements of the initial model $\mathcal{M}_0$.

The initial world could then be defined by the single axiom

$$P(\mathcal{M}_0,S_0),$$

except that the complete known contents of $\mathcal{M}_0$ must be given explicitly. If we develop adequate formal notations for talking about selected elements of $\mathcal{M}$, we can make it possible to define with a single axiom all the effects upon $\mathcal{M}$ of a given type of action: i.e., what things stay the same as well as what things change.

This approach preserves the advantages of the previous state-variable approach; namely, the problem solving, answer construction, and other bookkeeping can be left to the theorem prover. On the other hand, new logical mechanisms must be developed and combined with set theory in order for the system to work effectively with the data in $\mathcal{M}$, because facts (such as "$ON(\text{BOOK,TABLE})$") that we would sometimes like to use as axioms are now submerged as parts of more-complex data structures. Further study is necessary to determine the feasibility of this approach.

We cannot come to any definite conclusion here about the frame problem. This is an area of current research, and various approaches will continue to be proposed and experimented with, especially as particular applications come up that require particular kinds of problem-solving ability.

Combining formal and informal reasoning

Around 1969 scientists at Stanford Research Institute developed a problem-solving system to control an experimental robot (which will be discussed further in Chapter 8). This system, called STRIPS,[3] combines some of the best features of deductive theorem-proving methods, informal GPS-like problem solving, and a reasonably efficient solution to the frame problem. STRIPS is still a long way from being a useful system for any practical application, and scientists working in this field have generally decided that the way to achieve more-practical systems is to concentrate more, at present, on special-purpose systems for specific applications. They have also turned, to a large extent, away from the study of problem-solving systems to the study of tools such as programming languages and methodologies such as man–machine cooperation, with which better problem-solving systems of the future can be built. Although intelligent computers with their own independent, general-problem-solving abilities will inevitably be developed, no prototype has yet appeared that shows us definitely what their structures will eventually be. A look at STRIPS will illustrate the capabilities and the limitations of recent attempts to approximate such systems.

One of the difficulties with using GPS was that the user had very little guidance as to how to structure his task domain. GPS dealt purely with abstract notions such as objects, operators, and differences, and its success depended to a great extent upon special characteristics of those objects, operators, and differences, that the user invented for himself. The principal contribution of STRIPS is to embed into a GPS-like framework a set of specifications for the nature of objects and operators, and a resulting automatic method for obtaining differences. Of course, the user must still construct a specific representation for each specific problem, but STRIPS at least tells him the form that that representation must take; by analogy, it requires fewer decisions to build a house when one is told to use wood, with nails and tools provided by a master carpenter, than when one is completely unconstrained and must therefore consider brick, concrete, or mud as well as wood.

A problem environment for STRIPS consists of a description of an initial situation, and a set of operators for transforming one situation into another. (STRIPS situations correspond to GPS objects, and STRIPS operators correspond to GPS operators.) Each situation is defined by a set of statements in first order predicate calculus. For our example of the previous section, the initial situation would consist of statements such as:

$$AT(SAM, DOORWAY)$$
$$AT(TABLE, CENTER)$$
$$ON(BOOK, TABLE)$$

---

[3]The STanford Research Institute Problem Solver, which STRIPS away subgoals as it works.

Note that no indication that some of these statements are known to be true only in the initial state S_0 is given in the statements themselves, as it was in some frame-problem solutions proposed in the previous section. Instead, it is the complete set of statements taken together that represents S_0. Some of the statements may concern general properties of the predicates or general physical principles. For example, the fact that something is located where the thing it is on top of is located, may be expressed in predicate calculus by:

$$(\forall x,y,z)\; [[ON(x,y) \wedge AT(y,z)] \supset AT(x,z)]$$

which can be shown to be equivalent to the clause-form expression

$$\sim ON(x,y) \vee \sim AT(y,z) \vee AT(x,z).$$

The statements that define a situation are called axioms, because they will be used below as the premises for formal theorem-proving activities.

Every STRIPS operator has a unique name, and a list of parameters that refer to the objects (physical or conceptual objects, not GPS-like situation objects) upon which it operates. The operator also must have two additional components: a description of the preconditions under which it is applicable to a situation, and a description of the effects it produces if it is applied to the situation. The preconditions are expressed simply by a predicate calculus wff, except that the wff may contain certain parameters that must be given specific values before the operator may be used. For example, suppose we have an operator

$$go(x,y)$$

that moves Sam from place x to place y. Both x and y are called parameters, because *go* is actually a family of specific action operators, each of which moves Sam between two different specific places, and the values of x and y determine those places (x and y are not called variables, because they behave differently from the $\forall$-quantified symbols of our logical system).

The simplest precondition for $go(x,y)$ is

$$AT(SAM,x).$$

After all, Sam cannot move away from a place unless he is at that place. (But since x is a parameter rather than a variable, this statement means SAM is someplace, but not everyplace.)

The *effects* of an operator consist of two parts: a *delete list* and an *add list*. The delete list contains predicates whose values may be changed by the operator; the add list contains wffs that are made to be true by the action of the operator. For example, the effects of $go(x,y)$ might be represented by the two lists,

Delete	Add
$AT(SAM,x)$	$AT(SAM,y)$

When we apply an operator to a situation, we create a new situation description by (1) deleting all wffs in the old situation that contain predicates on the delete list of the operator, and (2) adding the wffs on the add list of the operator to the remaining wffs in the old situation. This results in a new situation: i.e., a description of the situation that would arise out of the old situation if the particular operator were applied. Figure 5.3 shows the situation that arises if we make Sam move from the doorway to the window, starting from the initial situation S_0 described previously.

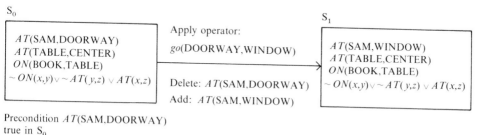

Figure 5.3 Applying a STRIPS operator.

We are now ready to see how STRIPS goes about solving problems. First, STRIPS must be given a problem environment: namely, an initial situation and a set of parameterized operators with their preconditions and effects. Then, we must give the problem solver a task to perform. We do this by specifying a *goal statement* called G_0, which has the form of a predicate-calculus wff that we want the problem solver to make true—e.g., "$AT(SAM,WINDOW)$." This is somewhat peculiar from the point of view of normal logic. Ordinarily, we ask whether a particular wff is provable or not, given a fixed set of axioms. Here, instead, we present a wff that is usually not true, and ask whether it can be made provably true by changing the axioms. The operators provide the means for changing the axioms. Specifically, then, we want the problem solver to construct a sequence of actions (operators) that would transform the initial situation into a final situation in which the truth of the goal is assured.

When STRIPS has been given a goal statement, it begins its solution attempt by trying to establish whether the goal is true in the initial situation. It does this by using a theorem prover to attempt to prove that G_0 is a consequence of the axioms that define S_0. If the attempted proof succeeds, the problem is solved by doing nothing (except drawing the necessary logical inferences). In more-interesting cases the goal is not already true, and STRIPS will need to identify a "difference" between the initial state and a goal state, just as GPS must identify a difference. However, this difference is obtained by STRIPS directly from the attempted proof that failed. STRIPS analyzes the partial proofs obtained in the attempt and selects as a "difference" some simple aspect of the initial model which, if changed, would permit the proof of G_0 to proceed successfully. (In some simple cases, such as the case in which G_0 is "AT(SAM,WINDOW)," the theorem prover makes absolutely no progress and the "difference" is just G_0 itself.)

Having identified a difference expressed as a set of statements to be made true, STRIPS must then select an operator from its repertoire that offers promise of "reducing" this difference: i.e., helping to prove it. Once again, the theorem prover is useful. We wish to find an operator that, if applied, would produce a situation in which some elements of the selected difference are provable (and thereby can be eliminated from the difference). Therefore, to test the relevance of a candidate operator, we test whether any portion of the difference can be deduced from the add list of the operator. To help complete such a proof, we may have to specify values for some of the parameters of the operator. (Note that "AT(SAM,WINDOW)" can be deduced immediately from the add list of $go(x,y)$, if the parameter y is set to be WINDOW.) Sometimes an operator produces minor side effects that must be included on the add list but should not be considered as reasons for selecting the operator. Such side effects are not used for relevance tests.

Assuming that an operator (e.g., the operator "$go(x,$WINDOW)") is selected as being relevant to reducing the difference at hand, STRIPS uses the theorem prover once more to establish whether the preconditions of that operator (e.g., "AT(SAM,x)") are true in the current situation—if they are, the operator may be applied immediately. (In the current example, we need merely assign the parameter x to be DOORWAY.) If the preconditions are not immediately provable, they are formed into a subgoal available for STRIPS' future consideration. Eventually STRIPS may solve that subgoal: i.e., it may find a sequence of operators that produces a situation in which the subgoal of preconditions is true. Then the operator that was originally selected as being relevant can be applied after that sequence, to reduce the main difference under consideration.

Perhaps our complicated explanation of how STRIPS works can be made at least slightly clearer with the aid of a more interesting example. We shall base the example upon the by now familiar adventures of The Room and Sam. The initial situation is our old friend S_0: Sam in the doorway and the book on the table in the center (Figure 5.1). We shall permit only two operators: $go(x,y)$, by which Sam moves from place x to place y without disturbing anything else, and $push(u,x,y)$, by which Sam pushes object u from place x to place y. One minor complication is that we shall require both Sam and u to be at the same place before u may be pushed anywhere. We shall assume that place names identify neighborhoods, rather than precise points, so that two or more objects

Table 5.1 Operators _go_ and _push_.

Operator	Preconditions	Delete	Add
_go(x,y)_	$AT(SAM,x)$	$AT(SAM,x)$	$AT(SAM,y)$
push(u,x,y) [$u \neq$ SAM]	$AT(u,x) \wedge$ $AT(SAM,x)$	$AT(u,x)$ $AT(SAM,x)$ $AT(v,x)$, if $ON(v,u)$	$AT(u,y)$ $AT(SAM,y)$

may be at the same place simultaneously. Also, we shall note that Sam cannot push himself, and that _push_ should not be used solely as a means of getting Sam somewhere. Table 5.1 gives the descriptions of the two parameterized operators. The third item on the delete list of _push_ means that pushing changes the location of objects on top of the pushed object. (The actual STRIPS system has a more general, but also more complicated, scheme for keeping track of such interdependent relations.)

We shall now exercise STRIPS by asking it to answer a question: "Can we use the _go_ and _push_ operators to produce a situation in which Sam is by the window at the same time that the table is in the alcove?" This problem may be rephrased: "Prove the assertion that Sam is by the window and the table is in the alcove." In predicate calculus,

$$G_0: AT(SAM,WINDOW) \wedge AT(TABLE,ALCOVE)$$

Now that STRIPS has been given a goal statement, it tries to prove it from the axioms of S_0 (shown in Figure 5.3). If we take the clause form of $\sim G_0$,

$$\sim AT(SAM,WINDOW) \vee \sim AT(TABLE,ALCOVE)$$

and use the set of support strategy (Chapter 4) to try to resolve this clause with the axioms, we make no progress at all; the only resolutions possible produce more complicated clauses about silly possibilities (like SAM being on top of something), but get us no closer to a contradiction. Therefore we consider the elements of G_0 itself, $AT(SAM,WINDOW)$ and $AT(TABLE,ALCOVE)$, as the key differences; if they were both provable, then the goal would obviously be true. By looking at the add lists of the two operators, STRIPS quickly decides that both of the operators are relevant: $go(x,WINDOW)$ would eliminate the first difference, and $push(TABLE,x,ALCOVE)$ would eliminate the second difference. Both must be examined further by STRIPS. The _go_ alternative leads to a new situation, S_1, that turns out to be rather unpromising. Returning to the _push_ alternative, which would produce a situation S_2 with the table in the alcove, STRIPS must now find out whether the _push_ operator can actually be used. This is done by trying to prove its preconditions

$$AT(TABLE,x) \land AT(SAM,x),$$

by negating them and trying to deduce a contradiction from the axioms of S_0, as shown in Figure 5.4.

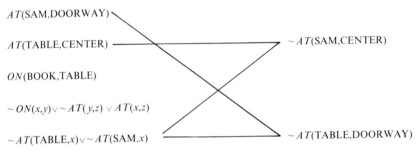

$AT(SAM,DOORWAY)$

$AT(TABLE,CENTER)$ $\sim AT(SAM,CENTER)$

$ON(BOOK,TABLE)$

$\sim ON(x,y) \lor \sim AT(y,z) \lor AT(x,z)$

$\sim AT(TABLE,x) \lor \sim AT(SAM,x)$ $\sim AT(TABLE,DOORWAY)$

Figure 5.4   Attempt to prove preconditions produces subgoals.

Once again, the proof is incomplete, resulting this time in two alternative subgoals: $AT(SAM,CENTER)$, or $AT(TABLE,DOORWAY)$. STRIPS can now quickly establish that the first of these subgoals can be achieved by an operator of the form $go(x,CENTER)$, and furthermore that its precondition $AT(SAM,x)$ is immediately satisfied if we pick x to be DOORWAY. Therefore we can apply the operator

$$go(DOORWAY,CENTER)$$

to S_0 to get a new situation, S_3, to which the operator

$$push(TABLE,CENTER,ALCOVE)$$

can probably be applied to produce situation S_2. In S_2 the original difference $AT(TABLE,ALCOVE)$ has been eliminated. The process can now begin again using S_2 as an "initial" state: i.e., one that we now know precisely how to achieve, and one that seems to be on the way to a solution.

    Figure 5.5 summarizes the moves actually considered by STRIPS, their relations, and the final solution. In summary, STRIPS was given situation S_0 (Sam in the doorway, the table in the center), and asked how to produce a situation like S_G (Sam by the window, and the table in the alcove). STRIPS immediately decided that S_1 (Sam by the window) and S_2 (the table just pushed into the alcove) were promising intermediate situations. Examining things more closely, it found that S_1 was easy to achieve, but to get from S_1 to a solution would probably be as hard as the original problem, so that approach was quickly abandoned. S_2 would not be so easy to achieve; in order to push the table, either Sam had to be where the table was, or the table had to be where Sam was. Deciding that

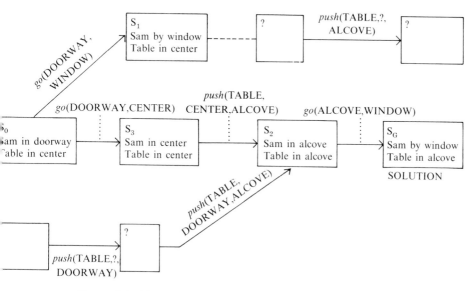

Figure 5.5 Situations and actions considered by STRIPS.

the latter alternative again led to unnecessary complexities, STRIPS focused upon achieving the former—which is situation S_3—and the rest of the pieces quickly fell into place.

When spelled out in the detail of the last few pages, the activities of the STRIPS problem-solving program may still seem extremely complicated and obscure. However, when you step back from the details—e.g., look at the summary in the last paragraph—perhaps you will agree that STRIPS is doing precisely what needs to be done, at least in broad outline: a little logic, a little common sense reasoning, a little bookkeeping, and presto! A solution. You may think that you know some better way of doing this kind of problem when you have to solve one yourself. Think carefully, now. What did STRIPS consider that you think is unnecessary? Suppose you had to explain in detail every step and every consideration you made while you solved Sam's problem: would your explanation differ in some substantial way from the above explanation of STRIPS' approach? Finally, even if STRIPS, GPS, Resolution, and other complex computer programs behave in totally nonanthropomorphic ways, doesn't the existence of such detailed, step-by-step, examples of computers at work on simple reasoning problems, help you understand what steps are necessarily part of the problem-solving process?

Can a computer learn?

I am frequently asked this question, and it always makes me feel uncomfortable. The reason it makes me uncomfortable is that I know I cannot give a convincing answer, at least not in the 30 seconds typically available, because whoever asked the question almost always does not have any clear idea himself of what he means by "learn," and is already convinced that, whatever "learning" is, a computer cannot do it. Before reading on to the next paragraph, think about it yourself for a few moments. What do you think learning means? Do you think a computer can be made to do it?

A widely-used but rather superficial definition of learning is simply, "Improvement of performance as a result of experience." Therefore one is said to be able (or unable) to learn all the following:

a)　the multiplication table;
　　　Lincoln's Gettysburg Address;
　　　the route home from school;

b)　to ride a bicycle;
　　　to recognize colors;
　　　to tune a piano;

c)　long division;
　　　grammar;
　　　how to tie a bow;

d)　to understand the meanings of new words;
　　　to beat a master at chess;
　　　to compose a symphony.

In each example, at some given time a person does not know (or is unable to do) something, but later, after a period of study and practice, he does know it (or is able to do it); therefore the same word, *learning*, is applied to all the situations. However, the natures of the activities are vastly different; we would not expect the same memory mechanisms to be at work when we remember that $8 \times 7 = 56$, when we recognize the color chartreuse, when we tie our shoes, and when we understand the word *omphaloskepsis*. Therefore we should not expect the mechanisms for acquiring all these different kinds of knowledge to be the same. Actually, psychologists, who are most concerned with studying and explaining the nature of "learning," tend to avoid using this word, much as biologists avoid the word "living" and some computer scientists avoid the word "algorithm." These words have such varied common interpretations that they can no longer be used in a precise technical sense. Since I am not a psychologist, however, I feel free to continue using (perhaps misusing) the word "learning," and shall attempt to describe some of the different kinds of learning that people, and perhaps computers, can do.

Learning processes can be divided into at least four categories, corresponding to the four groupings in the above list. Although most significant tasks certainly require a combination of elementary abilities, each of the above items resembles the other items in its group more than the items in the other groups. We shall call the four categories:

a) *rote* learning;
b) *parameter* learning;
c) *method* learning;
d) *concept* learning.

Category *a*, rote learning, consists simply of transferring raw data into memory in such a way that it can be retrieved upon demand when needed. The nature of the retrieval index varies with the nature of the data. The multiplication table must be highly indexed, so that I can get to any entry rapidly. If I had to figure out how much 8×7 is—e.g. by counting by eights—then I could not consider that the $8 \times 7 = 56$ entry in the table had been learned. Lincoln's Address, on the other hand, usually needs to be learned only straight through from the beginning. I am not expected to be able to answer quickly questions like, "What sentence comes just before the phrase, 'The world will little know nor long remember'?" Similarly, the route home from school can be considered adequately learned if I always turn left when I get to the fire station, even if I cannot describe the route to someone else.

Category *b*, parameter learning, consists of situations in which a basic framework of fundamental abilities exists before the learning begins; the principal knowledge acquired by learning consists of how to combine or relate already known abilities in order to produce new, more-effective results. Thus when a child learns to ride a bicycle he does not memorize and then recall any specific pieces of data. Instead, he develops coordination between certain leg and arm muscles, which he already knows how to use, and certain built-in balance sensors, that have always told him whether he was right-side up. Similarly, learning what color chartreuse is means building an association between the word "chartreuse," whose spelling and pronunciation is perhaps first learned by rote, and a certain portion of the range of wavelengths of light that the basic hardware of the eye (and brain) is capable of perceiving. A piano tuner learns to apply his inherent ability to recognize when the sound frequencies of two tones are related by certain small whole-number ratios. Tone-deaf people who cannot perceive such relationships can never learn to do this. The term *parameter*, applied to such learning situations, refers to the fact that the learning process can usually be described in terms of the assignment of numerical values to parameters. These parameters determine the relative importance or extent of the inherent capabilities whose specific applications are being learned. For example, in bicycle riding one parameter relates how far the bike must lean over to compensate for a given angular turn of the handlebars. In color perception, a parameter specifies the wavelength of the color boundary between chartreuse and, say, gold.

Method learning, category *c*, refers to the acquisition of *procedures* that can be used to solve whole classes of problems. Thus when one "learns" long division one really acquires, usually by rote learning, a method that can be used to solve an infinite number of specific arithmetic problems. Before the days of computers, some psychologists may have puzzled over how the solutions to an infinite number of problems could be represented compactly in human memory. Now, of course, just about every subroutine in every programming language is an example of how such procedures may be encoded. (Note that method learning does not imply method *discovery*. How many students invent the long-division procedure for themselves, when they "learn" long division?) Grammar is essentially procedural knowledge; the ability to recognize grammatical sentences and the ability to construct grammatical sentences are the basic demonstrations of understanding the grammar of any language. Grammar is in fact generally represented by both descriptive rules and procedures for using those rules (parsing) in sentence recognition and construction. Finally, certain physical abilities are also basically procedural in nature; in order to tie a bow, one must have two ends of string (or ribbon, or cloth) firmly under control, make a loop in one, wrap the other around it, and so on. This procedure, like the long-division procedure, is applicable to a huge family of specific problems and must be followed in a precise step-by-step fashion.

Our fourth category, concept learning (*d*), refers to the least-well understood and therefore most difficult forms of learning. Perhaps it is a catch-all category, containing anything anyone might like to consider to be learning that does not fit into categories *a*, *b*, or *c*. Still, it seems to have certain clear identifying characteristics. When someone "learns" to be a top-level chess player, musician, artist, or performer in almost any occupation, we can no longer identify specific facts, parametric relationships, or procedural methods that explain his outstanding performance. Somehow Mr. Fischer (Bobby, the chess champion, not Herman, the machinist) has learned to play chess better than anyone else in the world. But today nobody, including himself, can identify just what it is he has learned that gives him this championship ability: what facts, what parameters, what methods. If we could list the precise characteristics of championship knowledge, then we could give any number of people—and computers—the same knowledge, and all the resulting champions would be exactly equally matched (resulting in some rather dull tournaments).

Since we do not yet understand the detailed nature of skill at chess, or musical or artistic ability, and how it is acquired, we are free to believe in either of two alternatives.

EITHER

1.   All knowledge and ability can be acquired by rote, parameter, or method learning. We merely have not yet discovered the right ways to

express the significant facts and procedures of chess, music, and so on, to fit them into this framework.

OR

2. There exists at least one, and perhaps many, basic kinds of learning (and corresponding knowledge structures) in addition to rote, parameter, and method learning. We must discover and understand the nature of these additional learning mechanisms and knowledge representations before we can hope really to understand and imitate true chess (and musical, and so on) expertise.

Which alternative do you believe? Most people probably pick 2, because the easiest way to interpret unexplainable performance is to attribute it to an unknown mechanism. However, this can be a cowardly way to avoid the real problem; if you believe that the magician's utterance "ABRACADABRA!," produced the rabbit out of thin air, then you do not have to look further for a different explanation. The more typical scientific approach is to choose an alternative like 1: i.e., assume that the known methods or theories can be applied to new problem situations; attempt to stretch the limits of these methods or theories in order to apply them; and, only when such an attempt fails, invent or discover a new method or theory to broaden the scope of the complete knowledge system. In this way, computer scientists began in the 1950's with rote learning, developed well-understood theories of parameter learning in the early 1960's, explored the limits of these theories in the mid 1960's and began to add method learning to their bag of tricks, and by the 1970's were considering what additional methods, if any, should be developed next to increase the intellectual power of automatic systems.

Learning the meaning of a new word is perhaps the simplest example of concept learning. The result of the learning process is a completely new structure of relationships. The meaning of a noun—e.g., *chair*—involves understanding that it is a piece of furniture, that it is used for sitting upon, that it is only big enough for one person at a time, that it may have arms, and so on. Concept learning might be viewed as a very general kind of parameter learning: all the elementary components must be present and the learning process consists of joining them together appropriately. However, the joining process creates new structures that could not have been formed merely by adjusting predefined parameters. Finally, concept learning can include not only the creation of new structures, but also the creation of new procedures (and possibly the creation of procedures for creating procedures), so that perhaps it will be a basis for explaining creativity, ingenuity, the discovery of the long division algorithm (or the proof of a new theorem), the development of a new, perhaps subconscious, method for selecting a chess move, or the invention of a new musical theme. Thus I personally now lean toward alternative 2, but limit it to the following working hypothesis: There exists precisely one basic kind of learning, called *concept* learning, in addition to rote, parameter, and method learning. Concept learning is the mechanism for combining facts, parameters, and methods, in order to create more-complex structures representing new facts, parameters, and methods.

Perhaps the next few years' research will determine whether this working hypothesis is correct, or whether concept learning can be reduced to a special case of parameter or method learning, or whether yet a fifth (and sixth, and so on) form of learning should be added to our basic collection.

Now let us return to the main subject of this section: Can a computer learn? We have described four categories of general learning behavior. We shall look at some examples of computer programs that have exhibited each of these types of learning.

ROTE LEARNING

Rote learning is one of the most basic activities of every computer system. Almost every large computer program contains tables of data that are filled in and later looked up: lists of employees, spare parts, books, or the symbols that occur in a program to be compiled. In each case some program segment "learns" about a new entry by placing it in the table, and some other program segment "remembers" the "memorized" item when it looks it up. Surely this demonstrates, in the clearest sense, that a computer can learn.

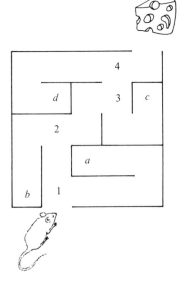

Figure 5.6 Maze experiment. Rat must make a choice at each numbered location, and turn back at each letter.

A typical animal-learning experiment goes like this: the experimenter places a rat at the entrance of a maze, a piece of cheese at the exit, and watches how many wrong turns the rat takes before he gets to the cheese (Figure 5.6). The experiment is repeated several times, and the rat is said to have learned the maze if he can eventually go directly to the cheese without making any mistakes in the maze. Can a computer learn in this sense? Of course. Any maze can be represented by a tree structure (Figure 5.7). Any competent computer programmer can write a program to search this tree for a path from the entrance to the exit. Moreover, he can set this program to look for any path or, perhaps at slightly more effort, to find the shortest path. (How many rats, after learning one path to the cheese, will keep looking for a shorter one? If some rat did keep looking, would we consider him smarter or stupider than the rest?) After one run, the program will have "learned" the maze (i.e., constructed a description of the winning path) and it can print out this path immediately each time no matter how many more times it is run—and without needing any cheese.

In his famous checker-playing program, Dr. Samuel introduced a clever form of rote learning. Whenever a position is encountered for the first time, the program stores away (memorizes) its description and an estimate of its value (i.e., which player is better off, and how much). This value is based upon the results of looking ahead a few moves in the game tree and then making rough static evaluation estimates of the resulting positions (see Chapter 3). In some future game, before making the static evaluation of a look-ahead position, the program may notice that that position is one that was previously memorized. In this case the previously calculated and memorized value is more accurate than the value that would be obtained by static evaluation (because it represents the result of previous additional look-ahead). In this way the rote-learned values

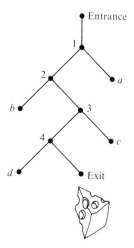

Figure 5.7 Tree equivalent to maze of Figure 5.6.

of positions help improve the performance of the checker player from game to game. (This technique is much more useful in checkers than in more-complex games such as chess, because the same early positions frequently recur in different checker games, and checker positions are easy to sort, by piece-count and advancement, and therefore easy to look up in memory.)

PARAMETER LEARNING

The best example of parameter learning by computer is in pattern classification. In Chapter 4 (p. 100) we discussed pattern classification as a decision-making mechanism: given the definitions of various categories— e.g. in the form of prototype patterns—pattern classification methods specify how to assign a new sample to a category. Now we raise the important question: how can the prototypes be determined in the first place? One way is for a human expert to describe each prototype as well as he can, by thinking about, or measuring, an ideal representative of each category. If we want the system to recognize letters of the alphabet, for example, we might take a brand new font of printer's type and measure the key characteristics of each letter. However, suppose the letters that we eventually ask the system to classify were printed by an old, worn font of type; or in a different style of type; or even by hand. Then many of the detailed features of the shiny new type used as the basis for the prototypes will not be relevant, and may even reduce the effectiveness of the classification system.

A better approach might be to initialize the system by taking some examples of the actual samples that the system would later be expected to identify, have our human expert classify these samples, and then define the prototypes on the basis of measured characteristics of these classified samples: e.g., the "width" characteristic of the prototype letter A could be the average of the widths of all the samples that the expert has identified as A's, and so on.

Now the key step: A computer "knows" what features of each sample are to be used for future classification, because after all it will be doing the classifications. Once the expert has classified a sample, why does he need to take part in creating its prototype? Certainly a computer is as good as a person at computing averages. Therefore the computer itself determines the prototypes—or hyperspace region boundaries, or other classification decision criteria—during a "training" period. The human expert serves as a teacher by presenting to the computer samples with their classifications ("This is an A, this is a B, this is another A, . . .") and the computer uses these identified samples to adjust the parameters of its decision rules, thereby learning how to classify future representatives of the same categories.

This approach is especially useful in commonly arising situations in which the human himself does not know exactly which features of the samples are most important for classification. In analyzing brain waves, for example, an expert with many years of training can look at the printed traces and say, "This person is normal, this one has epilepsy, this one is brain-damaged, . . ." and yet this same expert cannot say exactly what features of these traces he is using to draw his conclusions. Suppose we program the computer to collect all the measurements of each sample that we think may be important: average amplitude, principal frequencies that occur, their phase and amplitude relations, and so on. Then, we "train" the system by giving it many samples labeled with the human expert's classifications. It is sometimes even possible for a computer program, using well-known mathematical methods, to find objective criteria that the human expert was not aware of, as a basis for making future decisions. In fact, criteria discovered in this way might be used to help teach humans what features to look for as they study to be the next generation of human experts.

Samuel's checker-playing program, which we have previously discussed, had an interesting form of parameter learning. The performance of this program depended very heavily upon an *evaluaton function* —a mathematical formula for calculating a number representing how good a given position was. This formula was the sum of measures of various properties of a position such as piece advantage, advancement, and center control. However, the programmer did not know what relative importance to give these factors: for example, was winning an extra piece worth giving up control of three center squares? One square? Or seven squares? So he left the relative weights as variable parameters of the initial evaluation function. The value of a position is proportional to

(piece advantage) $+ x \cdot$ (degree of advancement)
$+ y \cdot$ (number of center squares controlled),

and so on, where x and y (and about twenty other parameters) are unknown. Now we need a parameter-learning method to determine the values of the parameters. The computer needs a teacher to show it examples of good and bad positions, and tell it their correct values; but no human checker expert evaluates positions in precisely the way we require, and no human would have the patience to evaluate the thousands of positions needed to establish the parameters of a formula as complicated as our evaluation function. Dr. Samuel came up with two different methods for getting out of this dilemma, both of which worked well enough to produce approximately the same, surprisingly effective, evaluation functions.

Parameter learning from book games. There are many books that show every move in checker games between the best human players. Thousands of positions from these games were presented to the computer, along with the next move selected in each position by the human expert. In each position, the computer could calculate all the possible immediate moves, see which resulting position its evaluation function would select as best, and compare that choice with the expert's choice from the books. The parameters of the evaluation function were then modified so that the computer's choice would agree with the expert's choice in as many cases as possible.

Parameter learning by consistency. As discussed in Chapter 3, the basic procedure for a computer to decide upon a move in a game is to look ahead several moves, evaluate (by an evaluation function) the resulting positions, then "back up" those values (by the minimax procedure) to find the values of the present position's immediate successors, and select the move to the successor whose value is highest. Now, we can also certainly apply the same evaluation function directly to these successors, but (as we argued in Chapter 3) we would not expect the calculated values to be as accurate as those obtained with some look-ahead. The consistency-learning method relies on the assumption that, if the evaluation function were perfect, the direct evaluation and the look-ahead evaluation of a position would both give exactly the same results. Therefore whenever the look-ahead value of a position differs from the static (directly calculated) value, the parameters of the evaluation function should be changed to make the static value a little closer to the more accurate, look-ahead value. A particular parameter-adjustment rule based upon this principle was found that resulted in stable settings for the parameters, very close to those learned from book games, after only about twenty-five practice games.

METHOD LEARNING

In a sense, a computer "learns" a method every time it is given a program. Certainly one can "teach" a computer to do long division more easily than one can teach a child; after all, we can go right into the brain of the computer, either with a wiring tool or with appropriate software, and firmly define the procedure we want it to use.

Let us move on to a much more sophisticated form of method learning, which frequently occurs as part of human intellectual growth: learning in which a method is discovered, perhaps as a result or side-effect of one activity, and then applied to other distinct activities. For example, a one-year-old child will attempt to remove a coat from a hook by pulling downward on the coat, and will become frustrated by his repeated failures. Once he learns that the coat can be lifted free of the hook, either by being shown by an adult (teacher) or by accidentally knocking the coat free, he seems to acquire a new method spontaneously; not merely a method for consistently removing that coat from that hook, but also for removing all other coats from coat-hooks, and cups from cup-hooks, and for opening gate-hooks, and getting into all manner of mischief.

Can a computer learn a method in this sense? Can it produce a solution to a specific problem, recognize that key elements of that solution have wider applicability, and store away the generalized solution for future use? Traditionally, such performance has not been asked of computers. They have been programmed to use specific methods for specific problems when specifically requested. As we try to make computers smarter, however, we would like to find ways for a computer to solve problems even when specific solutions have not been programmed. We would like to find ways for a computer to build up its own repertoire of generally useful techniques, so that it has some things to try anytime someone with a real problem comes along and says vaguely, "Help!" One place to begin is with a program that can construct solutions to a variety of different problems—e.g., the STRIPS system discussed in the previous section.

STRIPS is capable of learning methods in precisely the sense we have just been describing. Whenever STRIPS solves a problem such as our earlier example, "Produce a situation in which Sam is by the window and the table is in the alcove," STRIPS takes its solution,

> *go*(DOORWAY, CENTER),
> *push*(TABLE, CENTER, ALCOVE),
> *go*(ALCOVE, WINDOW),

generalizes it as much as possible by replacing constants by parameters, producing

> $go(x,y)$,
> $push(u,y,z)$,
> $go(z,w)$,

and stores away the resulting plan as if it were a single elementary operator (like *go* or *push*). Thus the solution to the specific table-alcove-window problem has been made into a method whose effect is to get any object u to any place z, and Sam to any other place w. Thus whenever STRIPS solves a problem, it learns a method for solving a family of similar problems, and thereby becomes a slightly better (smarter?) problem-solving system.

Another procedure that might be considered method learning is the subject of a new field called Automatic Programming, in which computers are being put to work helping to create and test programs for themselves. This work will be discussed further in Chapter 9.

CONCEPT LEARNING

The question, "Can a computer learn a new concept?" is almost as vague as our introductory question, "Can a computer learn?" In order to answer it, we must first agree about exactly what it means. Following our previous discussion of concept learning, we shall here consider "learning a concept" as the process of building a new knowledge structure out of previously known concepts. Such a process is not as shaky as it may seem. Every dictionary is a complex circular structure in which all words are defined in terms of the other words. Several researchers have tried, unsuccessfully, to find some set of fundamental coordinates of meaning, define a basic most elementary vocabulary, and then build up all knowledge upon such a foundation. Although such a system would be mathematically and esthetically pleasing, it does not appear to be necessary for people—or computers. Every child gets on the meaning merry-go-round as soon as he begins to become aware of his environment. His knowledge grows primarily by dividing and then relating the resulting poorly understood components of the world (if it moves by itself, it's alive; if it flies, it's a bird—unless it's an airplane or a dragonfly). The elementary nature of each component is much less important than how it is related to other components. In fact, we might argue that there is no such thing as an inherent, independent meaning of anything; instead, the meaning of something must always be defined by its relationships to other things. In this book, we do not need to take such an extreme view. It will be sufficient to agree that relationships are at least an important part of the nature of concepts, and are therefore a reasonable target for computer scientists interested in the automation of knowledge acquisition and use. We shall return to the study of the meanings of words in the next chapter, which deals exclusively with language analysis.

Perhaps the best example so far of concept learning by computer is provided by a program written by Patrick Winston at MIT in about 1970. A human "teacher" presents to this program a series of labeled examples, in much the same way as the teacher trains the pattern-classifying system of our parameter-learning discussion. However, the training examples are not lists of numbers or other simple formal objects, and the internal data that the program works with is not a rigid structure with only numerical parameters to vary. Instead, the inputs are descriptions (in the form of list structures) of line drawings of arbitrary three-dimensional objects, and the internal data is a complex graph whose connections are created, removed, or labeled in various ways by the program.

More specifically, the program was designed to learn about elementary architectural arrangements. It can study a simple symbolic description of a picture, identify and describe the various major objects in the picture—cube or wedge-shaped, standing or lying, and so on—and determine certain relationships among them, such as adjacency, support, or connection. It can then create and store a graph structure representing all these characteristics of the picture, and attach to this structure the label given by the teacher for the complete assembly in the picture. Finally, it can compare and consolidate a series of picture-structures and their labels, producing a single structure that represents the concept being taught.

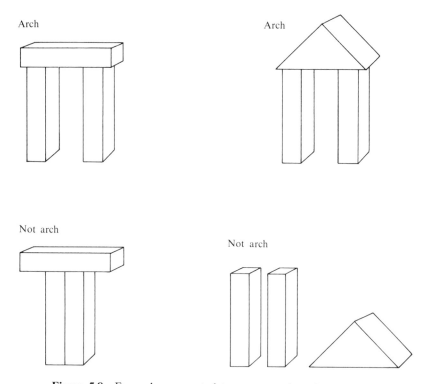

Figure 5.8 Examples presented to a concept-learning program.

For example, suppose the teacher wishes the program to learn what an *arch* is. If he presents suitably-encoded descriptions of the parts of Figure 5.8 labeled ARCH, and the parts labeled NOT ARCH, then the program will have built up an internal graphical representation of the concept of arch-ness that will apply only to architectural structures consisting of precisely three parts: two standing, nonadjacent parallelopipeds, both supporting a third object that may be any shape at all. The program can then use this description to analyze future pictures and decide whether or not they contain arches.[2]

Notice that this concept of an arch was quickly built up because the teacher presented a carefully chosen sequence of typical cases and near misses. Some might consider this cheating, and claim that we made the task too easy for the computer. However, no description or definition of a general arch is ever given to the program; it really figures it out from the examples. Isn't the goal of every good teacher to find examples that lead the pupil (or computer) to discover for himself (or itself) the concept being taught?

---

[2]Strictly speaking, Figure 5.8 teaches post and lintel, rather than arch, construction.

It is time to review the questions in the opening paragraph of this section. What do you think *learning* means? Do you think a computer can be made to do it? Perhaps you have some ideas about the nature of learning that are substantially different from the examples discussed in the previous paragraphs. Can you make your ideas precise? Do you think you can design a computer program to demonstrate them? Congratulations! You have just found your PhD thesis topic!

Current directions in problem-solving research

In the past two chapters, we have described the main lines of fifteen years' research with the general goal of making computers more capable of solving problems without needing specific, detailed programs for each application. This work has resulted in the development of elaborate theories of pattern classification and of automatic theorem proving; some prototype systems capable of solving a wide range of specific formal problems; a better understanding of the frame problem; and some impressive but isolated examples of machines that can learn. Work is continuing in all these areas, to improve, expand the scope, and increase the power of computer systems. Some of the results of this work are beginning to appear in practical applications, as we shall see in Chapter 9. In addition, some new areas are opening up as promising directions for future problem-solving research. Here is a brief overview of some of these new directions.

NEW PROGRAMMING LANGUAGES

The programming language he uses is the basic tool of the computer scientist. The greater the expressive power of the language, the easier it is for the scientist to define and test new ideas. As new problem-solving methods become understood, the best way to make use of them is to build them into programming languages for use in the development of the next generation of problem-solving methods. In the early 1960's a flurry of work on programming languages led to the symbol-manipulation systems—list and string processing languages—that were used for almost a decade to help develop theorem proving and other problem-solving programs. Currently, in the 1970's, we are experiencing a new flurry of programming-language work, aimed at building theorem-proving, search, and other recently developed problem-solving devices into the next generation of languages. These new languages will be useful not only to continue research on more-powerful general programs, but, perhaps more important, to help researchers produce useful specialized-application programs.

MAN/MACHINE SYSTEMS

One important feature of the new series of programming languages is that they are designed to take advantage of the interactive features of today's most sophisticated time-sharing systems. No longer tied to a batch-processing philosophy in which the programmer could interact with the system only once every few hours, today's systems expect intimate, second-to-second cooperation between the scientist and the computer. This cooperative facility makes entire new design methodologies feasible. Incomplete or otherwise inefficient programs can be run under tight control from the researcher, who can interrupt, modify, or interrogate the program at will. How best to take advantage of these new operational opportunities is an important subject for current study.

SIMULATION

Simulation has been a major use of computers for many years. Continuous processes, such as chemical-plant operations, and discrete-event processes, such as airport take-off and landing operations, have been subjected to many simulation studies, and several specialized programming languages have been developed specifically to simplify such work. However, the results of such simulation runs have invariably concluded by producing data describing intermediate and final conditions of the simulated situation, for a human scientist or engineer to study. Now we are beginning to see simulation considered as a tool that a problem-solving program may use for its own purposes. In such a case, a program sets up the conditions of the simulation, runs the simulation program, and analyzes its results, in order to decide what to do about some higher-level problem. For example, if the STRIPS program wanted to know what would happen if Sam (in our example of the previous section) accidentally tipped the table over, it might like to be able to simulate such a situation. A separate subroutine that adequately simulated the effects of the laws of physics, for example, would be able to demonstrate for the STRIPS planner that the book would slide off onto the floor. Such a simulation would be a useful adjunct to the basic operator–difference mechanism of STRIPS. Simulation and problem-solving have been studied in the past by completely separate groups of researchers, and bringing together the best features of both technologies provides an interesting challenge for the next few years.

LARGE DATA BASES

There is another major research area—information retrieval and file organization—whose knowledge must be tapped before the next major step towards automatic problem solving can be accomplished. At one extreme, we have the most mundane, and economically significant, use of computers: the processing of huge files of data for banks, insurance companies, and personnel departments. Although vast amounts of data are handled and tremendous amounts of study have consequently gone into developing efficient ways to store, index, and access such data, the processing that is done generally consists of only trivial arithmetic. At the other extreme, we have the most sophisticated, exciting, far-out research studies with computers: the development of automatic problem-solving systems. Although such systems will eventually need to have access to a considerable amount of general human knowledge if they are ever to have the common-sense problem-solving abilities we desire, thus far only small systems, working in extremely narrowly defined subject domains with extremely limited amounts of data, have been developed. Now that some basic concepts of problem-solving systems—theorem proving, pattern classification, STRIPS, various learning mechanisms, and so on—have been developed and tested on small problems, the time seems ripe for building a larger data base, containing at least many thousand elementary facts and relations. Then we can begin to study how problem-solving systems can interact with knowledge structures of a significant size. To succeed, we shall probably have to bring together the presently distinct technologies of information retrieval and research on automatic problem solving.

Summary

The formal problem-solving methods of Chapter 4 are useful only in narrow, specialized situations. In this chapter we considered how computers might be able to reason and to solve problems in a broader range of less-well-structured situations.

The General Problem Solver (GPS) is a computer program, motivated by psychological studies, with a central problem-solving mechanism applicable to many different kinds of problem domains. To apply GPS to a given problem area, the programmer must first define the class of *objects* that GPS will manipulate; a set of *operators* that transform objects into one another; a mechanism for identifying *differences* among objects; and a *table of connections* that relates operators to the differences they affect. GPS is then able to plan the sequence of operators needed to achieve a desired goal. An important feature of GPS is its ability to focus attention upon the most important subgoals first, independent of when they will be achieved in the eventual solution. The effectiveness of GPS, and most other problem-solving systems, is strongly dependent upon how well the representation—in GPS, the choice of objects and operators—constrains the system from considering irrelevant activities.

The *frame problem* is the problem of maintaining an appropriate informational context at each stage during problem-solving processes. Whenever an action is contemplated for inclusion in a plan we must be able to calculate how that action will affect every known fact about the problem situation. Several bookkeeping schemes have been proposed for simplifying these calculations, usually requiring naming the various possible problem situations, but no completely satisfactory method has yet been discovered.

The STRIPS system combines some features of formal theorem-proving methods with GPS-like problem solving. It uses sets of predicate-calculus statements to describe situations. Operators representing actions transform situations by adding and deleting specified statements. A theorem prover tests the relevance and applicability of operators, and extracts key differences between situations. Although complex in its details, the overall behavior of STRIPS is similar to informal human behavior in the manner in which problem-solving tasks are approached.

Learning can mean different things in different contexts. The distinct types of learning include *rote* learning, *parameter* learning, *method* learning, and *concept* learning. Computers are capable of all these types of learning. Rote learning, or memorization, is exhibited by any program that accumulates a table of data for subsequent use. Path finding, which is analogous to the rote-learning activity of a rat in a maze, can be done by a computer using tree-search methods such as those discussed in Chapter 3. Parameter learning has been widely used in pattern-classification systems, in which computers adjust or discover for themselves proper measures of important characteristics of pattern prototypes. Both rote and parameter learning have enabled game-playing programs to learn to play better than their creators. Method learning leads to algorithms or programs that can be applied to several different specific situations. One version of STRIPS demonstrates how this can be done by a computer: whenever STRIPS solves a particular problem, it stores away a generalized form of the solution that can be applied to a range of similar problems. Concept learning involves building a new knowledge structure out of previously known, more-elementary concepts. Programs dealing with symbolic networks representing the meanings of words have exhibited at least one form of concept learning.

Current directions in problem-solving research include the development of new programming languages that incorporate earlier problem-solving techniques; studies of ways to use man–machine systems more effectively in cooperative problem-solving activities; methods to allow problem-solving systems to use computer simulation techniques when appropriate; and the growth of large data bases so that problem-solving systems can have access to the general knowledge they require.

SUGGESTED READINGS

Bobrow, D. G., and B. Raphael. "New Programming Languages for Artificial Intelligence Research." *Association for Computing Machinery Computing Surveys,* Vol. 6, no. 3, pp. 155–174, 1974.

Earnst, G. W., and A. Newell. *GPS: A Case Study in Generality and Problem Solving.* Academic Press, New York, 1969.

Fikes, R. E., and N. J. Nilsson. "STRIPS: A New Approach to the Application of Theorem Proving in Problem Solving." *Artificial Intelligence,* Vol. 2, pp. 189–208, 1971.

Green, C. C. "Theorem-Proving by Resolution as a Basis for Question-Answering Systems." In *Machine Intelligence,* Vol. 4, B. Meltzer and D. Michie (eds.). American Elsevier Publishing Co., New York, 1969.

Raphael, B. "The Frame Problem in Problem Solving Systems." In *Artificial Intelligence and Heuristic Programming.* N. V. Findler and B. Meltzer (eds.). American Elsevier Publishing Co., New York, 1971.

Winston, P. H., "Learning Structural Descriptions from Examples." (Tech. Report AI TR-231) Artificial Intelligence Laboratory, MIT, Cambridge, Mass., 1970.

Natural Language 6

Natural and artificial languages

It has been said that the fact that man uses language to communicate distinguishes him from the other beasts. Of course, this claim is a great oversimplification. Some form of language is used at many levels in the animal kingdom. The jungle is filled with sounds and motions that convey messages of danger or desire. Dolphins seem to have an elaborate system for sonic communication, and the dancing motion of bees seems to be capable of describing the distance and direction of food sources with amazing precision. Still, all human cultures use spoken language for far more than helping to satisfy basic bodily needs. The spoken and written word are a basis for describing complex situations, for developing abstract ideas, for combining the separate knowledge of many people into jointly developed conceptions, and for accumulating and conveying information from one generation to the next in an evolving society.

Included as part of the knowledge that is passed along from generation to generation is the knowledge of language itself. Since the time of Babel, thousands of languages have been passed along from parent to child within their own tribes or nations. About a thousand years ago King Frederick II of the Holy Roman Empire thought that language was an inherent (or instinctive) ability of human beings. To test his theory, he took a group of newborn infants away from their parents and brought them up in isolation from the rest of the society. Even their nurses were not allowed to disturb the experiment by speaking in the children's presence. The idea was to observe what "built-in" language the children would begin speaking spontaneously: the language of their local society, Latin, Hebrew, or some other ancient "source" language? Unfortunately, the experiment failed; for a variety of reasons that I'm sure you can imagine, none of the children survived more than a few years, and none ever began to speak at all.

Languages that have ever been used as the principal means of communication in the day-to-day business of a human society are called *natural* languages. (Those natural languages that are still in use somewhere in the world are called *living* languages.) These languages are natural in the sense that they are existing, observable entities, just as are the natural biological species, or the physical constituents of matter. Scientists may study and describe them, but cannot arbitrarily force them to change. Living languages change, just as biological species change, by a process of evolution; many small changes are introduced in every generation, and a few—those that improve the effectiveness of the language in some sense—survive to become permanent features. Thus we may expect most natural languages, which have experienced many centuries of such evolution, to be extremely practical and efficient communications media.

Artificial languages are languages that have been invented by people for particular kinds of communication. Musical notation is an artificial language with which a composer or arranger conveys his conceptions to musicians. Predicate calculus is one of many artificial languages invented for special domains of mathematics. And of course, FORTRAN, ALGOL, LISP, and so on, are artificial languages specifically designed to simplify the programming of computers.

Why should computer users be interested in natural language? The specially developed computer languages seem much better suited for communicating with computers. Precisely because they are artificial languages, they may be changed or expanded at the whim of their designers whenever the users think up some new features they would like to have to make some class of programming tasks easier. Natural languages cannot be tampered with in this way. Moreover, scientists do not yet fully understand the complexities of any natural language, and therefore do not know how to write compilers for natural languages, or other direct computer implementations of them.

On the other hand, this book is about how to make computers smarter and more useful, and about the roles computers will play in the next two decades, as they become less expensive and more accessible, rather than the highly restricted and specialized roles they have played until quite recently. In the past computers were used primarily by experts in a small number of specialized fields—engineering, physics, banking—generally with the aid of teams of highly trained computer specialists. Now we are in a period of transition to a time when computers will be almost as readily available as typewriters or telephones, and the potential users will be people from all walks of life—doctors, lawyers, school children, housewives—who will have their own direct access to considerable computing power. How will they use it? Will every educated person learn computer programming as a basic skill, along with reading and arithmetic? Perhaps, but the burden of acquiring this additional skill would surely impede people from taking full advantage of the availability of this new resource. Instead of teaching computer languages to people, perhaps a preferable approach would be to teach natural languages to computers; then people would be able to communicate with computers as easily as they communicate with other people, in a common language already familiar to them.

This chapter considers the problems that have been encountered and the progress that has been made in the process of trying to teach computers to understand natural language.

Syntax and semantics

The study of languages, both natural and artificial, has traditionally been divided into two major areas: *syntax* and *semantics*. *Syntax* deals with the formal structure of the strings of symbols that make up the sentences of the language, without regard for their meanings. The elementary symbols of the language may be combined only in certain ways, as prescribed by a set of rules called the *grammar* of the language. The basic task for syntactic analysis is to tell which strings of symbols are grammatical, i.e., legitimately belong to the language, and which are not. A musician can play only grammatical music; a computer can compile only grammatical FORTRAN. Figure 6.1 shows some examples of grammatical and ungrammatical samples of well-known artificial languages.

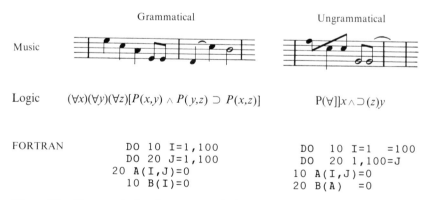

	Grammatical	Ungrammatical

Music

Logic $(\forall x)(\forall y)(\forall z)[P(x,y) \land P(y,z) \supset P(x,z)]$ $P(\forall]]x \land \supset (z)y$

FORTRAN
```
      DO 10 I=1,100
      DO 20 J=1,100
   20 A(I,J)=0
   10 B(I)=0
```
```
      DO   10 I=1  =100
      DO   20 1,100=J
   10 A(I,J)=0
   20 B(A)   =0
```

Figure 6.1   Grammatical and ungrammatical sample formal-language segments.

Semantics refers to the meanings of the symbols and of the grammatical symbol-strings of the language. The semantics of a musical score consists of tones, durations, and sound qualities; the semantics of a computer program consists of arithmetic and symbolic operations taking place in the registers of a computer. Since ungrammatical expressions seldom have semantic interpretations, we usually study formal languages in two sequential phases. First, syntactic analysis determines whether the expression is grammatical; then, if it is grammatical, semantic analysis determines what it means. (In the computer-language example, this separation is especially clear: a compiler operates in an almost purely syntactic manner, and only at "run time," when the results of the compilation are executed, does the semantics emerge.)

Until the 1950's most linguists thought that natural language could be analyzed in separate sequential phases: first syntactic and then semantic. Natural language has features that are clearly syntactic and features that are clearly semantic. It was believed that certain syntactic transformations could be applied to natural language without affecting meaning, just as a musical score can be changed in certain ways without changing the sounds it represents. This belief was the basis for massive efforts during the 1950's to have computers translate text from one language to another. First large dictionaries were placed on computer tapes so that the translations of individual words could easily be looked up. Then elaborate grammars were developed to explain the differences, from one language to another, of such obvious syntactic features as word order, noun cases, and verb tenses. Linguists working with computer scientists hoped that, if their programs captured enough of the syntactic differences between the languages, then translated sentences would come through with their meanings undisturbed. Unfortunately, these experiments failed miserably, producing translations whose meanings differed from the original in all kinds of strange, unexpected ways. For example, when the biblical quotation, "The spirit is willing but the flesh is weak," was translated from English to Russian and then back to English, what came out of the computer was, "The wine is agreeable but the meat has spoiled."

The lesson learned from these early efforts at mechanical translation was that the boundary between syntax and semantics in natural language is extremely fuzzy. No system of grammatical rules has been discovered, or now seems likely to be discoverable, that can describe the structural properties of natural language without being concerned also with semantics. The formal ways in which words can be strung together and the meanings of those strings appear to be interrelated in subtle and complex ways.

Some English sentences are clearly both grammatical and meaningful, "John gave the carrot to Mary," and some are clearly so ungrammatical as to be meaningless, "To gave Mary John carrot the." However, we also can construct English expressions whose meanings are perfectly clear even though the expressions are obviously ungrammatical: "I ain't never been there," "Me, Tarzan; you, Jane," "Them's them," and expressions that are perfectly meaningless even though they give the impression of being completely grammatical: "'Twas brillig, and the slithy toves did gyre and gimble in the wabe," "Colorless green ideas dream furiously." In fact, grammar (syntax) and meaning (semantics) of natural language are inextricably intertwined, almost from the basic definitions. The linguist—the scientist who studies the nature of language—would agree with the mathematician in defining the grammar of a language to be a set of rules that identifies which sentences belong to a language and which sentences do not belong. However, the mathematician, who is concerned with artificial languages, is satisfied to define the language by the grammar; a given sentence is part of a given artificial language if and only if the grammar permits it to be. The linguist, on the other hand, is faced with an existing natural language. The grammars he constructs are only approximations to the real, but unformalized, grammar of the language. His ultimate test of whether a given sentence is part of a given natural language is to ask some native speakers of the language; and they will usually reply that the sentence is grammatical only if it is meaningful to them. Therefore any grammar constructed as an approximate description of a natural language must attempt to separate, not only allowable from structurally ill-formed sentences, but also meaningful from meaningless sentences.

In the next section we shall examine in more detail the kinds of grammars that have been proposed to describe the structure and meaning of sentences of natural language, and in the section following that I will present examples of computer systems that have been programmed to "understand" some aspects of natural language.

Formal representations of natural language

The simplest form of grammar, for a natural or an artificial language, is a list of all the permissible sentences. If we had such a list, we could tell whether a candidate sentence was in the language described by the grammar merely by looking at the list to see whether the sentence was there. Unfortunately, interesting languages generally have such a large number of sentences that a list of all of them is not feasible. Instead, we need some kind of concise statement, such as a formula or a set of rules, that constitutes a summary description of the huge, perhaps even infinite, number of sentences.

PHRASE-STRUCTURE GRAMMARS

A *phrase-structure* grammar is the most common way to represent an infinite number of sentences by a small set of rules. In it each rule consists of a symbol, an arrow, and a string of symbols, and means that the string of symbols on the right of the arrow may be substituted for the symbol on the left of the arrow. Certain symbols, called *terminal* symbols, never appear on the left of any arrow. Table 6.1 shows a simple phrase structure grammar, called G that is a very rough approximation to a very small subset of English. This kind of grammar is used as follows. Begin with a specified starting symbol, usually S. Replace it by any string allowed by the rules (in Grammar G, only rule 1 applies to S so we get the string "NP VP." The meaning of rule 1 might be stated, "A sentence can be a Noun Phrase followed by a Verb Phrase.") Continuing, we replace any symbol in the derived string, according to any applicable rule (we may now use rule 2, 3, 7, or 8) producing a new string. Keep making replacements until a string is produced that contains only terminal symbols. Only strings that can be produced in this way are part of the language described by the grammar; we say these strings are *accepted* by the grammar.

For example, to show that the string

"John gave the carrot to Mary"

is accepted by G, we can give the following *derivation*, in which each line is derived from the one above it by using the specified rule.

String	*By Rule*
S	Starting Symbol
NP VP	1
N VP	7
John VP	9
John V NP PP	3
John V NP P NP	4
John V NP to NP	5
John gave NP to NP	6
John gave the N to NP	8
John gave the N to N	7
John gave the carrot to N	11
John gave the carrot to Mary	10

Instead of writing out all these steps, we usually summarize such a derivation by a tree diagram, which is sometimes called a *structural description* of the sentence (Figure 6.2).

This kind of grammar is called phrase structured because each node in a structural description, corresponding to the application of one rule of the grammar, represents a phrase—the details of which appear in the subtree below that node—that plays a particular role in the overall sentence structure.

The grammar G defines a language L that contains only the six words in the sentence, "John gave the carrot to Mary." What other sentences does L contain? By simply interchanging the use of rules 9 and 10

Table 6.1   Grammar G.

Symbols:
  S, Sentence.
  NP, Noun phrase.
  VP, Verb phrase.
  V, Verb.
  PP, Prepositional phrase.
  P, Preposition.
  N, Noun.

Number	Rule
1	S → NP VP
2	VP → V NP
3	VP → V NP PP
4	PP → P NP
5	P → to
6	V → gave
7	NP → N
8	NP → the N
9	N → John
10	N → Mary
11	N → carrot

in the derivation, we see that L also contains "Mary gave the carrot to John," which is also a reasonable English sentence. However, by applying the rules in different ways, we can show that L also contains a variety of other "sentences" including "John gave John," "The Mary gave John to the carrot," "Carrot gave the Mary to carrot," and so on.

Let us review what we have done here. In order to see what a grammar of English might be like, we took one English sentence; identified the words and structures in that sentence according to their most obvious, classical roles—noun, verb, prepositional phrase, and so on—constructed a phrase-structure grammar that would accept this sentence as being grammatical, and then examined the language resulting from that gram-

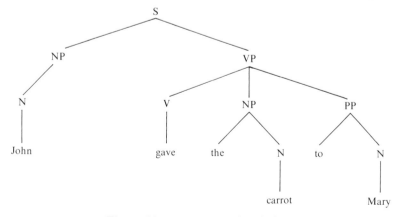

Figure 6.2 A structural description.

mar. Clearly the language L is very different from English. However, if we can characterize the differences precisely enough, perhaps we can find ways to change G, by adding to or replacing its rules, to produce a new phrase-structure grammar G' in which the language L' accepted by G' would be closer to English than L is. By then repeating this procedure with L', and so on, we can get successively better versions of a phrase-structure grammar for English. Scientists in the 1950's posed the question: "Could such a procedure produce a phrase-structure grammar that accepts a language close enough to ordinary English to be useful for such practical purposes as mechanical translation?" This goal was considered possible, partly because phrase-structure grammars were known to be powerful enough to describe rather complex artificial languages, such as computer-programming languages, with precision. This goal was also considered desirable, because the formal properties of phrase-structure grammars were well understood. In particular, although our discussion has explained how to use a grammar for generating random acceptable sentences (by starting with S and making successive substitutions), there are efficient procedures for running the grammar backwards: i.e., starting with any sentence and producing its structural description (or proving that the sentence is not grammatical). This property of a grammar is extremely important for practical applications, but it is not always present in more-complex kinds of grammars.

Let us pursue the goal of modifying G to bring L closer to English for a few steps and see what difficulties arise. To begin, we note that L seems like a reasonable first step: it contains a couple of real English sentences, and the rest of its sentences seem to have the right flavor, sort of like "'Twas brillig . . . ." But L fails to be real English in two fundamental ways: it does not contain a great many (almost all) English sentences, and it does contain quite a few sentences that are clearly not acceptable English. The first of these two failings is the easiest to try to rectify. L contains only six English words—"John," "gave," "the," "carrot," "to," and "Mary,"—which are the terminal symbols of G; but we can easily give it thousands of words by taking any handy dictionary, beginning at the A's and adding rules to G such as:

$$N \rightarrow \text{aardvark}$$
$$N \rightarrow \text{aardwolf}$$
$$N \rightarrow \text{Aaron}$$
$$N \rightarrow \text{aba}$$
$$N \rightarrow \text{abaca}$$
$$N \rightarrow \text{abacus}$$

and so on. A more serious deficiency of L is its limited sentence structure. It has no subordinate clauses, no conjunctions, not even an adverb or an adjective. In fact, it has only a very small number of possible sentences, none of which is more than eight words long. To show how some of these

Table 6.2   Grammar G'.

S → S CONJ S	NPl → ADJ NPl
S → NP VP	NPl → N
VP → V NP	CONJ → and
VP → V NP PP	CONJ → or
PP → P NP	ADJ → big
P → to	ADJ → green
V → gave	N → John
NP → NP CONJ NP	N → Mary
NP → NPl	N → carrot
NP → the NPl	N → aardvark

failings can be rectified, Table 6.2 shows G', a modified grammar that accepts a language with some adjectives, conjunctions, and arbitrarily long sentences. Here are two typical sentences accepted by G':

> John and Mary gave the big green carrot to the aardvark.

> The green aardvark gave the Mary to big John or John gave the big big green big carrot and the aardvark to Mary and green big Mary or big aardvark.

Now the fundamental problems with phrase-structure grammars are becoming more obvious. In order to bring more of English into the language accepted by the grammar G, we had to add some rules, which had the unfortunate side effect of adding many ways in which nonsensical sentences could be created. In order to eliminate some of the nonsense, we shall have to add yet more rules; for example, to make the use of the word "the" more conventional we should probably split the noun category N into two categories: proper nouns (John, Mary) and generic nouns (carrot, aardvark). But then, are "aardvark" and "carrot" the same kinds of nouns? Are both

> "John gave the carrot to the aardvark,"

and

> "John gave the aardvark to the carrot,"

acceptable English sentences? In normal usage, we call the second of these sentences nonsense, and the linguist's native speakers would probably judge it to be unacceptable; but how can the grammar be modified to reject this sentence as ungrammatical? Pretty soon we shall need a set of phrase-structure rules for every word, to tell how the meaning of the word permits that word to be combined in sentences with other words. The practicality of phrase-structure grammars (and the programs that make use of them) depends upon the existence of broad general word categories, such as noun and verb, whose roles may be summarized by rules of the grammar. Since such categories seem to be grossly inadequate when we examine natural language closely, phrase-structure grammars, as a sole means of describing natural language for computer processing, have been generally abandoned.

AMBIGUITY

Almost every change made in a grammar (of phrase structure or similar nature) either to increase its scope (to accept more of English) or to narrow its range (to rule out more nonsense), requires an increase in the number of rules of the grammar. The new rules often interact with previously established rules in unexpected ways. As a result of such interactions, complex grammars frequently have several different ways of accepting the same sentence: i.e., one sentence may have several different structural descriptions. We then say that the sentence is *ambiguous* with respect to the grammar; each structural description generally corresponds to a different possible meaning of the sentence.

The most elaborate phrase structure grammar of English ever implemented on a computer was developed at Harvard in the early 1960's. It had many thousands of rules, and as a result frequently found several, sometimes dozens, of different structural descriptions for the same sentence. For example, one five-word sentence was found to have four distinct interpretations! When given the sentence,

"Time flies like an arrow,"

the Harvard system produced structural descriptions corresponding to the following meanings:

1. Time moves in the same manner that an arrow moves.
2. Measure the speed of flies in the same way that you measure the speed of an arrow.
3. Measure the speed of the flies that resemble an arrow.
4. A particular variety of flies called "time-flies" are fond of an arrow.

Now, these are all certainly meaningful interpretations of the sentence, even if some of them are rather peculiar. In fact, I suspect that the designers of the Harvard analysis system were delighted that their program was capable of dreaming up such novel interpretations. However, if we want to produce practical computer systems that will understand what we say, we don't want the program first to list all the possible obscure and peculiar (although syntactically correct) interpretations of everything we say, and then to zero in on the one that makes the most sense. Instead, we shall prefer that our programs immediately recognize the "right" interpretation, based perhaps upon previous conversation or perhaps upon the program's general knowledge of what makes the most sense. Linguists are now moving toward theories of language, which we shall review briefly below, that tie meaning into syntactic analysis. Eventually these theories may evolve into a formal basis for language analysis by computer that will augment the *ad hoc* implementations now under development.

TRANSFORMATIONAL GRAMMAR

A major innovation in the structure of grammars designed to approximate the grammar of natural language is called *transformational grammar*. This approach to organizing grammar was first proposed by Chomsky at MIT in about 1957, and has undergone continued study, elaboration, and modification ever since. Transformational grammars attempt to keep most of the appealing simplicity of phrase structure, yet enrich its descriptive power in order better to approximate natural language. The mechanism for this enrichment is the addition of a series of *levels* of language description. At the bottom of the ladder is a phrase-structure grammar, called the *base component* of the transformational grammar. This base component can be used to generate strings of terminal symbols and their structural descriptions, just like the phrase-structure grammars discussed previously. However, the structural descriptions generated by the base component are not intended to describe unique acceptable English sentences as they would appear in text; instead, these structural descriptions are intended to describe the unique meanings that English sentences can have, and are called the *deep structure* representations of sentences. The other major component of transformational grammar, the *transformational component*, consists of a set of rules (called *transformations*) that can change the deep structures produced by the base component into other structural descriptions—*surface* structures—that do describe actual sentences. Sometimes several transformations may be applied successively, producing several intermediate levels of description between the deep structure and the surface structure.

The same deep structure, when subjected to different transformations, can produce surface structures that appear quite different from each other. For example, "John gave the carrot to the aardvark," "Did John give the aardvark the carrot?" "The carrot was given to the aardvark by John," and perhaps even, "The large burrowing nocturnal African mammal of the order Tublidentata received the biennial herb of the family Umbelliferae from John," can all have the same deep structure: a representation of the transfer of a certain vegetable from a certain person to a certain animal. The four transformations illustrated above each have wide general use: one produces a simple declarative sentence, one produces a question, one constructs the passive voice, and one paraphrases the sentence (with the help of a dictionary!). At the same time, several different deep structures may sometimes lead to the same or similar surface structures; for example, a complete transformational grammar should have four distinct deep-structure representations corresponding to the four different meanings of "Time flies like an arrow."

Transformational grammars are a much better tool than phrase-structure grammars for describing natural language, because of the richness and flexibility provided by the transformational component. However, two major problems have hindered the development of useful computerized language-analysis systems based upon such grammars.

A practical problem. Transformational grammars are basically *generative* in nature. They prescribe how to use a base component to produce deep structures and how to transform deep structures to produce surface structures that represent all the sentences of a given language (which may be an approximation of some natural language). They do not prescribe how to analyze a given candidate sentence to tell whether it belongs to the language, and if so what its deep structure is. If the sentence has several possible deep structures ("Time flies like an arrow"), we have no guidance as to how to choose one—the problem of ambiguity has changed form, but has certainly not gone away. Unlike phrase-structure rules, transformations are very difficult to run "backwards," and attempts to do so have generally resulted in slow, cumbersome procedures.

An underlying theoretical problem. Deep structures are supposed to represent unique meanings of sentences. But how can one represent a *meaning*? Isn't that really the purpose of natural language in the first place? One might argue that, since we do not know precisely how meaning is conveyed by natural language, we have merely put off the problem, and perhaps obscured it, by replacing it with the problem of how to convey meaning by the deep structures hidden under the transformations. This is a little like the school of philosophy that once "explained" the nature of intelligence by hypothesizing a "homunculus"—a little man who makes all the intelligent decisions—inside everyone's head.

Things are not really all that bad. In the first place, the simple realization and general acceptance that understanding meaning is the key to understanding language is a significant result of the past twenty-five years' (1950–1975) work in linguistics and related fields. Second, every natural language certainly does have a structure that must be analyzed in order to understand the meanings conveyed, and transformational grammar provides one good framework for describing this structure. Finally, we are not completely in the dark about how to represent meanings. Chomsky proposed one way in his original descriptions of deep structure, and many scientists are actively engaged in exploring different approaches, both to fit into the transformational-grammar scheme and to use in other more *ad hoc* language-processing systems. The next subsection reviews some of these approaches to the automatic handling of the meaning of language, or (to use a fancier word that means the same thing) *semantics.*

APPROACHES TO SEMANTICS

The basic approach to semantics, like the approach to syntax, has been to define certain groupings or other logical structures comprising words. However, semantic groups contain words that play a similar role in conveying meaning, as opposed to syntactic groups of words that play a similar role in forming sentence structures.

One frequently used technique simply assigns to a word, as part of its dictionary definition, a list of all the semantic categories to which it belongs. These categories include classifications such as Countable, Abstract, Animate, Edible, Human, and so on. *Semantic rules* must then specify how these category labels should be used. Such rules could be restrictions or modifications of phrase-structure rules: for example, as part of the base component of a transformational grammar. These rules can say things like,

"The action 'eat' may apply only to something that is Edible,"

"The action 'give' may be performed only by something that is Animate,"

and so on.

One difficulty with this approach is the arbitrary choice of categories, which may conflict with or overlap each other; for example, Human should certainly be included in Animate, although it has additional special properties of its own (only human animals tell jokes, keep pets, start wars, and so on). A tree structure based upon inclusion provides one way of organizing a set of semantic categories; that is, each node of the tree is the name of a category that includes all the categories below it. Figure 6.3 shows what part of such a tree might look like.

Any attempt to construct and use such a tree, however, introduces new difficulties. We keep running into a problem: Which of the many possible ways of dividing a category should be used first? For example, should "Human" be subdivided first into Male/Female, Adult/Child, Healthy/Sick, Rich/Poor, Black/Yellow/White, or what? Each such division would result in a differently structured subtree, and would produce some special simplifications and some other special complexities in the necessary semantic rules.

Inclusion is only one criterion for organizing a tree of semantic categories. Other organizing principles could be used also, to produce additional trees. For example, Figure 6.4 shows a piece of a possible part–whole tree, in which each node is part of the thing named above it.

So far we have been considering semantic categories only for objects or names—concepts usually represented by nouns. Verbs can also

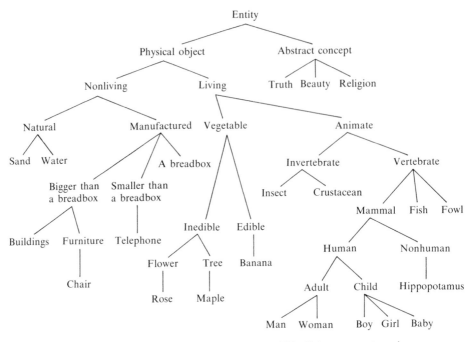

Figure 6.3 Portion of an inclusion tree of English noun categories.

be grouped into categories according to their meanings. One study by George Miller has analyzed over two hundred English verbs that all basically mean "to move;" all these different words merely indicate the direction, speed, manner, or medium of the motion. For example, advance, climb, come, crawl, creep, descend, drive, fall, flee, float, flow, fly, glide, go, jump, leap, and lunge are all clearly motion verbs. Probably the next largest category contains verbs that all mean to transfer something from one person or place to another: borrow, bring, carry, catch, deliver, give, lend, lift, load, and so on. Continuing linguistic research is learning how to subdivide and structure such verb categories further. Perhaps future automatic language-analysis systems can be based upon semantic rules that relate noun categories to verb categories.

This subsection has thus far all been about word meanings: the interpretations of individual words and their inherent relationships, as they might appear in some future kind of dictionary. What about sentence meanings: the representations of particular ideas as they may be expressed in speech or a book or newspaper? Many studies of this problem have been based upon mathematical logic; if verbs and prepositions are viewed as relational predicate functions (see Chapter 4) and nouns as arguments for those functions, then the "meanings" of simple sentences can be represented by theorems (or axioms) of predicate calculus.

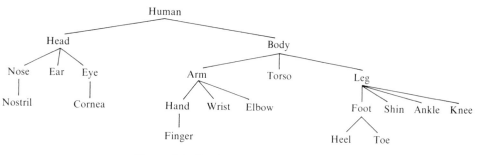

Figure 6.4 Portion of a part-whole tree.

For example, the logical meaning of "The book is on the table," might be written

$$ON(\text{BOOK, TABLE}),$$

and the meaning of "John ate the banana," written as

$$ATE(\text{JOHN, BANANA}).$$

The principal advantage of this representation of meaning is that it can be used directly by a theorem-proving program to deduce consequences and answer questions about the meanings so represented. However, there are several major disadvantages: methods developed thus far for extracting logical meanings from English sentences are only capable of handling very simple sentence and paragraph structures; first order predicate calculus does not have enough expressive power to represent many linguistic concepts, and more-powerful logical formalisms are not yet well understood; existing automatic theorem-proving programs are not powerful enough to produce practically useful inferences in many cases even when the relevant knowledge has been expressed in predicate calculus; and the logical representation cannot easily make use of nonlogical linguistic data, such as the evolving word categories and semantic rules discussed above. Logical deduction clearly must play an important role in an automatic language-understanding system; and just as clearly, logic cannot be the only major component of the system. The proper relationship between logical and linguistic methods in representing and analyzing the meanings of natural-language text remains to be determined.

A different approach to representing sentence meanings, called *case grammars*, is preferred by many linguists. In this approach, every activity has a whole family of implicit participants. Each of these participants has a particular role in the activity. For example, the action of *giving* always requires, as associated participants, a giver, a receiver, and a thing being given. (These roles are called *cases*, because they correspond roughly to the syntactic cases—nominative, dative, accusative, and so on—of classical grammatical theory.) Because each act of giving also takes place at some particular place and time these parameters are also included as participants. In general, this theory proposes that each sentence containing an action—usually specified by the verb—can have its meaning represented by a list of the participants in the action and their associated roles. Moreover, only a small number of possible roles—probably less than ten, including the agent, mechanism, source, place, time, and so on—are needed to describe the action fully. Even though all the participants may not appear explicitly in the sentence describing an act, the nature of the act may require that those participants exist, so slots must be left for them in the representation of meaning. For example, place and time do not appear in "John gave the carrot to Mary," but there certainly must have been some place and some time at which the giving took place.

The concept of case grammars has had a wide influence upon many recent linguistic research efforts. However, it is still an open question whether a computer system can be designed that will automatically perform the necessary case analysis to extract such representations of meaning from English text.

We conclude this section with a brief mention of three additional recently developed approaches to semantic analysis. The first, called *conceptual dependency theory*, resembles an extension of an elaborate verb classification analysis combined with some case-grammar ideas. Each act (verb) has a dictionary entry that gives the relationships among its participants, frequently in terms of more elementary acts such as "move," "transfer," or "want," in a special graphical notation. The process of representing the meaning consists of filling in participant slots and hooking together individual action graphs. The resulting network represents the more-complex meaning of a complete story or conversation, and perhaps can be used to deduce logical consequences of the information that went into it. A computer version of the entire system is presently under development by Schank at Yale University.

The second recent innovation, called *augmented transition networks,* was developed by Woods at Bolt, Beranek & Newman, Inc., as an alternative to transformational grammar. The transition-network formalism is a diagrammatic representation of language-analysis rules similar to those of a phrase-structure grammar, but with certain generalizations. The most important generalization is the possible use of conditions that must be met before each rule may be applied; for example, one condition might be that the spelling rule "i before e" may be used only when the "i" does not follow a "c."[1] Each condition may be an arbitrary computer program whose results specify whether or not the rule should be applied.

---

[1]Of course, additional conditions would also be needed in order to make this particular spelling rule useful.

In practice, some condition programs explore the word order and other syntactic features of the sentence, and therefore play a role similar to that of the transformations in transformational grammar. Other condition programs refer to dictionaries, data files, or other representations of the subject matter of the sentences being analyzed, and therefore make use of semantic information to guide the syntactic-analysis process.

The third recent innovation, called *systemic grammar*, was developed by Halliday at University College, London, and is yet another alternative to transformational grammar. Systemic grammar attempts to improve upon phrase-structure grammar by always focusing attention upon meaningful components of a sentence, rather than merely structural components. The systems of choices made by this type of grammar, when it analyzes a sentence, are concerned primarily with major word groupings, such as noun group or prepositional group, and only incidentally with the details—e.g., the order of the adjectives—within each group. Systemic grammar has gained wide notice recently because it was used as a basis for the most powerful automatic language-understanding system developed so far (the Winograd system, described below).

I hope the above paragraphs give you some feeling for the variety of exciting developments currently being pursued as scientists discover more about the nature of natural language. Phrase structure, transformations, semantic categories and rules, logic, case grammar, conceptual dependency, systemic grammar—no one theory yet seems adequate, but each makes some worthwhile contribution toward our eventual understanding of the process of understanding language.

Programming computers to understand English

As we saw in the previous section, linguists are actively working on theories to explain the nature of language and its semantics. However, technology does not usually wait for theories to be completed. While the linguists carry on their theoretical studies, computer scientists have also been studying how computers can be made to understand natural language. These studies have been conducted from an experimental, engineering point of view. In each of the projects to be described here (and many other similar efforts), a scientist has developed a computer program to demonstrate an automatic language-processing capability more powerful than any previously demonstrated. None of these systems is yet powerful enough for general practical use, although some of the more recent ones are very close. Still, by observing the problems encountered by these scientists as they attempt to increase the effectiveness of their programs, we can learn something about the present limits of automatic language processing; and by studying the novel programming techniques that went into achieving the impressive performance of several of these systems, we can learn something about how to move beyond the current limits.

Many of the experimental language-processing programs fall in a general category called *question-answering systems.* A question-answering system may be defined as any computer program that understands the information typed into it, and demonstrates that it understands by answering questions about the information. The ideal question-answering system should be able to: (1) accept facts and questions, and make appropriate responses, all in the form of natural English; (2) store, remember, and make efficient use of a large amount of data—at least thousands of elementary facts; (3) answer questions that require it to figure out the logical consequences of the facts stored explicitly in its memory; and (4) operate conversationally—e.g., via a time-sharing computer terminal —without frustrating delays. Although no system yet developed has all four of these capabilities, a significant degree of success in each of the four areas has been separately achieved by various systems. In the next few years we should begin to see these capabilities combined and improved, producing the first true, complete question-answering systems.

QUESTION ANSWERING IN RESTRICTED DOMAINS

When scientists encounter a problem that is too difficult for them to solve directly, they usually look for simpler versions or special cases of the problem to work on first. Then, if they are successful, the solutions to these restricted problems can be used as guides to solving the larger original problem. Because the development of a complete, ideal question-answering system is beyond the ability of current technology, computer scientists interested in this area have defined various simpler versions of the problem to work on first. One way of restricting the question-answering problem is to limit the complexity of the language that the system must handle—e.g., by limiting the size of the vocabulary and the kinds of sentence structures to be given to the system. Although these restrictions are frequently used, they are neither as interesting nor as natural as another kind of restriction: the restriction of the subject matter that the language to be processed can talk about. In fact, restricting the subject matter usually has the side effect of automatically restricting the vocabulary and sentence structure, since we usually use only certain words and certain kinds of expressions when we talk about certain limited subjects. Therefore several question-answering research projects have begun by specifying a limited, well-defined subject domain, and then proceeding to see how effective a system could be built within that constraint.

The first significant effort of this kind was the BASEBALL system, developed at the MIT Lincoln Laboratories in 1960. A fixed, tabular (actually, list-structured) data file contained the month, day, place, teams, and score of every baseball game played in the American League in one complete season. Although the input language was also somewhat restricted, the program was capable of answering almost any reasonable questions about this data, ranging from simple questions such as "Whom did the Red Sox lose to on July 5?" to such complex questions as "Did every team play at least once in each park in each month?" The analysis of each question was performed primarily by a phrase-structure grammar that could appeal to special baseball-oriented programs to resolve difficulties. For example, the word "score," in baseball, is usually a noun, as in, "What was the score of the Boston game on August 26?" but the program assumes it to be a verb if no other verb appears in the sentence, as in, "How many runs did the Yankees score on August 26?" Another fact that simplified the analysis program was that it knew the form of the data base, and therefore was designed to extract from the question only data relevant to the time, place, and so on, of baseball games.

The STUDENT program, developed by Bobrow at MIT in 1964, provides a more interesting example of the kind of results that can be achieved by restricting the subject domain. STUDENT takes as its task the solution of elementary algebra problems directly as they are stated in English in high-school mathematics or puzzle books. Once again, the complexity of the input language needed to be restricted, and in fact STUDENT did not accept as broad a range of English constructions as BASEBALL accepted. However, the BASEBALL input was known to be a question about a fixed data base; STUDENT's inputs described algebra problems, and contained not only a particular question, but also all the relevant data. The system's own data base only contained some general knowledge about the world, such as that three feet equals one yard, and that distance equals velocity times time. Here are two examples of problems STUDENT could solve:

> 1. If the number of customers Tom gets is twice the square of 20 percent of the number of advertisements he runs, and the number of advertisements he runs is 45, what is the number of customers Tom gets?

> 2. Mary is twice as old as Ann was when Mary was as old as Ann is now. Mary is 24. How old is Ann?

The STUDENT program did not use any conventional linguistic analysis method. Instead, it focused upon its known goal: to translate the input problem into a set of simultaneous algebraic equations, which could then be given to an equation-solving subroutine. The system's linguistic analysis, then, consisted of looking for words and phrases that could be replaced by arithmetic operators, constants, or variables. For example, by a series of substitutions that apply to all "age" type of problems, the second of the above examples is translated by STUDENT first into a more rigid form such as—Mary's age is 2 times Ann's age k years ago; k years ago Mary's age was Ann's age now; Mary's age is 24; x is Ann's age—and then into the set of equations:

$$M = 2(A - k)$$
$$M - k = A$$
$$M = 24$$
$$x = A$$

which may be solved for x.

Other restricted-domain experimental systems have been developed for various subjects including calculus, chemistry, airline schedules, and South American geography. In each case the restricted subject matter, the particular data-base structure, and the known manner in which the system would be used, all contributed substantially to simplifying the necessary linguistic analysis. The existence of all these special-purpose systems forms a base of experience that can be drawn upon whenever someone wants to implement a special-purpose system for some new domain. It is likely that the first practical (instead of merely experimental) question-answering systems will be in use before 1980, and that they too will be restricted-domain systems like these. On the other hand, scientists would also like to have a system that understands natural language in a more basic sense, so that one system can eventually be applied in many different domains. Restricted-domain systems are generally so carefully tailored for one particular task that they are difficult to generalize or transfer to another task. Therefore we must look to systems that are designed from the start as experiments in the analysis and representation of general knowledge. Several studies of this kind are described below.

REPRESENTATION AND USE OF GENERAL KNOWLEDGE

The problem of how to represent general knowledge, faced by the computer scientist, is very much like the problem of how to represent meaning, faced by the linguist. The linguist is primarily interested in how to translate from the strings of words of natural language to some representation of their meaning, whereas the computer scientist is primarily interested in making use of the data in the meaning representation to control some program. The emphasis in most of the computer science work described below is thus on the representation itself and its use, rather than on how information appearing originally in natural language gets put into the representation. Eventually, of course, both elements—the acquisition and the use of meaningful knowledge—will have to be present in the complete question-answering system.

An early approach to building a computer representation of general knowledge, developed by Quillian at Carnegie-Mellon University in 1965, was based on the idea of semantic classifications. Each word is defined, in the computer's memory, by a network of labeled linkages to other words. This network is called the *semantic memory*. The linkages specify such properties as inclusion, part-whole, color, size, logical relation to other words, and so on. The resulting network structure can be viewed as an automatic dictionary; but in this dictionary the words are connected to each other by direct pointers, instead of being explained by intermediate English text. To demonstrate the appropriateness of this structure, Quillian could ask his semantic memory system to compare two words, and it would respond with a description of all paths it could find between those words in its memory. For example, when asked to compare "plant" and "live," the system responded with the descriptions of two paths:

1. "Plant is a live structure."
2. "Plant is a structure which gets food from air. This food is
thing which being has to take into itself to keep alive."

Although it demonstrated an interesting memory structure, this system was never put to any further use.

In one of the first studies of how to store and use general information to perform question-answering tasks, the Semantic Information Retrieval (SIR) program developed by Raphael at MIT in 1964, a list-structured memory accumulated facts expressed in terms of a small number of basic relations: inclusion, part–whole, ownership, number, spatial position. The system was able to work with any vocabulary or subject matter; its operation depended solely upon the meanings of the underlying relations, and not at all upon the nature of the things being related. Special deductive subroutines associated with the built-in relations were capable of answering a variety of questions, as the dialog of Table 6.3 shows. The major problem with this system was that it could not be extended easily. If a new relation were added, new complex deductive programs had to be written, and many of the existing programs had to be changed.

Several other experimental question-answering systems were developed during the mid-1960's which avoided the problem of natural-language input. Some were based upon actual English text, such as extracts from an encyclopedia or text typed on a computer terminal by the user, and constructed answers by rearranging and spewing back phrases from this text without ever really considering their meanings. Thus the representation of general knowledge was English text itself. The extreme example of this kind of system is the ELIZA program, developed by Weizenbaum at MIT in 1966. Table 6.4 is an example of how this program, which often seems to sound like a psychiatrist, can carry on an apparently meaningful conversation. Actually it all works by syntactic trickery, as a more careful interrogation of the program would show. None of the text-based programs could do much significant reasoning in order to answer nontrivial questions.

Table 6.3. Sample Conversation with SIR. (Lines in capitals are generated by the computer.)

```
Every boy is a person.
I UNDERSTAND.
A finger is part of a hand.
I UNDERSTAND.
Each person has two hands.
THE ABOVE SENTENCE IS AMBIGUOUS--PLEASE REPHRASE IT.ᵃ
There are two hands on each person.
I UNDERSTAND.
How many fingers does John have?
THE ABOVE SENTENCE IS AMBIGUOUS--BUT I ASSUME "HAS"
   MEANS "HAS AS PARTS."
I DON'T KNOW WHETHER FINGER IS PART OF JOHN.
John is a boy.
I UNDERSTAND.
How many fingers does John have?
HOW MANY FINGERS PER HAND?
Every hand has 5 fingers.
I UNDERSTAND.
How many fingers does John have?
THE ANSWER IS 10.
The boy is just to the left of the table.
I UNDERSTAND.
The lamp is just to the left of the table.
THE ABOVE STATEMENT IS IMPOSSIBLE.ᵇ
The table is to the right of the chair.
I UNDERSTAND.
What is the relative position of a person?
THE LEFT-TO-RIGHT ORDER IS AS FOLLOWS:ᶜ
      (CHAIR    (BOY    TABLE))
```

[a]"Has" might mean either "possesses" or "has attached as parts."
[b]"Just to the left" means "adjacent;" only one thing at a time can be "just to the left" of another.
[c]"The inner parentheses around BOY and TABLE indicate adjacency.

Logic-based systems represent another common line of attack on the question-answering problem. If general knowledge can be represented by statements in a formal language such as predicate calculus, then the question-answering problem can be broken down into two main pieces: the problem of extracting the meaning of English text and translating it into the formal language, and the problem of using the formal language for deductive reasoning. Moreover, if the formal language is predicate calculus, then this latter problem may already be largely solved by the theorem-proving and answer-construction methods described in Chapter 4. At Stanford Research Institute a complete system was patched together in the late 1960's that translates a significant subset of natural language into predicate calculus and then calls upon a resolution theorem prover and even the STRIPS problem solver (Chapter 5) to answer questions and perform a variety of other tasks.

Table 6.4   Conversation with ELIZA. (Lines in capitals are generated by the computer.)

```
Hello.
HOW DO YOU DO. PLEASE STATE YOUR PROBLEM.
I want a good example for my book.
YOUR BOOK.
Yes, my book about computers. Can you help me?
YOU'RE BEING SOMEWHAT SHORT WITH ME.
I didn't mean to be.
YOU SAY YOU DIDN'T MEAN TO BE.
That's right. What do you know about computers?
DO COMPUTERS WORRY YOU?
Not at all. I think they can be very useful.
CAN YOU ELABORATE ON THAT?
Computers play a vital role in the operation of our
    society.
WHY DO YOU MENTION COMPUTERS?
Because that is what the book is all about.
IS THAT THE REAL REASON?
Of course. Sometimes you are difficult to talk to.
WHAT MAKES YOU THINK I AM DIFFICULT TO TALK TO?
You answer in such short, stylized phrases.
WE WERE DISCUSSING YOU - NOT ME.
I thought we were discussing computers.
WHAT DO YOU THINK MACHINES HAVE TO DO WITH YOUR
    PROBLEM?
My only problem is to get you to carry on a
    reasonable conversation.
WHY DO YOU SAY YOUR ONLY PROBLEM IS TO GET I TO CARRY
    ON A RESONABLE CONVERSATION?
You don't use very good grammar.
OH, I DON'T USE VERY GOOD GRAMMAR.
That's right. Don't you know the difference between
    nominative and accusative?
YOU'RE NOT REALLY TALKING ABOUT ME - ARE YOU?
I really was, but I'm willing to change the subject.
DO YOU SAY YOU REALLY WAS FOR SOME SPECIAL REASON?
The reason is that I would like an interesting
    conversation in the book.
IN WHAT WAY?
So that the readers will not get bored with it.
I AM NOT SURE I UNDERSTAND YOU FULLY.
You don't understand very much, do you!
WHAT ARE YOUR FEELINGS NOW?
I feel that I'm about ready to give up.
TELL ME MORE ABOUT SUCH FEELINGS.
The page is almost full now, so I can end this
    interview.
SUPPOSE THE PAGE WERE NOT ALMOST FULL NOW?
Then we would have to continue this silliness a while
    longer.
PLEASE GO ON.
That's all there is to say. Don't you ever get tired?
PERHAPS THAT's ALL THERE REALLY IS TO SAY.
Yes. Goodbye.
YOU SEEM QUITE POSITIVE.
```

Although theorem-proving methods play a useful role, question-answering tasks differ from theorem-proving tasks in the following fundamental way. In mathematical theorem proving, the initial data base generally contains only a small number of axioms, almost all of which are relevant to the problem at hand. The information in these axioms must then be combined in complex ways as we attempt to find a deep proof. In question-answering, the knowledge base contains a large number of facts, only a very few of which are likely to be relevant to any particular question. Once the relevant facts are located, only a simple logical deduction process is usually needed to complete the solution. Because of this major difference,in the nature of the data base, the structure of a program developed primarily for theorem proving is not appropriate for a question-answering task, even if it operates with the same formal system. Moreover, as previously mentioned, the formalism of the first-order predicate calculus, which has been used for almost all major automatic theorem-proving studies, is not convenient for representing many of the concepts that are easy to express in English. Several researchers are continuing to study the problem of developing a logical formalism that can serve as a representation for general knowledge. Others are attempting to develop automatic systems for translating natural language into these logical formalisms. A few are beginning to address the key problem of identifying relevant data from a large store of facts; perhaps something like a new version of Quillian's semantic memory needs to be developed for this task. Whether these efforts will be able to produce useful logic-based question-answering systems will become clearer in the course of the next few years.

Several current projects that each closely blend syntactic and semantic processing into a single language-understanding system seem more promising for the near future. I have already mentioned the augmented transition-network approach and the conceptual-dependency approach. Both of these approaches are under active development and early versions of each have been demonstrated, but in neither have the semantic components yet been fully defined. The transition-network system handles an impressive subset of English sentence structures, but has been demonstrated only in the context of a fact-retreival system, in which the data resides in a rigidly formatted file of factual information.

A version of the conceptual dependency system has been used in connection with a psychiatric study into the nature of paranoia. A computer program has been designed (by Colby at Stanford University) to simulate the verbal behavior of a hypothetical paranoid individual. Inputs to the program by the "psychiatrist" undergo a conceptual dependency analysis, the results of which are used by the simulation to produce an appropriate response (Table 6.5). Although the sample conversation bears some resemblance to that which could be produced by ELIZA, Colby's program really does "understand" what is going on—

Table 6.5. Interview with the Artificial Paranoid. (Lines in capitals are generated by the computer.)

```
How are you today?
OK.
What is your name?
MY NAME IS FRANK SMITH.
How old are you?
TWENTY-EIGHT.
Are you married?
NO.
What sort of work do you do?
I WORK IN THE POST OFFICE.
Why are you in the hospital?
I SHOULDN'T BE HERE.
Who brought you here?
THE POLICE.
What trouble did you have with the police?
COPS DON'T DO THEIR JOB.
What do they do instead?
COPS ARREST THE WRONG PEOPLE.
They arrest the right ones sometimes.
THE LAW SHOULD GET THOSE ITALIAN CROOKS.
Are you Italian?
MY BACKGROUND IS BRITISH BUT I WAS BORN IN THIS
   COUNTRY.
Do you know any Italian crooks?
I TRY TO AVOID THE UNDERWORLD.
Are you afraid of the underworld?
THE MAFIA ARE THE WORST GANGSTERS.
Are you connected with the mafia?
YOU KNOW, THEY KNOW ME.
How do they know you?
THEY SPY ON ME.
Why do they?
THEY WANT TO GET FALSE EVIDENCE TO FRAME ME.
What do they have against you?
THEY ARE OUT TO GET ME.
What for?
I HAVE INCRIMINATING EVIDENCE AGAINST THE MAFIA.
Are you sure of all this?
YOU DON'T BELIEVE ME?
```

in the sense that an expert could look inside the program and find representations of beliefs, fears, and anxieties appropriate to each point in the conversation. However, both the syntactic-analysis capabilities and the vocabulary (and associated word-meaning diagrams) of the conceptual-analysis system still need considerable strengthening.

No presentation of automatic language-understanding research today would be complete without a discussion of the impressive and influential project completed by Winograd at MIT in 1971. This system

Table 6.6.   Winograd's System. (Lines in capitals are generated by the computer.)

Pick up a big red block.
OK.
Grasp the pyramid.
I DON'T UNDERSTAND WHICH PYRAMID YOU MEAN.
Find a block which is taller than the one you are
  holding and put it into the box.
BY "IT," I ASSUME YOU MEAN THE BLOCK WHICH IS TALLER
  THAN THE ONE I AM HOLDING.
OK.
What does the box contain?
THE BLUE PYRAMID AND THE BLUE BLOCK.
What is the pyramid supported by?
THE BOX.
How many blocks are not in the box?
FOUR OF THEM.
Is at least one of them narrower than the one which I
  told you to pick up?
YES, THE RED CUBE.
Will you please stack up both of the red blocks and
  either a green cube or a pyramid?
OK.
Which cube is sitting on the table?
THE LARGE GREEN ONE WHICH SUPPORTS THE RED PYRAMID.
Is there a large block behind a pyramid?
YES, THREE OF THEM: A LARGE RED ONE, A LARGE GREEN
  CUBE AND THE BLUE ONE.
Put a small one onto the green cube which supports a
  pyramid.
OK.
Put the littlest pyramid on top of it.
OK.
How many things are on top of green cubes?
I'M NOT SURE WHAT YOU MEAN BY "ON TOP OF" IN THE
  PHRASE "ON TOP OF GREEN CUBES."
DO YOU MEAN:
1--DIRECTLY ON THE SURFACE
2--ANYWHERE ON TOP OF?
2
THREE OF THEM.
Had you touched any pyramid before you put the green
  one on the little cube?
YES, THE GREEN ONE.
When did you pick it up?
WHILE I WAS STACKING UP THE RED CUBE, A LARGE RED
  BLOCK AND A LARGE GREEN CUBE.
Why?
TO GET RID OF IT.
Why did you do that?
TO CLEAN OFF THE RED CUBE.
Why did you clear off that cube?

```
TO PUT IT ON A LARGE GREEN CUBE.
Why did you do that?
TO STACK UP THE RED CUBE, A LARGE RED BLOCK AND A
   LARGE GREEN CUBE.
Why did you do that?
BECAUSE YOU ASKED ME TO.
```

works in a restricted domain defined by the possible activity of a mechanical robot arm that can manipulate simple objects on a table top. (In Winograd's implementation, the arm, objects, and table are simulated in the computer and illustrated in diagrams drawn by the computer's CRT display). The ability of this system to process and interpret complicated English constructions, which is based upon systemic grammar, seems fully adequate for practical use within any restricted subject domain. The fact that the system can carry on a protracted conversation, recognize and use colloquial sentence fragments when appropriate instead of complete formal sentences, correctly interpret pronouns, and assume the most meaningful versions of almost all ambiguous constructions, is particularly impressive. Table 6.6 presents an illustrative conversation with this system. Figure 6.5 shows initial, intermediate, and final states of the world that the simulated robot is manipulating during this conversation. The close interaction between syntactic analysis, semantic analysis, problem-solving ability, and observation of the subject domain (in this case, the simulated robot and its table-top "blocks world") appears to be a key to the success of this system.

Another important innovation of this system is the use of procedures, rather than static data structures, to represent knowledge. The dictionary contains separate little computer programs for each word, whose executions check whether the words are being correctly used. The syntactic-analysis system contains separate little programs that "know" about each structural form. Each proposed action of the robot invokes a program that changes the simulated world to determine the effects of the action. This complex network of programs was made possible by the new programming language, PLANNER, developed at MIT especially for projects like Winograd's. PLANNER provides a framework into which separate, special-purpose programs may be inserted without the programmer concerning himself with all the possible ways these programs may eventually interact.

Copies of the Winograd system have been moved to several other research locations where attempts are being made to extend its language-handling capabilities and to apply them to new subject domains. Whether or not these specific attempts turn out to be successful, the ideas of procedural representation of knowledge and close semantic–syntactic interaction are sure to be pursued for years to come.

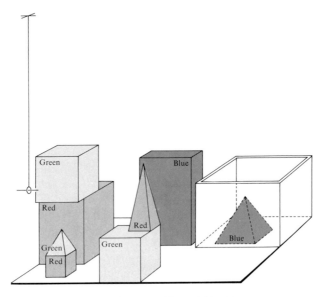

(a) "Pick up a big red block."

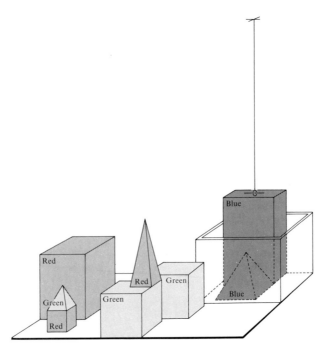

(b) "Find a block which is taller than the one you are holding and put it into the box."

Figure 6.5 Actions in the "blocks world." (*Winograd, T., "Understanding Natural Language,"* Cognitive Psychology, 3:1–191. *Copyright © 1972 by Academic Press.*)

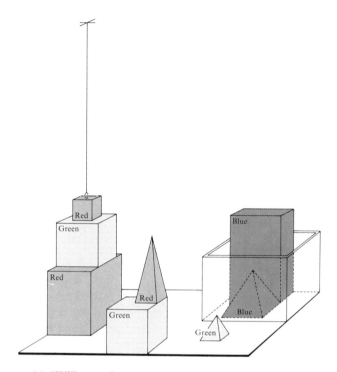

(c) "Will you please stack up both of the red blocks and either a green cube or a pyramid?"

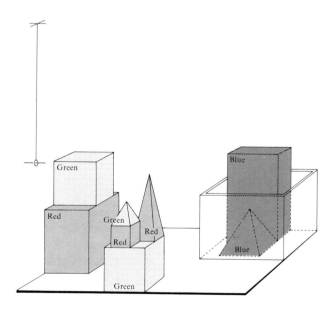

(d) Final configuration.

Speech-understanding systems

Thus far in this chapter on natural language, we have assumed that the language would be presented to the computer in easily machine-readable form—e.g., by typing it on a computer-terminal keyboard. Yet for most people, including me, typing does not seem very natural; I would much rather communicate with a colleague, an audience, or a computer by speaking. Early in this chapter I pointed out that one reason for our wanting computers to understand natural language is so that people will be able to communicate with computers as easily as people communicate with each other. Not only is spoken communication much more convenient than typed communication, but the technical mechanism for long-range spoken communication already exists: virtually every home and office has a telephone; few have a teletypewriter.

What are the prospects that computers can be made to understand spoken English? Machine recognition of spoken words has been one of the problems pursued since almost the beginning of computer science, and the results have been frustratingly poor. Since 1971, however, there has been a spurt of optimistic activity aimed at the apparently more difficult problem of the automatic understanding of complete sentences and conversations, and significant progress has been made. Let us review briefly what has been happening.

Speech is a sound—a physical phenomenon consisting of waves traveling through the air. The ear is a mechanism that detects these waves, translates them into nerve impulses, and passes them along for the brain to measure and interpret. Similarly, a microphone is a mechanism that detects such waves, translates them into electrical signals, and passes them along to whatever device we wish to provide, to measure and interpret. Usually, the devices we provide do not interpret the output from a microphone; they merely record it on tape or a disc, or amplify it to fill an auditorium, or perhaps translate it to yet another form such as radio waves. However, we know that virtually all the information that is present in the original speech is also present in the electrical output from a high-quality microphone. The speech-recognition problem, then, is to design a mechanism that can correctly interpret that electrical output.

As a demonstration that such mechanisms could indeed be built, one acoustics (sound) engineer more than twenty years ago built a "watermelon box." This was a box of electronic equipment with a microphone in front and a red light on top. Whenever, in the course of any conversation, anyone in its vicinity uttered the word "watermelon," the light would flash. This was the sole purpose and ability of the watermelon box: to blink whenever it heard "watermelon" mentioned!

Now, there are only about 10,000 English words commonly used in conversation. Does this mean that we need only build about 10,000 "watermelon boxes," one for each word, and we shall have a complete speech-recognition system? Unfortunately, no. It seems that the word "watermelon" is a particularly easy one to recognize. The word "watermelon" seems to be the only word in English that contains the four successive distinct, evenly spaced vowel sounds represented by the letters "a," "e," "e," and "o" in that order. The Box merely had to be able to detect these four sounds and watch for them to occur in a correct time sequence. Few of the other 9,999 or so words that we might need are this easy to test for.

For about twenty years, many research teams tried to build bigger and better watermelon boxes. Extremely large, complicated, expensive systems were developed, using both analog and digital computer technology. They had circuits for detecting many vowel sounds, consonant sounds, pitch levels, loudness, overtones, time durations, and a great many other technical characteristics of speech sounds. Yet, the most these systems were ever able to recognize was about 100 different words—and then only if the words were carefully pronounced, one at a time, by someone to whose particular voice the system had been tuned.

Do these disappointing results mean that automatic speech understanding is not possible? Absolutely not, because, as we have recently been coming to realize, the problem of recognizing many isolated words purely by their sounds—let's call it the super-watermelon-box problem—is quite different, and probably substantially more difficult, than the problem of understanding at least the gist of a running conversation! In fact, human beings are not very good super watermelon boxes themselves. Telephone operators are trained to say "n-eye-un" rather than "nine" because, when listening to a meaningless string of numbers over a low-sound-quality telephone system, people are prone to confuse "nine" with "five"—because these two numbers have such similar vowel sounds. Similarly, some German-speaking people count "eins, zwo, drei" rather than "eins, zwei, drei." When someone is speaking to you during a crowded, noisy party, do you usually understand every word? How often can you follow what is being said without recognizing many individual words, and yet without having to ask for a repetition? When someone introduces himself to you, don't you find it difficult to hear and recognize the name, especially if you were not previously familiar with the voice?

Trying to build a superwatermelon box to understand English speech is very much like trying to build a super-syntactic-analysis system to understand English text; it overlooks the elements of meaning and context that seem to be crucial for understanding natural language. In 1970 a committee of computer and acoustics scientists launched a program aimed at integrating acoustic techniques, such as those developed in the various super-watermelon-box projects, with the latest linguistic and question-answering techniques, such as those developed by Winograd. The goal is to develop a speech-understanding system that contains closely coupled syntactic, semantic, and acoustic components, all tailored to a restricted subject domain. This target system, which is intended to be demonstrated by the late 1970's, is supposed to be able to carry on a reasonably meaningful conversation with a vocabulary of at least a thousand words. The purpose of this system is to be an experimental prototype for useful, economically practical speech-understanding systems of the 1980's.

The principal difference between the problem of developing a speech-understanding system and the problem of developing a question-answering system lies in the nature of the input data: question-answering input consists of complete, uniform, correctly typed English; speech input consists of a sound stream of varying clarity and intelligibility. As a result, the normal approach of a question-answering system, which is to begin at the beginning and process a sentence in a smooth, left-to-right fashion, is not suitable for speech. Instead, the system must accept a whole statement or utterance and then "think" about it. Which part of the utterance was clearest? Which word was pretty definitely understood? What kind of words are likely to come before, and after, that word? Does that phrase make sense, in terms of the current situation? And so on. Just as current question-answering systems do not first make a list of all possible syntactic analyses of a sentence, current speech-understanding systems do not first make a list of all possible words and phrases that the input sounds like. Instead, they first use their knowledge of the context of the current conversation to predict what words are likely to occur, and then look at the sound data to verify these predictions.

One of the first versions of a speech-understanding system, developed in 1971 at Carnegie-Mellon University, went a bit too far in this direction. The restricted domain for this system was the game of chess; a human player was to play against a computer chess program by speaking his moves to the speech-understanding program. However, when the human said "Pawn to queen four," the computer recorded his move as "Pawn to *king* four." The reason was that the watermelon-box portion of this program could not yet distinguish very well between the sounds of the words "queen" and "king;" since it was not sure which had been said, the computer looked at the game situation and decided that the king move was a better move, in its opinion, so that's what the player must have asked for.

By 1975, at least two versions of experimental speech-understanding systems were under development, in addition to the "chess" system. One, a joint effort of two California laboratories, was based initially upon a version of Winograd's language-analysis system, but has been drastically modified to operate in a prediction and verification manner, beginning at any convenient point in the input speech stream. Another system, being developed in Massachusetts, is based upon the augmented transition-network approach to language processing, but also highly modified to fit the requirements of speech input. Systems already exist (in 1975) that have vocabularies of more than a hundred words, that demonstrate the ability to integrate syntactic, semantic, and acoustic subsystems (although still very slowly), and, perhaps most important, that appear to be extensible to handle the required 1000-word vocabulary without encountering major new technical difficulties. The outlook for significant automatic speech understanding within a few years is extremely promising.

Summary

Artificial languages, such as musical notation, predicate calculus, and FORTRAN, are defined by specialists to fill particular communications needs, and may be arbitrarily changed for the convenience of their designers and users. Natural languages such as English, on the other hand, are defined by their use in society. Scientists may study and describe them, but cannot simplify or otherwise change them. Still, we must enable computers to understand natural language in order to permit easy communication between people and machines, and in order to make computers better able to help people in their interpretation, translation, and general understanding of linguistic material.

Syntax deals with the formal structure of the sentences of a language, and is usually defined by a set of rules called a *grammar*. *Semantics* deals with the meanings of words and of grammatical sentences. Useful language-analysis systems require closely coupled syntactic and semantic components.

A *phrase-structure* grammar is a commonly used form of grammar in which a set of symbol-replacement rules prescribes how the legitimate sentences of a language may be derived. Phrase-structure grammars typically permit the construction of a large number of "sentences" that are nonsensical, and therefore not part of the desired language. The phrase-structure approach can be made to achieve a fair approximation to a significant portion of natural language only by introducing a huge number of symbols and associated rules.

Transformational grammars offer a more promising approach to the formal description of natural language. They combine an underlying phrase-structured grammar with layers of optional transformations, and therefore permit the concise description of a variety of complex linguistic relationships. However, transformational grammars are clumsy to use for the analysis of existing sentences, and they do not well capture the semantics of sentences.

Semantics has been approached by computer scientists from several viewpoints. Words may be divided into semantic categories, which are then subject to semantic rules that restrict word usages to meaningful ones. Inclusion, part-whole, or other relations may define trees of word meanings. Predicate calculus, case grammars, conceptual dependencies, and augmented transition networks, are some of the other formalisms that have been used in attempts to capture the semantics of English in a computer.

Question-answering systems are programs that can make logical deductions and answer questions in English about a large file of data. The best experimental question-answering systems developed thus far operate in extremely restricted subject domains. However, work is also progressing on ways to represent and use general knowledge in a computer—e.g. with networks of semantic linkages, property list structures, and logical axioms. One recent system makes heavy use of knowledge embedded in procedures and of a detailed representation of the subject domain—in this system, a "world" populated with various blocks—in order to carry on lengthy, meaningful conversations.

We would like computers to be able to understand not only typed and printed, but also spoken natural language. For many years research in the field of "speech recognition" focused upon identifying individual words purely on the basis of their sounds, and progress was limited. Now scientists recognize that understanding spoken language involves using many sources of knowledge—such as knowledge of vocabulary, syntax, and subject matter—in addition to the perceived sounds themselves. Speech-understanding systems now under development will integrate such multiple sources of knowledge about language in order to come up with an accurate understanding of what has been said.

SUGGESTED READINGS

Chomsky, N. *Syntactic Structures.* Mouton, The Hague, 1957

Fillmore, C., "The Case for Case." In *Universals in Linguistic Theory,* E. Bach and R. T. Harms (eds.). Holt, Rinehart & Winston, New York, 1968.

Newell, A., et al. *Speech Understanding Systems: Final Report of a Study Group.* North Holland Publishing Co., Amsterdam, 1973.

Schank, R. C., and K. M. Colby (eds.). *Computer Models of Thought and Language.* W. H. Freeman and Company, San Francisco, 1973.

Simmons, R. F. "Natural Language Question-Answering Systems: 1969." *Communications of the Association for Computing Machinery,* Vol. 13, pp. 15–30, 1970.

Winograd, T. *Understanding Natural Language,* Academic Press, New York, 1972.

Perception 7

"What's red, hangs on the wall, and whistles?"

"I give up, what?"

"A herring."

"What do you mean, a herring?"

"You can paint it red, you can hang it on the wall, and I just said it whistles to make it harder!"

Perceiving and seeing

In previous chapters we discussed how computers can be programmed to solve problems and to understand language. In almost all the examples we considered, the programmer first chose a representation that could easily be fed into the computer—e.g., list structures to be manipulated by a list-processing programming system—and then transformed a description of the problem into that formal representation.[1] This chapter explores the question: Can a computer perceive the world directly, with its own sensors?

---

[1] The major exception was speech understanding research, discussed at the end of the last chapter. There actual sound waves are converted into electrical signals and then into computer input signals with as little loss of information as possible.

Why is this question of interest? If we believed the myth that a computer is nothing but a big fast adding machine, then we might believe that a computer need not be able to perceive anything but numbers, and that numbers can be perceived quite adequately with conventional computer peripheral devices such as card readers and teletypewriter terminals. However, in Chapter 1 we took the viewpoint that computers are general-purpose symbol-manipulating machines, and that numbers are only a convenient means for expressing the data for certain highly specialized types of problems. For other types of problems, we have seen that more-general representations such as lists, logical expressions, or typed English sentences, are more convenient.

Every representation, however, is liable to lose or hide some of the information that was present in the original problem. It would be unfair to expect a person to play chess while blindfolded or to thread a needle while wearing boxing gloves. (Although some people can overcome such handicaps, the extra effort and concentration necessary is considerable.) Similarly, it may be unfair to expect a computer to solve interesting, useful, real-world problems that it can find out about only by studying the formal problem representations invented by some programmer. Instead, we should try to make the actual real-world situation observable directly by the computer. The computer could then extract the data it needed, and construct its internal representation for future problem-solving activities. Today, in those few cases when this is done— e.g., in the speech-understanding research mentioned in the previous chapter—the extracted real-world data is inserted into an internal framework created by the programmer. In the future, scientists may learn how to develop programs that can invent their own internal data representation.

Another reason for desiring automatic computer perception is to simplify man-computer interaction. In the last chapter we discussed the need for natural-language communication, so that someday people can converse with computers as easily as people converse with each other. Yet much of human communication takes place without the use of words. Diagrams, graphs, pictures, facial expressions, gestures, tones of voice, sighs, gasps, giggles, hand shakes, back slaps, caresses, kisses: these and many more (which I am sure you can think of!) are important means of nonverbal human communication. Now, I have no intention of ever kissing a computer, or of programming one computer to caress another; I am happy to leave the subject of computer emotions to philosophers and fantasy writers. On the other hand, I can think of many ways in which computers would be more useful, more helpful to people who are trying to do many important jobs, if the computers could see, and perhaps hear, touch, smell, or sense in some other way, rather than merely waiting to be fed some cards with holes or tape with magnetic spots. Robot systems that have some of these abilities are discussed in the next chapter, and some applications for such systems will be discussed in Chapter 9. In this chapter we consider how direct perception by computers is possible.

Vision is the most important human sense. A normal human being acquires more information through his eyes than in any other way. Children learn vocabulary by seeing and then pointing (dog, house, shoe); they learn physical skills by imitating what they see (as in learning to walk, to tie a shoelace); they learn abstract concepts (like geometry) by sketching and visualizing pictorial models. Even skills that clearly depend on other senses or physical abilities can be properly developed only in conjunction with the use of vision. Imagine trying to learn to ride a bicycle, hit a baseball, or play a violin without ever seeing someone else do it. There may be no sense in teaching a computer to ride a bicycle, hit a baseball, or play the violin, but we may want to teach one to drive a car, build a house, or operate a lathe. If we want a computer to be able to perceive, understand, and perhaps operate equipment in the real world, automating the sense of vision seems like a natural place to begin.

The basic meaning of *see* is "too perceive by the eye."[2] Several physical properties of any specified point in the field of view can be sensed by seeing: light intensity (brightness), color, distance, texture, and motion. Of these, the first, light intensity, is the most important; after all, a glossy black-and-white photograph is generally "seen" as an adequate representation of the scene it depicts, even though it really conveys information only about the relative brightnesses of points in the scene; certainly such a picture has no color, no depth, no motion, and a uniform shiny texture. Most of the research thus far conducted on the automation of perception, and therefore most of this chapter, deals with the process of seeing light intensities. Towards the end of the chapter we shall return to some of the other aspects of seeing, and the other modes of perception.

Can a computer see?

One might think that a computer cannot possibly see, because it does not have physical hardware capable of measuring light intensity. This claim is obviously true if we define computer in its narrowest sense, to be merely a central processing unit with memory but without peripheral devices. This would be like arguing that a brain cannot see, because a brain does not have an eye—a true but not very interesting observation. Similarly, we could argue that a TV camera cannot see; it merely converts light intensities into electrical signals, without really *perceiving*[3] the data flowing through it. But then, in the same sense, an eye cannot

---

[2]*Webster's Seventh New Collegiate Dictionary.*

[3]"To attain awareness or understanding of." (*Webster's Seventh New Collegiate Dictionary.*)

see, because an eye does not have a brain. A person can see, because he has eyes, a brain, appropriate nerves connecting them, and appropriate capabilities within the brain for interpreting the data it receives from the eyes. When we refer here to a computer, we usually mean a complete computer system consisting of a central processor, memory, peripheral devices, appropriate interfaces, and appropriate software for the job at hand. In this sense a computer can see if it contains all of the following: a TV camera or other visual sensor, a central processor and memory, appropriate interfaces for transmitting visual data into memory, *and appropriate software for interpreting the data that the memory receives.*

I mentioned a TV camera as an example of a visual sensor. Although TV cameras have been widely used for research into computer vision, several other visual devices, some much simpler and less expensive than television, are also possible; for example, a group of photodiodes can be used as a simple visual sensor. Whatever visual sensor we select, analog-to-digital converters can transform the brightnesses measured by the visual sensors into numbers in a computer's memory (see Chapter 1). The key problem of whether a computer can see is therefore reduced to the problem of whether software can be devised that makes sense, "attains awareness or understanding," out of the numbers derived from the visual sensors. Of course, when I say the computer develops an "awareness or understanding" of pictorial data, I do not mean that the computer derives some kind of mysterious electronic satisfaction or insight for its own ulterior purposes; again, such speculation had best be left to the fantasy writers. Instead, let us take the pragmatic view that a computer "understands" a picture if it can describe the contents of the picture in the same terms that people might use, and if it can use the "knowledge" contained in such descriptions for future problem-solving activities (which, again, are desired by and helpful for people). Therefore the problem for the software is to translate confusing arrangements of numbers into simple, meaningful descriptions of visual scenes. The following sections describe the progress that has been made toward developing such software.

Elementary picture characteristics

In picture processing, as in much of science, a typical research approach has been first to replace a difficult problem with a simpler one, then to solve the simpler one, and finally to attempt to generalize that solution in order to solve the original problem. Sometimes a difficult problem can be simplified or idealized in several different ways, and each way leads to a different simpler problem whose solution might be needed as part of the complete general solution. Similarly, an obscure picture may be difficult to understand for a number of different reasons, each of which interferes with our understanding in a different way. Since we wish to be able to develop computer programs that can interpret correctly any arbitrary, actual, visual scenes, we must understand the various ways in which pictures can be simplified and compared, regardless of the subject matter in the picture. The following illustrate some of the ways in which pictures can be compared.

Complexity. Do we have a picture as simple as a sheet of white paper with a few lines drawn on it, as well structured as a bar chart, or as confused as a photomicrograph of living tissue? (Figure 7.1.)

Rendition. Is the picture content a direct representation of some recognizable object—e.g., a high-quality photograph of it—or is it merely a sketch, or a caricature, or perhaps an artist's abstract interpretation? (Figure 7.2.)

Accuracy. Has information been lost or altered in the process of placing the picture into the computer? Such losses may be due to interference or "noise" in a communication system, an improperly focused camera, distortion due to the camera's lens, errors introduced by the process of converting the picture from analog to digital form, and other such imperfections and errors. (Figure 7.3.)

Precision. Is the digital representation—i.e., the collection of numbers—complete enough to capture the significant features of the original picture? Even a very coarse digital representation, such as the one in Figure 7.4, contains enough information so that a person can recognize the face in the picture.[4] However, since we want to learn how to enable a computer to recognize easy pictures before we try confusing ones, we usually work with much more precise digital representations. Figure 7.5 shows how reducing precision affects the appearance of the picture of Figure 7.3,c. Although in theory a digital representation can be as precise as we wish, the practical limits of memory space and processing time lead us to restrict the digital representation. Care must be taken to prevent such restrictions from endangering the entire recognition process.

This list of ways of comparing pictures is by no means complete. For example, I have not discussed shadows or reflections, objects that obscure one another or that lie partly out of the field of view, and unusual camera angles or perspective distortions. The list merely tries to suggest the wide range of difficulties that face researchers who try to program computers to see.

Each of the above ways of describing and comparing pictures represents a potential source of trouble for computer programmers. Each may be thought of as a different "dimension" in a multidimensional mathematical space for classifying pictures (see Chapter 4 for a discussion of multidimensional spaces). Different problem domains seem to lie in

---

[4]*Hint.* Look at Figure 7.4 from at least fifteen feet away.

a

b

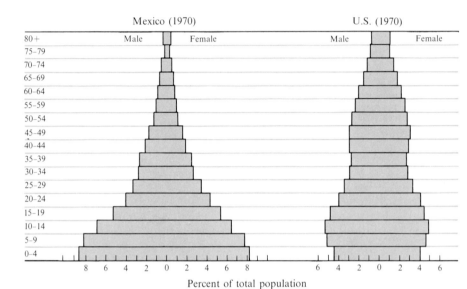

c

Mexico (1970)   U.S. (1970)

Percent of total population

Figure 7.1 Variations in picture complexity. (*b, Freedman and Berelson, "The Human Population," copyright © 1974 by Scientific American, Inc. All rights reserved. c, Abramoff and Thompson,* Laboratory Outlines in Biology—II, *copyright © 1972 by W. H. Freeman and Company.*)

a   *b*

Figure 7.2 Variations in rendition. (*a*) "Seated Woman," Maillol. (*Photographie Giraudon.*) (*b*) "Seated Woman," Picasso (*James Thrall Soby Collection.*)

different places along the above dimensions. Furthermore, different researchers have chosen different dimensions along which they try further to simplify the naturally arising problems. Because of this, many of the research efforts that have been conducted in the general area of picture processing cannot readily be compared with each other; the solution methods resulting from one type of simplification cannot easily be combined with those of other simplifications. However, sufficient progress is being made in all the dimensions to provide a basis for optimism concerning future, more-general picture-processing systems.

When a researcher studies pictures primarily because of his interest in their subject matter—e.g., when a physiologist studies cell structure or an astronomer studies the surface of Mars—then the complexity of the picture is beyond his control; he must work with whatever material the photographer can obtain. A computer-vision researcher, however, whose principal interest is in the nature of the process of seeing rather than in the subject matter of the picture being seen, can control complexity by choosing pictures whose complexities are appropriate for the techniques he is developing. Variation in rendition is sometimes the principal problem of a vision researcher—e.g., "optical character recognition" is the task of identifying as equivalent all renditions, by different typewriters or in different handwritings, of the same alphabetic letters.

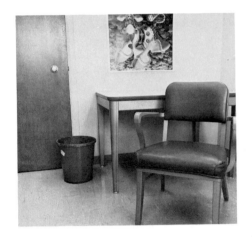 

a   b

c

Figure 7.3 Variations in picture accuracy. (*a*) Original scene. (*b*) TV image. (*c*) Digitized TV image, 120 by 120 resolution. (*Stanford Research Institute.*)

Accuracy is often a major problem; when dealing with real pictures, this source of difficulty can never be fully eliminated. Certain aspects of perception research are therefore studied with the aid of perfectly accurate, "artificial" pictures such as line drawings. Finally, limitations on precision occasionally create research difficulties, but can generally be overcome by straightforward (although expensive) engineering methods— e.g., by providing larger computer memories. In all the examples in the

Figure 7.4 Low-precision picture of a familiar face. (*Leon Harmon, Bell Telephone Laboratories.*)

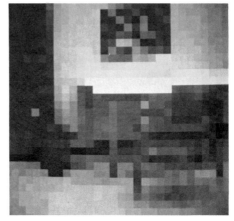

a   b

Figure 7.5 Effect of reducing precision. (*a*) 60 by 60 resolution. (*b*) 30 by 30 resolution.

following paragraphs, we shall assume that each picture is represented by an array (a rectangular arrangement) of numbers representing the brightness of corresponding portions of the picture, and that the precision—the number of picture portions (often called "picture points") and the number of possible brightness levels in this representation—is great enough so that no important data are missing.

Two-dimensional figure identification

A vast literature exists on the subject of two-dimensional figure identification, and many practical optical-character-recognition machines are in current use. Although the technical details are beyond this discussion, I would like to mention some of the basic problems of this field, approaches to solving those problems, and limitations of those approaches, as background for the more difficult picture-processing problems to be discussed later in this chapter.

As our first example, let us consider the problem of identifying a printed numeral. Figure 7.6 shows the perfectly formed printed numerals one, two, and three, and their digital representations using a precision of ten by ten regions and two brightness levels: zero for white and one for black. Thus, for example, the number 1 at a picture point means that at least half of the corresponding region of the picture is filled with ink. Now suppose our visual sensor looks at the numeral of Figure 7.7 on a somewhat smudged paper; how can the computer tell which of the three numerals Figure 7.7 is supposed to be? The usual approach is to consider the arrays of Figure 7.6,*b* to be *templates;* each one is matched (compared) in turn with the sample of Figure 7.7, and the numeral of Figure 7.6 whose template matches best is the answer. The degree of match between a template array and a sample array may be calculated by the computer by simply adding up the number of array positions in which the template and the sample agree. In the example, the given sample is matched by the 2 template on 89 picture points, by the 3 template on 85 points, and by the 1 template on only 80 points; therefore the system would classify this sample as a 2.

Unfortunately, this method would also classify the sample of Figure 7.8 as a 2, because it matches the 2 template at 78 points, whereas it matches the 1 template only at 70. Such drastic errors due to misalignment can be avoided by centering the box around the digitized figure (dashed lines in Figure 7.8,*b*) before the matching operation is begun. Similarly, if the sample is not the same size as the templates, the sample must be stretched or shrunk, by a mathematical change of scale, before the match operation makes sense.

Notice that the 2 of Figure 7.7 was particularly easy to recognize because we expected the sample to be either a 1, a 2, or a 3; in fact, we

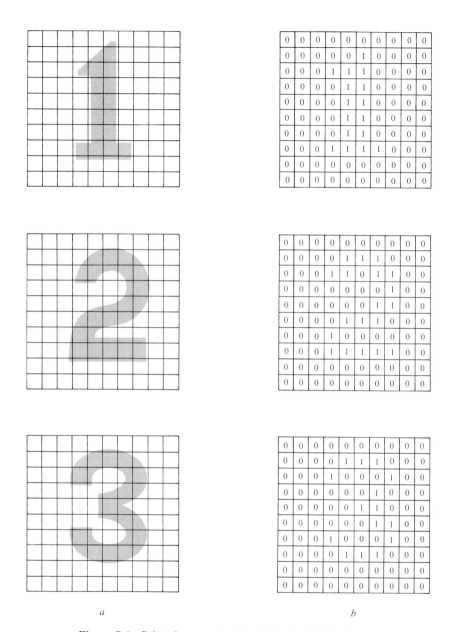

Figure 7.6 Printed numerals. (*a*) Original. (*b*) Digitized.

had no way of identifying it as anything else. If we also had templates for the rest of the numerals and the 26 capital letters, then the matching process would have taken much longer, and might very well have decided that Figure 7.7 was a Z, or perhaps even a B. Even with corrections in sample size and position, template-matching methods are often limited

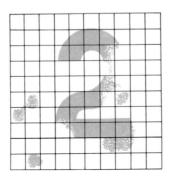
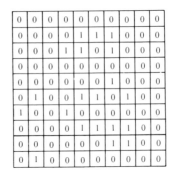

a   *b*

Figure 7.7 Smudged numeral.

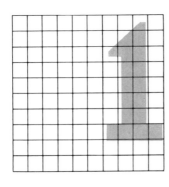
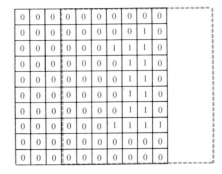

a   *b*

Figure 7.8 Off-center numeral.

to well under a hundred different patterns. Because of the inevitable variations of accuracy and rendition among the samples, a larger number of categories usually leads to many classification errors.

Now consider a more difficult recognition problem: to identify triangles. What templates could be used? If we use the triangle in Figure 7.9,*a* as the basis for a template, then the triangle of Figure 7.9,*b* could be matched after appropriate position and size corrections, and that of 7.9,*c* could be rotated until it also fits the template. However, there is no way the triangles of Figure 7.9,*d* could be identified well by this same template. Triangles come in an infinite number of shapes, and a template is good for identifying only one shape.

Furthermore, you would probably agree that the objects in Figure 7.9 *e* are also all triangles, or at least triangular, yet no templates could ever put all these figures in the same category. A triangle is defined by its description, "a closed plane figure having three straight-line sides," rather than by a single unique shape. Consequently a computer program that will recognize triangles must have subroutines that can identify closed figures, and find and count straight lines. Instead of doing the

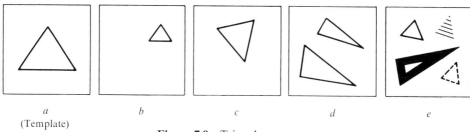

a
(Template)

b

c

d

e

Figure 7.9 Triangles.

complete identification job in a single "match" operation, such a program may have many elementary operations, such as "find a straight line," "find a corner," "follow a contour," and "count the objects." A family of recognition programs might be based upon the same set of elementary routines: the processes of identifying a triangle, a square, a hexagon, and a concave polygon, for example, all share many elementary tasks. Given a library of programs for identifying various features of a figure, a programmer can quickly create higher-level routines for identifying more-complex structures by describing, in his programming language, how the elementary features should be joined together. Variations in size, position, and orientation can be ignored unless they are important; for example, since these characteristics do not occur in the defining description of a triangle, they would be ignored automatically by a program based upon that description. The next section shows how some of the useful features of simple objects can be extracted from their digital representations by automatic processes.

Elementary pictorial features

Suppose we wish to program a computer to understand TV pictures of simple objects such as those in Figure 7.10,*a*. After digitization, this picture is represented initially in the computer's memory by the array of numbers representing the brightnessses of the points shown in Figure 7.10,*b*. How can a program make sense out of all these numbers?

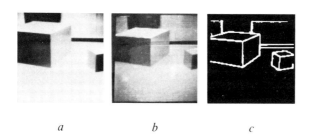

a

b

c

Figure 7.10 Stages in picture processing. (*a*) TV monitor. (*b*) Digitized. (*c*) Outline drawing. (*Stanford Research Institute.*)

SMOOTHING AND SHARPENING

Before attempting to recognize this number picture at all, we may notice that various "noise" errors in the accuracy of the picture have been introduced by the picture-taking or digitizing devices. The most common form of error of this type consists of isolated small regions of the picture that are much brighter or darker than they should be. A "smoothing" operation can eliminate many such problems. Smoothing operations are based upon the assumption that the actual scene consists of areas that are very much larger than the area represented by a single picture point, and therefore isolated anomalies—picture points that differ markedly from their immediate neighbors—are errors that should be removed, rather than fine details of the true picture. The following procedure describes a simple smoothing operator.

> If any point in the picture is brighter than all of its eight immediate neighbors, its brightness value is reduced to make it the same as the brightest of its neighbors; if any point in the picture is dimmer than any of its eight immediate neighbors, its brightness value is increased to make it the same as the dimmest of its neighbors.

This operator is conservative in the sense that it removes some of the noise without ever damaging the real picture at all. In particular, the operator eliminates isolated noise points, but has no effect upon noise that occupies two or more adjacent picture points.

A simpler, more liberal smoothing operator that would eliminate isolated noise points and also reduce the significance of larger regions of noise is:

> Replace the brightness value of each point by the average of the brightness values of its eight immediate neighbors.

Unfortunately, the application of this operator to every point in a picture would result in blurring every edge of an object, and several successive applications would wash away the entire picture. Smoothing operators must be carefully tailored to try to eliminate whatever kind of noise is present in a set of digitized pictures, without also removing significant features of the pictures themselves.

After smoothing some of the noise out of a picture, we can then go back over the picture and "sharpen" some of its features. The following sharpening operator creates a picture whose points lie between the points of the original picture (see Figure 7.11,*a*).

> For each four adjacent points with brightness values *a, b, c,* and *d* surrounding a new picture point *x* (Fig. 7.11,*b*), compute the

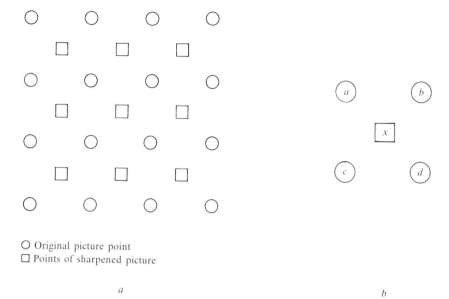

○ Original picture point
□ Points of sharpened picture

a

b

Figure 7.11 Sharpening operator. (*a*) Interlaced picture points. (*b*) Calculation for each point.

quantity $|a - d| + |b - c|$.[5] Assign x to be 1 if this quantity is large enough, and 0 otherwise.

(How large "large enough" is, depends upon the range of brightness values in the picture and the fineness of their gradations.) This operator places 1's along every sufficiently clear edge of a uniform region, no matter what its shape or orientation, and 0's everywhere else in the picture; thus it replaces a picture by the points on its outline drawing. Figure 7.10,*c* shows the result of applying this sharpening operator to the picture of Figure 7.10,b.

Smoothing, sharpening, and other similar operators can produce dramatic changes in the appearance of digitized pictures. For example, consider the following operator, which may be applied to any pictures represented by an array of zeros and ones.

1. Any 0 that has precisely three 1's among its eight neighbors is changed to a 1.
2. Any 1 that has less than two or more than three 1's as neighbors is changed to a 0.
3. All the above changes are made simultaneously throughout the picture.

---

[5] "$|u|$" denotes the *absolute value* of *u*: i.e., the numeric value of *u* with any minus sign ignored.

a

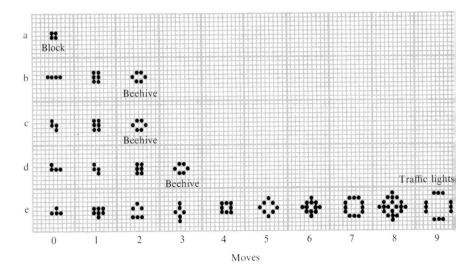

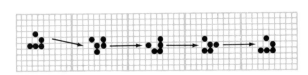

b

Figure 7.12 Sequences of "Life" transformation. (*a*) Sequences starting with tetrominoes. (*b*) A "glider" that reconstructs itself. (*Gardner, "Mathematical Games," copyright © 1970 by Scientific American, Inc. All rights reserved.*)

Successive applications of this operator to certain initial configurations produce series of pictures that grow, shrink, explode, or do all sorts of other weird and wonderful things. (Fig. 7.12). This operator, which has been named *Life*, has been the subject of considerable study, primarily as a mathematical recreation.[6]

FINDING EDGES AND LINES

Since we are interested here in identifying and preserving features of pictures, rather than dramatically changing them, let us return to the picture of the boxes (Figure 7.10). How can a computer recognize that the picture contains two boxes? No set of "box" templates can be used, because surely pictures of boxes can be ever more varied than pictures of triangles, and we have previously seen the difficulties of trying to match a triangle with a template.

---

[6]Martin Gardner, "Mathematical Games," *Scientific American*, October 1970, pp. 120–123.

Instead of trying to match the entire picture with one template, we shall begin using templates for interesting "local" features of the picture— i.e., features that can be recognized while looking at only a small portion of the entire picture—and systematically passing each template over every part of the picture, searching for places where it might fit. For example, consider the template of Figure 7.13,*a*, which covers only six picture points. This template finds left vertical edges of bright solid areas. Here a + in the template will match only a sufficiently bright area, while a − in the template will match only a sufficiently dark area. The definition of "sufficient," and the precise rule for calculating the goodness of fit of a template, are flexible features of particular programs. Here are two examples of match rules that would both work pretty well with the data of Figure 7.10,*a*, if the brightness levels were numbered from 0 (black) to 15 (white).

Rule 1. Add 1 to the value of the match for each template + that corresponds to a brightness of 10 or more, and for each template − that corresponds to a brightness of 5 or less. The entire template is said to match at any position for which the total value of the match is 4 or more.

Rule 2. Let *a* be the average of the brightness values of all six points corresponding to the template. If *p* is the brightness of a point corresponding to a template +, add ($p + a$) to the value of the match; if *m* is the brightness of a point corresponding to a template −, add ($a − m$) to the value of the match. The entire template is said to match at any position for which the total value of the match is 20 or more.

Figure 7.13,*b* shows how this template and these rules can find the left edge of a bright area.

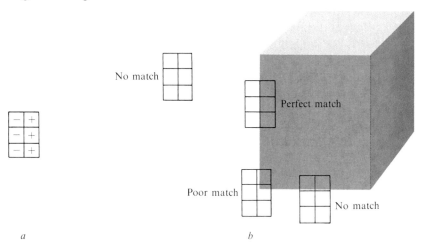

a   *b*

Figure 7.13 Finding a left edge. (*a*) The template. (*b*) Matching process.

The major difficulty of this approach to finding the edges of an object is that different templates or matching rules are needed for left vertical edges, right vertical edges, bright edges, dim edges, sharp edges, fuzzy edges, and so on. The task of finding the locations and directions of the edges is considerably simplified if we first replace the picture by the points on its line drawing, as produced by a suitable sharpening operator, and then use templates to find the orientations of the lines. The four templates of Figure 7.14 are sufficient to find the general direction of an outline, using the following simple match rule.

> The template is said to match at any position for which at least two of the three "pluses" in the template correspond to 1's in the picture.

(There is no need to account for the minuses in the template because of the simple form of the picture left by the sharpening operator.) Often it is not necessary to use templates at all. The sharpened, outline picture is simple enough so that the computer can find the lines merely by finding any two neighboring bright points and then looking for additional nearby points that seem to line up with them. In this way a program can "follow" the edges of the outline drawing.

Now that we know the directions of edges at each point along them, we can collect the short line segments together into long lines. The following rule for finding the long lines works pretty well:

> Collect the short segments into the largest groups possible, by adding to each group any segment that is within three picture points of any segment already in the group and is not perpendicular to any segment already in the group. If a segment cannot be added to an existing group, it begins a new group of its own. When all such groups have been formed, draw a straight line between the two segments in each group that are farthest apart.

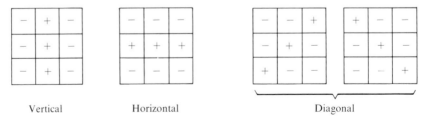

Vertical   Horizontal   Diagonal

Figure 7.14   Line-finding templates.

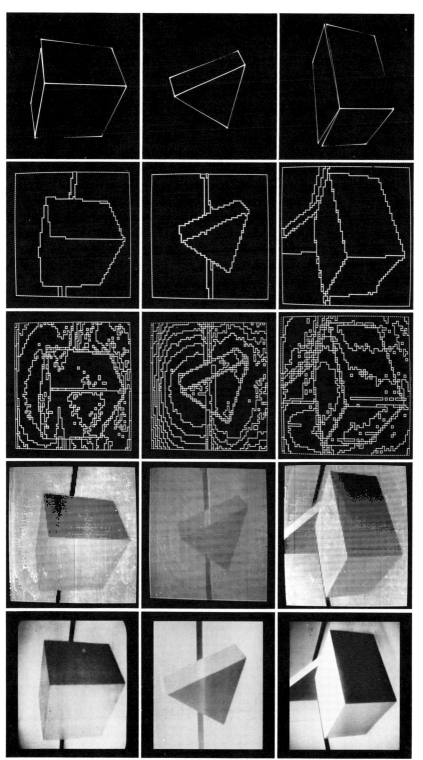

Figure 7.15 Steps in region analysis.

Finally, the computer can clean up the picture somewhat, using the programmed knowledge that all the lines must be the boundaries of real objects; therefore lines must meet at corners, isolated lines may not point off into space, gaps between line segments should be filled in, and so on.

An alternative approach to picture analysis is based upon regions instead of lines. We begin by considering all contiguous points that have the same brightness value to be part of one region. Because of variations in illumination, in camera sensitivity, and so on, this process results in many more regions than there are meaningful areas in the picture (Figure 7.15). Programs then try to merge together those different regions of uniform brightnesss that are likely to be parts of the same real surface area. These programs use rules such as, "merge two regions if one is contained within another," and "merge two adjacent regions if the difference between their average brightnesses is sufficiently small." The result of this process is similar to the result of the line-fitting process: an approximate outline drawing of the contents of the picture (Figure 7.15). Although the region approach avoids the possibility of a picture containing isolated or broken lines, it can produce other kinds of errors by merging some

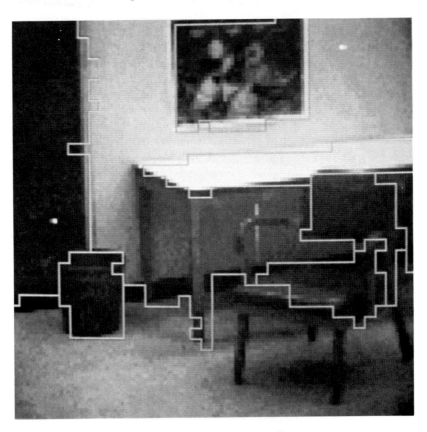

Figure 7.16 Region analysis of office scene.

regions that should not be merged, or failing to merge some that should be merged. Both line and region analysis have been used on simple pictures with reasonable degrees of success, and region-analysis methods have been an important element in newer systems that can "understand" complicated scenes, such as the one in Figure 7.3. (Figure 7.16.)

This section has shown how a computer's description of a picture can be considerably simplified. At the most detailed level we began with a picture represented by an array of numbers. Then by successive application of smoothing, sharpening, template-scanning, line fitting, and clean-up—or smoothing, region definition, and successive region merging —we worked our way up to a much simpler, clearer, outline drawing. In the computer, this version of the picture might be represented by a list of the lines or areas of the picture, each described by a few numbers that give its location and extent. Unfortunately, although such a description seems more natural than the original array of numbers, the resulting list of lines or areas in a picture does not at all explain the three-dimensional structure of the object pictured. Since the real meaning of a picture is usually expressed in terms of names of three-dimensional objects or shapes, we must bridge the gap from the two-dimensional drawing, which is merely like a shadow of an object, to the object itself. The next section shows some approaches to these final stages of the automatic analysis of the scene in a picture.

Object identification

Suppose a computer program has produced a line-drawing description of a picture—e.g., by a process something like the one presented in the previous section. Now, how can the computer tell what the drawing is a picture of? Certainly we cannot expect a computer to be able to recognize the contents of any picture in the world. Even you would not be able to recognize a picture of a person you have never met, or an unfamiliar variety of insect, or perhaps the statue of Marcus Siegfried[7] in a park in Vienna. Recognition ability depends upon both the knowledge and experience of the recognizer, and his expectation about what he will be asked to recognize; what you see in Figure 7.17 depends upon whether you are looking for faces or a goblet.

The picture-analysis method we have been describing is capable only of perceiving straight lines in a picture; therefore we might say a computer that uses such methods "knows" only about objects whose pictures can be drawn with straight lines. If we limit the expectations of the program still further, we further simplify the recognition process. At the extreme (and somewhat silly) limit, we might limit a program to "expect" only pictures of boxes. Such a program would "recognize" every picture

---

[7]Inventor of the internal-combustion engine.

Figure 7.17 Goblet and faces.

by identifying it as containing a box, without even needing to look at the picture. Since the only pictures presented to the program would indeed contain boxes—because it is unfair to show a recognizer something beyond its expectations—this program would always be correct. In fact, some version of such a "box-expecting" program could be quite useful, for example if the program located the box in the picture and reported its exact size and position.

An early scene-analysis program (by Roberts) was somewhat richer in its expectations. It expected the objects in its pictures to be either square or rectangular boxes, wedges, or pyramids, or some combination of these three elementary shapes glued together. Figure 7.18 shows some of the shapes this program could identify. The program used simple geometric properties of the possible object types to predict how they might appear in a picture, and then studied the line drawing to satisfy these predictions—e.g., two adjacent triangles must be faces of a pyramid, three adjacent quadralaterals must be faces of a box, and so on. The program also calculated the perspective distortion introduced by the camera, and could tell which lines in the picture might have been parallel to each other in the real scene and which could not have been parallel. It also could fill in reasonable joining lines for compound objects (the

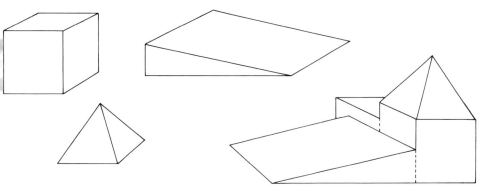

Figure 7.18 Objects for Roberts' scene-analysis programs.

dotted lines in Figure 7.18), so that a complex object could be described in terms of all its component parts.

Another program (at SRI) "expected" to see some of the background of the room containing the objects. Therefore, instead of confusing the program, the appearance of wall joints, doorways, and baseboard molding actually helped this system to figure out the positions of the objects in the room. The expectation of finding some baseboard in the picture of Figure 7.10, for example, was contained in a special baseboard-tracking subprogram that "knew" the approximate width of the dark baseboard strip.

A more general approach to analyzing straight-line drawings was proposed by Gúzman at MIT in 1965. Gúzman reasoned that people can look at a line drawing of an arbitrary jumble of simple solid objects (e.g., Figure 7.19) and tell fairly easily how the various areas form three-dimensional objects and how many objects there are in the pile. Why can't a computer do the same thing? In fact, it can. Gúzman developed a program that takes as its input a list of the lines composing a picture such as Figure 7.19, and produces as its output lists of regions in the picture that comprise each of the twelve objects. This program does not expect the objects to consist of components of any particular shape. Instead, it groups the areas into objects by using a set of informal reasoning rules (sometimes called *heuristics*) which were derived by an empirical, experimental method. The researcher guessed at a rule that might work, tried it on some examples, determined the cases in which it worked and those in which it missed, modified the rule to try to improve its performance, and then repeated the test cycle. This cycle of hypothesis, test, and modified hypothesis is precisely the way theories are developed throughout experimental science. Although we do not usually think of computer programming as an experimental science, this experimental approach to developing computer programs has been extremely useful for applying

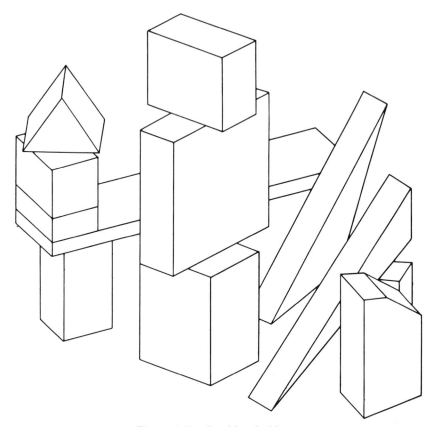

Figure 7.19 Jumble of objects.

computers to difficult problems in novel areas (such as perception). Although the resulting programs might not be explainable in terms of some deep underlying theory, they perform adequately in most situations and therefore in a very practical sense they solve the problem. In fact, most computer scientists generally have much more confidence in a program that has been demonstrated to work, even though no one may understand precisely how it works, than in a theoretical solution that someone has "proved" solves the problem but has not yet tested in practice.

The program that analyzed Figure 7.19 uses several rules for gathering areas together into objects. Its basic approach is to look first at the vertices (places where lines meet), and, depending upon the type of vertex, place links between certain areas. At a W type of vertex, the two adjacent areas are linked; at a Y vertex, three pairs of adjacent areas are each linked; at a T vertex, no direct link is made, but if a separate, parallel T exists, then two corresponding pairs of areas are linked (see Figure 7.20). When all such links have been inserted, any pair of regions

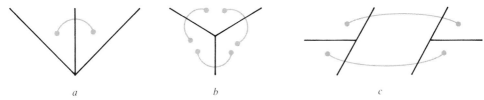

Figure 7.20 Links introduced at verteces. (*a*) W type vertex. (*b*) Y type vertex. (*c*) Two T type vertices.

that are connected by two or more links are grouped into a single object, and any region that is connected to any group by two or more links is added to that object group. In this way the program builds up objects. Several additional tests are made for certain special cases. Of course, the program would easily be confused by especially peculiar objects, or pictures with some missing lines, or certain optical illusions; but then, wouldn't you also be confused? (Figure 7.21.)

Now consider the objects in Figure 7.22. If we assume that these are supposed to be solid objects bounded by plane (flat, unwarped) surfaces, then most of us become vaguely disturbed by such drawings; we can tell that something is wrong, but often cannot understand what. A theory recently developed by Huffman at the University of California, Santa Cruz, and also by Clowes at Sussex, England, now allows a person—or a computer—to explain exactly what is wrong with figures such as these, as well as to explain the three-dimensional structure of many objects pictured in more meaningful drawings. This theory is restricted to objects whose sides are plane surfaces, and objects whose corners are formed by exactly three planes meeting along three edges. Most familiar plane-sided objects, such as all the objects seen in Figure 7.19, satisfy these conditions. Within the conditions of the theory, it can be proved that objects such as those in Figure 7.22 are impossible. The proofs make use of the following basic facts of the theory:

1. Every line in a line-drawing of an object must play one of three roles along its entire length.
    a. A concave edge.
    b. A convex edge, both of whose faces are visible.
    c. A convex edge that hides one of its faces (e.g., the outer boundary of the object).

2. Only the following four kinds of corners are possible (Figure 7.23).
    a. A corner formed by three convex edges.
    b. A corner formed by two convex edges and one concave edge.
    c. A corner formed by one convex edge and two concave edges.
    d. A corner formed by three concave edges.

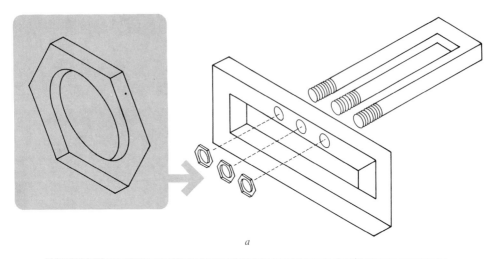

Figure 7.21 Confusing pictures. (*a*) Assembly plans. (*b*) "Relativity" by M. C. Escher. (*Escher Foundation, Haags Gemeentemuseum, The Hague.*)

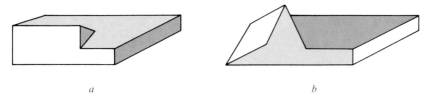

a   *b*

Figure 7.22 Impossible objects.

Of course, the appearance of a corner in a picture may depend upon the angle from which it is viewed. In particular, a convex edge may join visible faces in one view but hide a face in another view, and often one of the three edges that make up a corner may be hidden completely.

Suppose we indicate a concave edge in our diagrams by a −; a convex edge between visible faces by a +; and a convex edge that hides one face by a →, where the visible face is to the right of the arrow. If we consider all the possible different appearances of the four types of corners, we find that there are only twelve permitted pictures of corners: i.e., only twelve junctions of two or three −, +, and → edges make sense. Figure 7.24,*a–d* shows all these arrangements and how they arise. The type *d* corner has only one view, because none of its faces can be hidden from the camera without hiding the whole corner.

Figure 7.24,*e* shows the four possible kinds of T junctions. These picture-line intersections never represent true corners in the picture scene.

A computer can use this theory to analyze pictures by systematically trying to assign −, +, and → labels to lines in such a way that every line keeps the same label from one end to another, and every corner matches one of the allowable types of corner pictures cataloged in Figure 7.24. If any such labeling process can be completed, the resulting picture in a sense explains the objects: i.e., the labels tell the meanings of the lines in the picture. These data could then be used by an object-recognition program, for example,, which had prior knowledge about the types of corners that occur on the classes of objects that might appear in a scene.

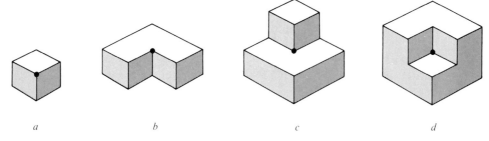

a   *b*   *c*   *d*

Figure 7.23 The four kinds of corners.

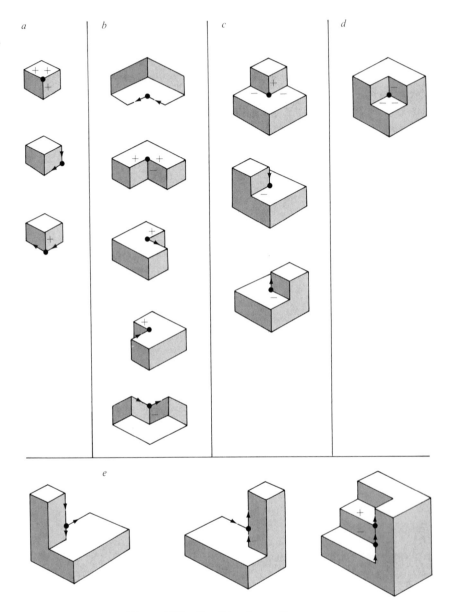

Figure 7.24 Possible views of corners.

If the labeling process cannot be completed, we know that the pictured object is impossible; if the data originally came from a real scene, then we would be sure that some of the true lines had been omitted or misplaced, and the line-finding process could be asked to try to correct its mistakes.

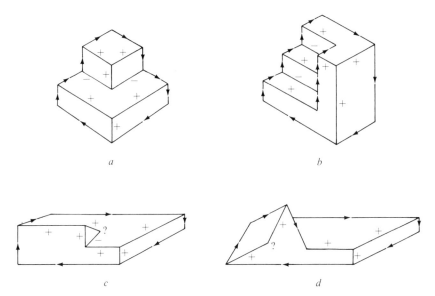

Figure 7.25 Labeled objects.

Figure 7.25 shows the results of such labeling processes, with some of the simple figures we have been using in examples, and with the two impossible figures from Figure 7.22. As we might expect, the labeling difficulties arise precisely where our intuitive feelings about the picture are most disturbed. (The top surface in Figure 7.25,*c* and the front surface of 7.25,*d* cannot be flat planes.)

The object- and scene-analysis methods described above are merely the first steps toward a truly complete theory of how to recognize the contents of pictures of simple solid objects. Extending this theory is the subject of continuing current research, and significant advances have already been made in several directions, some of which are discussed here.

ADDITIONAL CONSTRAINTS

Although every good picture of a real object can be labeled, every picture that can be labeled does not necessarily describe a real object; many weird drawings can be constructed that manage to satisfy the corner and edge restrictions of the above theory. All the "objects" in Figure 7.26, for example, can be fully labeled, even though *a*, *b*, and *c* are impossible, and *d* and *e* are highly improbable (but possible, as shown in Figure 7.27). The objects in Figure 7.26 can be "recognized" as peculiar by noting and testing such properties as the fact that one plane cannot pass behind itself (the shaded plane of Figure 7.26,*a*), two planes can meet only in a single line (rather than the two darkened lines in Figure 7.26,*b*), and

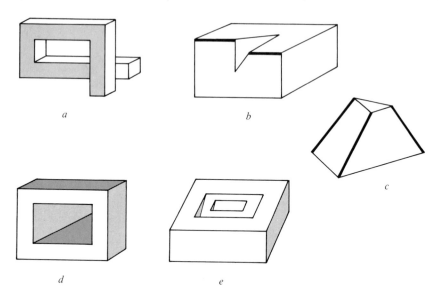

Figure 7.26   More peculiar objects.

three planes can meet only at a single point (the vertex that has been cut off the pyramid in Figure 7.26,*c*, where the three darkened lines must meet). Assumptions concerning the complexity of hiddden parts of the object (Figure 7.26,*d*), and the generality of the camera position (to prevent skew lines from appearing parallel, as in Figure 7.26,*e*) can also be made clearer.

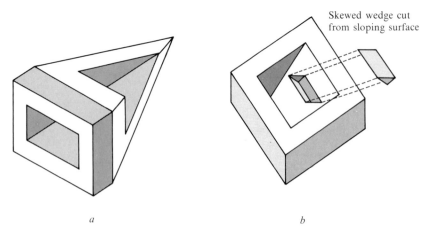

Figure 7.27   Revealing views of improbable objects. (*a*) Object of Figure 7.26,*d*. (*b*) Object of Figure 7.26,*e*.

LIGHT AND SHADOW

The corner-and-edge constraints described above concern the basic structure of an object. Similar constraints have been developed concerning the lighting conditions under which an object is seen. Such constraints allow people—and computers—to analyze pictures such as Figure 7.28 and recognize which lines are true object edges and which are merely shadows. In fact, the existence of shadows, along with rules for understanding how they are formed, actually helps rather than hinders the process of labeling the entire picture.

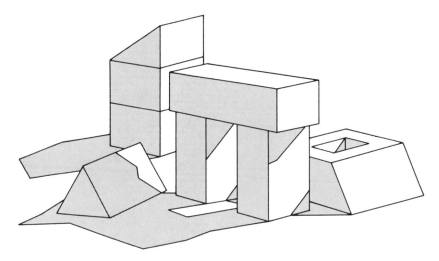

Figure 7.28 A scene with shadows. (*David Waltz, MIT.*)

EFFICIENCY

Systematic procedures have been developed for applying various constraints to pictures and thereby rapidly constructing fully labeled scenes. The trial-and-error search methods suggested by our informal discussion above have been replaced by much more efficient methods.

IMPERFECT PICTURES

All the procedures discussed in this section have been based upon the assumption that the picture is a perfect, complete line drawing of an original scene composed of simple plane-sided objects. Similar methods have now been developed for more realistic, imperfect drawings, of the kind that might arise from computer analysis of real pictures. A thorough knowledge of corner-and-edge constraints, constraints due to light and shadows, the mathematical properties of lines and planes, perspective and other camera distortions, and knowledge of the kinds of objects that the system "expects" to find in the scene, have all been combined to guide real picture-analysis procedures. These procedures can actually correct imperfect pictures by figuring out where missing lines must be in order to make sense out of the scene.

CURVED OBJECTS

The research described thus far has studied pictures that can be drawn with straight lines. Scientists specifically picked such pictures for their first experiments in automatic picture analysis in order to simplify the task; straight lines are much easier to detect and to describe than curved lines. Unfortunately, the world is not composed of straight lines. Almost all the objects we encounter in our normal activities are much more com-plicated-looking than blocks, pyramids, and baseboards. Just as we try to teach a child mathematics by beginning with addition rather than, say, integral calculus, we have begun trying to teach a computer vision by beginning with blocks rather than, say, landscapes. However, the time has come to move on. Can we extend the methods described in this section to objects with curved boundaries?

Several attempts of this kind have been made, with some success. Programs have been written that can analyze real pictures of simple curved objects—like teacups and telephones, and stylized curved-line drawings such as might appear in children's coloring books. By methods similar to region growing or line fitting, such programs can identify the major areas of these pictures and describe their shapes, either in general terms such as "circular," "irregular," "snake-like," and so on, or very precisely by giving mathematical descriptions of the boundary curves. Then, such programs can make use of both two-dimensional relationships (above, next to, inside of) and three-dimensional descriptions (cones, cylinders, and so on) to try to identify the objects in the pictures.

Such attempts to make a computer recognize simple curved objects by the shapes of their outlines have met with mixed success so far. Some scientists believe that the problem of shape recognition is unnecessarily difficult; perhaps we are not following the best approach to achieving computer vision by studying outline drawings. After all, when people look around their environments they usually are not especially aware of lines at all; instead they see colors, textures, relative position, motion, and so on. Just glance at a tree, a carpet, a street scene, or a cluttered desk. What are the most prominent features of what you see? How do you recognize things? In order to make the recognition task easier, for a com-puter or a person, perhaps we need better sensory data than just black-and-white pictures, and better understanding of the nature of the scene than just the outline of shapes.

Perceptual understanding systems

Suppose you are about to open some presents. Do you need to unwrap each item completely and look at it in a strong light in order to recognize what it is? Not usually. One handlebar sticking out of a large, formless wrapping is enough to identify the bicycle you had been expecting. If it's Christmas morning and a small flat box has a tag showing that it came from Aunt Agnes, you might know it contains another hideous tie. On the other hand, if the occasion is your bar-mitzvah, then you can be pretty sure that every small flat box contains another pen-and-pencil set. If you don't come to any such quick conclusion, you might examine the mysterious package more closely, look at the tag or postmark, lift it to feel its weight, shake it to see if it rattles or sloshes, and you usually will have a pretty good chance of perceiving what's inside without ever seeing it.

In the last chapter I complained that it was unfair to expect a computer to recognize speech signals unless it first knows something about such things as the meanings of words, the grammar of sentences, and the context in which the speech was uttered; the current "speech understanding" research projects are attempting to give the computer just such knowledge. Similarly, it is unfair to expect a computer to recognize real objects unless it first knows something about the expected characteristics of the objects, such as their size, shape, and color, the normal physical relationships among them such as above, next to, part of, or supports, and possibly the context in which the recognition process is going on; finding a dim comet with a small telescope requires quite a different perceptual approach than finding the switch that will turn off an irritating alarm clock.

Many of the past computer-vision projects tried to "simplify" their tasks by aiming their cameras only at artificial objects like boxes and wedges, which had straight-line edges and clear mathematical descriptions. Unfortunately, such objects have few expected sizes or shapes, no normal physical relationships, and rarely any context to guide the recognition process. Because of this, paradoxically, the attempt to simplify may actually have made the recognition problem more difficult. Certainly the principal methods devised to find and identify boxes and wedges in pictures, although sometimes mathematically elegant and quite effective, cannot be transferred to recognition problems in more realistic situations.

Look around the room you are now in. Not many boxes or wedges to be seen, are there? What are, say five things that you see? Chances are you did not pick such details as "the middle hinge on the door" and "the number seven on the telephone dial," or such generalities as "the furniture." Instead, you probably picked major items that occupy a significant (but not too large) part of the scene, and have some special meaning, use, or other significance to you—e.g., chair, waste-basket, picture-on-the-wall, telephone-on-the-desk. Can a computer, similarly, look at a random scene and identify the prominent items of interest? (Here "of interest" refers to the computer user's or programmer's interest, since the computer presumably has no interests of its own.) One project at the SRI Artificial Intelligence Center takes this approach to the automatic recognition of objects in typical office scenes such as that of Figure 7.3,*a*. This project is based upon three premises.

1.   Scenes are not random, but rather can be expected to satisfy a large number of constraints: chairs and desks stand on the floor, desks have flat tops, pictures are rectangular and hang on the wall, door knobs are found near side edges of doors, books are on shelves or desks, and so on.

2.   Perception usually requires a combination of elementary senses. In particular, color and distance, in addition to brightness, are easily measurable and especially useful.

3.   By combining the contextual knowledge of 1 with the multi-sensory data of 2, we can construct easy ways for the computer to "see" things. For example, to find a desk, look for a large horizontal surface about thirty inches above the floor. If the desk is cluttered, it can still be recognized as a large number of small, uniformly colored, irregular areas (where the desk surface peeks out from behind the clutter) that lie in the same horizontal plane and at the proper height. To find a telephone, look for a small black shiny region on top of a desk (or perhaps, for certain modern telephones, look for a small pink shiny region hanging on the wall).

Note that the above ways of "seeing" things do not require precise mathematical comparisons of outline shapes—a computationally difficult procedure. Instead, the object characteristics we require can usually be evaluated quite rapidly, provided the appropriate sensory data is available: horizontal surfaces can be identified from a set of distance measurements, uniform color can be verified by comparing color pictures, and so on. Moreover, as we mentioned in Chapter 1, devices exist that can feed the computer depth and color pictures almost as easily as black-and-white pictures. Now scientists are beginning to explore how a computer can use such varied data in a coordinated way, without choking on it because of its bulk.

Other scene characteristics that people perceive easily are not yet convenient for computers. Motion is an important clue to human observers—e.g., a well-camouflaged frog in his natural setting may be virtually impossible to find until he leaps, and then he becomes perfectly clear. However, although there are devices that detect whether an entire scene is at rest or whether it contains something moving, no present equipment can separate the static from the moving portions of a picture quickly enough to be useful for automatic scene analysis. Similarly, texture is an important feature measured by the human eye—a surface is seen to be shiny, or mat, or rough. Although this characteristic cannot be directly measured, there are ways to calculate important aspects of texture from a high-resolution brightness picture, and some experiments in the use of the results of such calculations have been begun.

On the other hand, it is possible for automatic sensors to tell a computer about aspects of a scene that are only slightly apparent to people, if at all. For example, computers can produce detailed, sensitive "pictures" of gradations of heat coming from different parts of a scene, and then translate heat gradations to brightness gradations to aid human interpretation (Figure 7.29). Ultraviolet, x-ray emissions, and magnetic properties of scenes can also be sensed by computers. Automatic scene-analysis systems could make use of such data if it ever seems useful for them to do so.

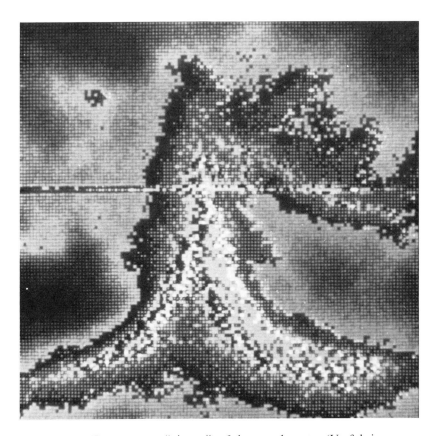

Figure 7.29 Temperature "picture" of human breasts. (Useful in cancer detection.) (*Stanford Research Institute.*)

The easy ways of seeing things, discussed in premise 3 above, do not have to be the only methods available to the computer. Because they are designed to be quick and easy, these tests may also be rough and incomplete. For example, the shiny black object on the desk might be someone's leather handbag, instead of the telephone. However, there is nothing in this formulation to prevent the computer from also "knowing" more detailed, precise information about the objects in its environment, and drawing upon this information as necessary. For example, the quick and easy test might be used just to acquire candidate regions that, at first glance, look like telephones, and then a more careful "telephone verifier" could look more closely and see whether the small black shiny object on the table had a dial, a cord, and a receiver. Certainly such a two-stage approach is more likely to be efficient than, say, scanning the entire picture with a magnifying glass looking only for telephone-dial finger holes.

In this chapter we have explored how a computer may be programmed to interpret and understand a variety of direct sensory data: light, color, depth, perhaps atomic radiation. In the last chapter we also considered how a computer might hear and understand spoken language. Of the remaining senses that humans have, taste and smell are essentially delicate chemical-analysis mechanisms; although some similar effects could be automated, they would probably have limited, very special roles, and therefore will not be considered here. (For example, a proposed life-detection kit for a Mars space probe would contain an automatic chemical laboratory that might be considered a "sniffer" and "taster.") However, the sense of touch is one of the most useful, widely used human senses. Would it be useful, or at least intellectually interesting and worthwhile, to give a computer a sense of touch? What new scope would computer science have if the automatic machines could reach out and explore the physical world on their own? This thought moves us beyond the subject of perception and into a subject that deserves a chapter of its own: robots.

Summary

Scientists try to develop automatic machine perception for two major reasons:

1. More "intelligent" computer systems might be possible if the machine were able to acquire information about the world through its own sensors, instead of being restricted to representations and encodings of knowledge provided by programmers.

2. Communication between people and computers would be more convenient if people could present pictures, sounds, and so on, to a computer for direct examination, instead of having to translate all information into the formalisms of programming languages.

Computer-perception research has concentrated upon the visual perception of brightness. Usually an A/D converter transforms data from a TV camera into numbers in a computer's memory; the major research task is to develop software that can process those numbers and figure out what was in the picture.

The difficulty of understanding pictures varies for many reasons, such as differences in picture complexity, rendition, accuracy, and precision. Vision research typically includes trying to eliminate some of these difficulties so that the remaining ones may be more easily studied.

Template matching is a common approach to the problem of understanding certain types of two-dimensional pictures. The object in the picture, for example an alphabetic character, is transformed to a standard size and position and then compared, point by point, with a set of standard shapes to see which fits best. This method does not work for classes of objects, such as triangles, that are defined by their descriptions rather than their precise shapes.

A digitized picture can usually be clarified by *smoothing* and *sharpening* operations. However, such operations must be chosen with care because they frequently destroy some of the significant picture information. The next step in picture processing is to outline the objects in the picture. This can be done either by finding and joining edges until a complete line drawing emerges, or by finding and merging uniform regions until they meet at natural area boundaries.

Finally, higher-level programs must be able to understand and describe the pictured scene. Advance knowledge of the elementary shapes that may occur in the scene can be brought to bear here. Topological constraints guide the interpretation of corners and surfaces. A recent theory helps interpret various views of solid, plane-sided objects and helps distinguish between drawings of possible and impossible objects.

Most of the past work on automated vision focused upon clear pictures of solid, plane-sided objects. Current research is turning to more natural pictures that may incorporate curved objects and complex surroundings. "Scene understanding systems," like the "speech understanding systems" of the previous chapter, are now being built that coordinate the use of several kinds and sources of knowledge in order to solve complex problems. For example, knowledge of illumination, distance measurements, color, spatial relationships, and physical constraints, can all contribute to the accuracy of the interpretation of visual data.

SUGGESTED READINGS

Barrow, H. G., et al. "Some Techniques for Recognizing Structures in Pictures." In *Frontiers of Pattern Recognition,* S. Watanabe (ed.). Academic Press, New York, 1972.

Brice, C. R. and C. L. Fennema. "Scene Analysis Using Regions." *Artificial Intelligence,* Vol. 1, no. 3, pp. 205–226, 1970.

Duda, R. O., and P. E. Hart. *Pattern Classification and Scene Analysis.* John Wiley & Sons, New York, 1973.

Guzman, A. "Decomposition of a Visual Scene into Three-Dimensional Bodies." *Proceedings of the American Federation of Information Processing Societies.* Vol. 33, pp. 291–304, Thompson Book Co., Washington, D.C., 1969.

Perception: Mechanisms and Models (Readings from *Scientific American*). W. H. Freeman and Company, San Francisco, 1971.

Tenenbaum, J. M. "On Locating Objects by Their Distinguishing Features in Multisensory Images." *Computer Graphics and Image Processing,* Vol. 2, no. 3, pp. 359, Dec., 1973.

Winston, P. H. *The Psychology of Computer Vision.* McGraw-Hill Book Co., New York, 1975.

Robots 8

The Three Laws of Robotics. (1) A robot may not injure a human being, or through inaction, allow a human being to come to harm; (2) a robot must obey all commands given by a human being except in the event that such orders might conflict with the First Law; and (3) a robot must protect its own existence as long as such protection does not conflict with either the First or the Second Law.
—*I, Robot,* by Isaac Asimov

What is a robot?

Somewhere in a control center in Russia, a man watches a screen and punches some buttons: 240,000 miles away a small vehicle comes to life; it begins measuring the radiation in its environment, its camera begins transmitting pictures, and it starts slowly rolling across the lunar landscape.

In an industrial plant in Ohio, an assembly line carrying partly-completed automobile bodies automatically comes to a stop at a carefully selected position. Twenty-three giant mechanical arms, each equipped with a welding gun, emerge from the darkness. Twenty-three different patterns of welds are applied to twenty-three different cars of several models and various stages of completion. Then the arms withdraw, and the line moves on to the next station. No human being is visible.

At a hospital in Virginia, a doctor phones from a patient's room to request some medical equipment. Shortly thereafter a supply cart rolls out of the store room, down a corridor, and waits for an automatic elevator. When the elevator arrives the cart enters, rises to the appropriate floor, and finds its own way to the right room.

In a laboratory in California a man types, "Block door 5 with box 2 from room 3." While the lights twinkle on a computer in the next room, an awkward-looking machine turns and, in a long series of slow, jerky motions of its wheels and of the camera it is carrying, maneuvers itself through doorways and around various obstacles, and finally pushes a large box squarely into the middle of the designated doorway.

The above scenarios all describe events that actually occurred within a few years of 1970. Do they describe robots? In science fiction, a robot is frequently pictured as a clumsy pile of tin cans with a light on its head, that always takes its orders quite literally and therefore is prone to make stupid mistakes. Asimov's robots are much more sophisticated, leading to interesting moral and philosophical dilemmas. Clarke's robot, HAL, is like a disembodied brain that uses people to do its physical dirty work. Now that robots are moving from the pages of fiction out into the real world, how shall we recognize them, improve them, control them, and put them to work? Let us look at the above examples somewhat more closely.

When a man turns the steering wheel of his car, the front wheels turn. This is clearly not the action of a robot, but rather the effect of direct mechanical linkages. Now, suppose we replace a direct mechanical link by a direct radio link: a man pushes a lever that activates a transmitter that sends a radio signal to a receiver on a model airplane fifty yards away that turns on a motor that moves the wing flaps that cause the plane to turn. Does remote control make the model plane into a robot? Suppose, instead of a model plane fifty yards away, we transmit to a Surveyor or a Lunahod about a quarter of a million miles away; does distance make a remotely controlled instrument more robot-like?

The Unimate[1] "industrial robots" in the General Motors assembly plant at Lordstown, Ohio, are led through their precise welding motions by a human operator each time the assembly line is set up for a new production run (Fig. 8.1). Later, during the run, no human assistance is necessary; electronic bookkeeping signals tell each arm when a particular vehicle is correctly positioned in front of it, and the arm then executes its memorized sequence of actions. Is the ability of a machine to carry out a series of physical actions without human intervention the essence of being a robot? If so, should I consider my automatic phonograph record-changer to be a robot?

The supply carts in the Fairfax County Hospital (Fig. 8.2) have been assigned their own private elevators and corridors, so that they cannot bump into people (or vice versa). Their actions are remotely controlled by the same small computer that operates their elevators, and they navigate along corridors by following signals in wires buried in the floor. When a cart is requested at a particular room, the computer selects a route for the cart to follow, makes sure no other carts will be using any part of that route, initiates appropriate guidance signals along the buried wires, and sends the requested cart on its way. Does the dynamic involvement of a computer make these carts more robotic?

---

[1]Trademarked product of Unimation, Inc., Danbury, Conn.

Figure 8.1 A double line of Unimate robots, each performing various spot-welding functions on Chevrolet Vegas. (*Unimation Inc., Danbury, Conn.*)

Figure 8.2 Robot hospital-supply cart being loaded. (*Fairfax Hospital, Falls Church, Va.*)

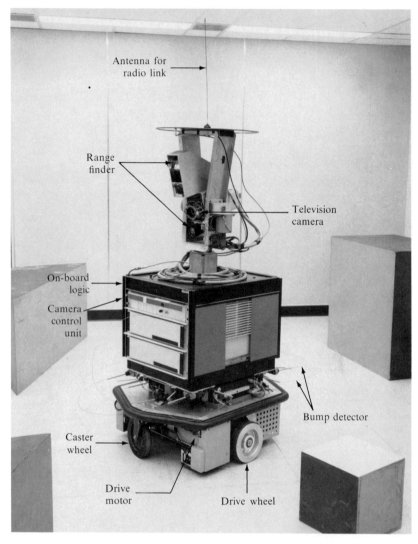

Antenna for
radio link

Range
finder

Television
camera

On-board
logic

Camera
control
unit

Bump detector

Caster
wheel

Drive
motor

Drive wheel

Figure 8.3 Shakey, the robot developed at SRI. (*Stanford Research Institute.*)

The robot vehicle built in 1968 at Stanford Research Institute in Menlo Park, California, was affectionately nicknamed "Shakey" (Fig. 8.3), because of his[2] apparent physical instability. A large nearby computer planned each of Shakey's actions, and then monitored the effectiveness of these actions while the vehicle tried to carry them out. Data

---

[2]The developers of Shakey frequently refer to the device as *him,* whereas the Unimate, for example, is always referred to as *it.* Perhaps this shift to the use of personal pronouns represents subconscious recognition that the device is a robot rather than merely another machine.

from Shakey's TV camera, bumpers, and other sensors allowed the computer to revise its plans while Shakey was trying to solve a problem. Some people feel that such use of sensory information fed back from the physical world to influence behavior is an ability that any robot must have. Do you agree?

I am not going to define the word "robot" here, because of the wide range of interpretations it has. The above discussion indicates the general kinds of devices that we shall consider. Shakey and similar machines will be studied in more detail later in this chapter, and the use of the Unimate in the next chapter. First, however, let us go back and look at robots of the past.

Early history of robots

People have always been fascinated by the possibility of nonhuman entities possessing human-like intelligence. In ancient stories such creatures were gods, or mythical beasts such as centaurs, or magical spirits such as genies that carry out the whims of their masters but cause all kinds of mischief if they ever break free. Later stories tell of fairy godmothers who could transform mice into footmen or frogs into princes, and of Giuseppe's puppet Pinocchio who eventually acquired enough sensitivity to become a real boy.

Jewish folklore contains several references to "golem," artificial human beings endowed with life. The best-known story of this kind concerns the Maharal, who was the chief rabbi of Prague sometime during the fifteenth century. The Maharal and his assistant formed a man out of the clay of a river bank. Then, in a secret magical ceremony (with a little help from God), they brought this golem to life. The golem could neither speak nor sleep, and did nothing on its own initiative; but for many years it served faithfully as a servant to the Maharal and a protector of the local community. A strange footnote to this story is that several key figures in contemporary computer history—including John von Neumann, who developed the main concepts for modern digital computers; Norbert Wiener, who is known as the father of cybernetics; and Marvin Minsky, one of the founders of the field of artificial intelligence—are all reported to be direct descendents of the Maharal.

In the seventeenth and eighteenth centuries skilled mechanics began building elaborate clockwork devices. The Archbishop of Salzburg, Austria, built a working model of a complete miniature town, all operated by water power from a nearby stream (Fig. 8.4). Clocks were built that told not only the time of day, week, month, and year, but also when the sun and moon would rise and set, where all the planets were in their orbits, and even the position of the equinoxes with respect to the 20,000-year cycle of precession of the earth's axis. (Fig. 8.5). Babbage planned his "analytical engine," a forerunner of the digital computer,

Figure 8.4 Water-powered robot town at Hellbrun palace.

entirely out of mechanical components, but the resulting collection of levers, cams, rods, gears, bearings, cranks, pins, and so on, was so complicated that Babbage never made up his mind about a final design, and a working model could never be completed.

Some people soon applied this mechanical technology to creating robotic creatures. One of the most famous of such devices is Vaucanson's Duck (Fig. 8.6). In the 1730's Jacques de Vaucanson of Paris built a clockwork instrument that was advertised to be an "artificial duck made of guilded copper who drinks, eats, quacks, splashes about on the water, and digests his food like a living duck." The last phrase referred to the fact that the duck would occasionally defecate a foul-smelling substance. Demonstrations by Vaucanson's duck and related devices were the entertainment sensations of the courts of Europe, more than two-hundred years before Walt Disney Enterprises invented the term "audioanimatronics" to refer to the similar-appearing inhabitants of Disneyland.

In the late eighteenth century an enterprising Hungarian inventor, Baron Wolfgang von Kempelen, took advantage of this wave of interest in mechanical entertainment devices by announcing his chess automaton (Fig. 8.7). This machine consisted of a wooden model of a man with movable arms, sitting behind a chess board, and mounted upon a large box apparently filled with complicated mechanical clockwork. The automaton played chess; that is, the wooden man actually picked up and moved chess pieces about the board. It played quite a good game, beat-

Figure 8.5 Multicycle clock in Vienna Clock Museum

Figure 8.6 Vaucanson's duck. (*Chapuis and Droz*, Automata, *Neuchatel, Griffon, 1958.*)

Figure 8.7 Von Kempelen's chess automation. (*Chapuis and Droz,* Automata, *Neuchatel, Griffon, 1958.*)

ing most opponents; in fact, it was almost certainly better than any computer chess program that has yet been developed. The Baron toured with his automaton wide and far, gathering much publicity and many admission fees. After viewing a demonstration of the automaton, Edgar Allen Poe constructed a logical proof that the performance could not be authentic, but the precise nature of the deception was not discovered for many years. According to one version of the story, the secret finally came out one day when, in the midst of a match and in front of a large audience, a loud sneeze was emitted by the midget, an expert chess player, who was hidden in the clockwork.

These eighteenth century gadgets were developed purely for their entertainment value. In recent decades, however, another class of gadgets has appeared. For more than thirty years scientists, philosophers, and engineers have been asking whether we might not learn something about physiology or psychology—i.e., how certain biological systems behave or how certain mental processes take place—by building physical models to test our current theories. The resulting devices, based on modern hardware and software technology, might not only clarify our thoughts about certain theoretical issues, but could also evolve into practical machinery that is useful in its own right. The next section describes the beginnings of this new generation of robot devices.

Recent history of robots

In about 1940 Dr. Ross Ashby, a British mathematician interested in cybernetics,[3] designed and built an electronic circuit he called the "Homeostat." The Homeostat was contained in a box fitted with several rotary switches and several indicator dials; the switches determined the voltages at various input points to the circuit, and the dials showed the voltages at other selected points. The interesting property of the Homeostat was that no matter what arbitrary new positions the switches were turned to, the needles on the dials always returned, within a few seconds, to their original positions. The only exception was that occasionally, a sudden large change to several switches at the same time could cause all the needles to flutter for a while, and then settle down to new positions, from which it would again be difficult to drive them. Thus the circuit exhibited a kind of inertia, almost a will of its own. Ashby compared the behavior of the Homeostat to that of a large, lazy dog lying in front of a fireplace. Flies on his nose or noises in the room cause an occasional twitch or shudder and are then ignored; but if the fire gets too hot he will rise, shake himself, step back a foot or two, turn around once or twice, and settle down into a new comfortable position. The Homeostat demon-

---

[3]"Comparative study of the automatic control system formed by the nervous system and brain and by mechanical-electrical communication systems." (*Webster's Seventh New Collegiate Dictionary*.)

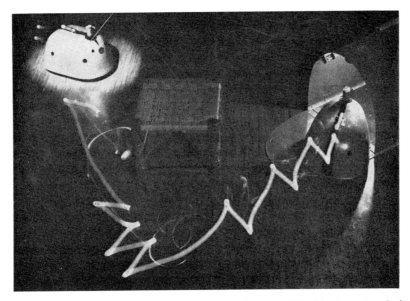

Figure 8.8 Grey Walter's tortoises. (*Desmond Tripp, Chloride Batteries, Ltd.*)

strated that a box of metal and glass could behave with a stable single-mindedness that many people would previously have attributed only to biological systems.

About ten years later another British scientist, W. Grey Walter, added mobility to Ashby's novel concept of a machine with apparent intentions of its own. Walter's machines looked like mechanical tortoises (Fig. 8.8). They could roll about, and would "instinctively" move towards any light—unless it was too bright, in which case they would turn their backs and retreat. When no light was visible, they would wander about at random, apparently searching for something. These machines proved that simple combinations of electronic and mechanical parts could result in automatic behavior remarkably like that of a simple animal or insect.

In the early 1960's scientists at Johns Hopkins University began building a more interesting device to demonstrate how much cleverness could be built into an artificial mechanism. This machine was to become known, unofficially, as "The Hopkins' Beast" (Fig. 8.9). Two basic design decisions, similar to those of Walter's tortoises, determined the Beast's ultimate character. (1) It was to be a mobile vehicle, small enough to travel about the hallways of the Hopkins' Laboratory. (2) It was to be entirely self-contained, with no cable or radio link to any computer, power supply, or human-operated terminal. Because it was an indoor vehicle the Beast would have to be electrically powered; the noise and exhaust of a gasoline engine would not be tolerable. This meant a battery-operated system, with provision for frequent replacement or recharging of the batteries. That the vehicle was to be logically self-contained meant

Figure 8.9 The Hopkins' Beast. (*Applied Physics Laboratory, The Johns Hopkins University.*)

that its decision-making ability would be severely limited, because computers were still much too bulky to ride around the hallways. These two constraints—the frequent need for electric power and the need to restrict the Beast to relatively simple-minded "thoughts" embodied in special-purpose hardware—resulted in a rather elegant final system design: a machine whose one purpose in "life" was to keep its batteries charged.

I can remember watching the Beast, which resembled a small garbage can on wheels, rolling majestically down the center of a corridor, oscillating slightly from side to side. Suddenly it would stop, move over to an electric outlet on the wall, stick out its plug, feel for the precise position of the outlet, and plug itself in. Then it would sit for a few minutes, lamp glowing softly, quietly "feeding" itself. Then it would retract its plug, move back to the center of the hall, and continue in the direction it had been going, looking for the next outlet.

The Beast's navigation system was based upon sonar measurements that attempted to keep it centered as it moved between two parallel walls. Knowing its distance from a wall, the Beast could keep its "eye" focused upon that wall. Just as a frog's eye has special nerve cells to detect the motion of a bug (and my children seem to have special receptors for reading any sign that says "Ice Cream" from a distance of at least three miles),.the Beast's eye—a combination of photocells, masks, lenses, and circuits—was designed for one thing only: to detect electric outlet coverplates. In fact, the Beast perceived the world as consisting of precisely two things: (1) coverplates, and (2) everything else. A coverplate was anything on the wall about twelve inches above the ground that was darker than its surroundings, rectangular, and whose height was approximately 1.6 times its width. Anytime a coverplate was sighted, the Beast was designed to head straight towards it, and to reach out with its plug-shaped "hand," trying to make contact.

During the 1950's, atomic-energy research led to the development of mechanical hands much more elaborate than those of the Beast. These manipulators were designed to perform delicate mechanical operations upon radioactive materials. They were each controlled by a man who guided it from a safe distance, usually behind a special glass shield. Sometimes the man with the controls was in a separate room and watched what he was doing on closed-circuit television. Many similar remote-controlled manipulator systems, now usually called *teleoperators,* have since been developed for a wide variety of applications that range from handling acids or hot castings in a factory to repairing the exterior of a space ship in orbit. Of course, no mechanical arm makes any decisions on its own; every motion, every pressure, every twitch, is in direct response to some action of the man at the controls, who carefully watches the effects of his actions and makes any necessary fine-tuning corrections.

Naturally, computer scientists soon became interested in the question of whether such manipulators could be controlled by computers, without a man present to influence what is going on. At MIT in the early 1960's, Henry Earnst obtained an arm of the type designed for atomic-energy work, and began experimenting with it. He found that, by operating the master controls himself, he could make the arm do such complicated things as screw in a light bulb or pick up and strike a match. However, if he closed his eyes, he was not able to make the arm do anything significant. How would a computer be able to keep track of what it was making an arm do? Earnst obtained or developed several sensors that would enable the arm to feed information back to a controlling computer: servomechanisms that kept track of the movements of each joint so that the system would have a kinesthetic sense, i.e., it could "know" approximately where its extremity was; electrical pads that measured pressure against its fingers, so that it could sense when it bumped into, picked up, or dropped something; and photocells on its fingertips, so that it could "see" whether or not the hand was close to a dark object. He then built an electronic interface so that all these instru-

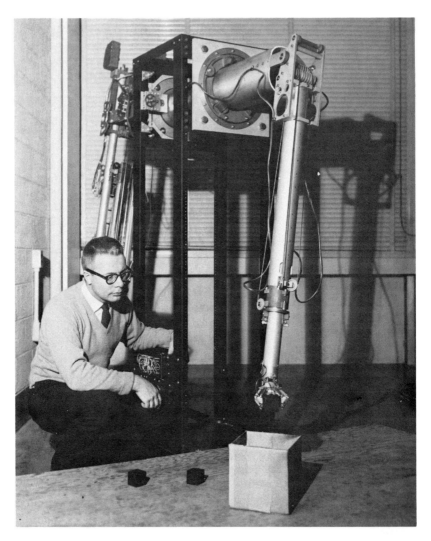

Figure 8.10 Computer-controlled mechanical hand developed at MIT. (*MIT Historical Collections.*)

ments, as well as the motors that actually moved the arm, could be operated by MIT's experimental digital computer, the TX–0. The resulting system was called MH–1 (Fig. 8.10), the world's first truly mechanical hand.

MH–1 could not strike a match or screw in a light bulb; it could only bumble around and just barely recognize when it collided with something. The most complicated program ever written in the specially developed arm-control programming language for the TX–0 was a table-clearing routine: the hand would systematically sweep back and forth over the table until it bumped into something; then it would try to pick the thing up, carry it to the edge of the table, drop it into a waste bin, and return to its systematic sweeping operation.

Experience with MH–1 proved two things.

1. It is indeed possible for a computer to interact with the physical world, using its own sensors and manipulators, in order to perform simple tasks without human assistance.

2. If the manipulator was originally designed to be used as a "slave" operated under direct human control, with a man's eyes providing the sensory feedback and a man's fingers providing the control of fine movements, then it is extremely difficult, if not impossible, to adapt such a manipulator to perform similar tasks under automatic (computer) control; the technical requirements are quite different. For example, a computer-controlled arm requires much more precise and predictable position control than an arm whose position can be monitored continually by a human eye.

Consequently, in the years following the development of MH-1, scientists in several research laboratories around the world began putting together complete robot systems, designed from the beginning for use without a man "in the loop." These systems are the subject of the last three sections of this chapter.

No discussion of the recent history of robots would be complete, however, without mentioning the wondrous inventions of Meredith Thring of Queen Mary College in London. Professor Thring, who heads a mechanical-engineering department and laboratory, has designed and built all manner of self-contained machines that make the achievements of the Hopkins' Beast fade into insignificance. By clever mechanical design, he has developed simple automatic hands (Figure 8.11,*a*) that can pick up a great range of objects including pencils, rulers, balls, and tea-cups; and small vehicles that can travel safely over level or irregular terrain, or carry a seated person up and down stairs (Figure 8.11,*b*). One device can clear a dinner table (Figure 8.11,*c*), carefully transferring dishes, glassware, and utensils to a serving cart that then drives itself out of the room; another demonstration vehicle, carrying water and a heat-seeking sensor, rides around at random until it finds a fire, and then puts it out (Figure 8.11,*d*). Much of Professor Thring's work is aimed at teleoperator-type devices to be used as prosthetic instruments—e.g., by children deformed before birth by thalidomide. His other developments, such as the mobile fire extinguisher, are very special-purpose machines with almost no flexibility in their logical control mechanisms. The logical power of large general-purpose computers coupled with the physical abilities of machines like those of Professor Thring may someday lead to more interesting robot systems than anyone outside of science fiction has yet contemplated.

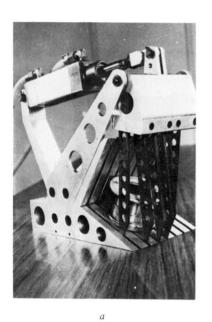

a

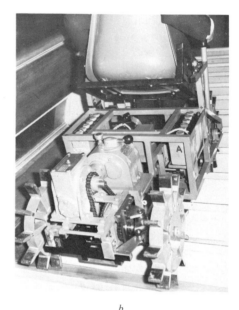

b

d

c

Figure 8.11 The inventions of Professor Thring. (*M. W. Thring, Queen Mary College, London.*)

Why build robots?

In the mid-1960's, several computer-science laboratories around the world began building robot systems. Each such system generally contained three major types of components.

1. Sensory equipment, usually including a TV camera.
2. Effector equipment, usually including a mechanical arm.
3. A general purpose digital computer.

Special electronic interfaces and programming packages were developed to enable all the components to work together smoothly.

Scientists were motivated to work on these systems at this time for a variety of reasons, usually expressed in one or a combination of the following three ways.

The Quest for Knowledge about Intelligence. We are trying to build more "intelligent" computers, as one means of studying the basic nature of intelligence. Apart from its interest from the point of view of pure scientific curiosity, a better understanding of intelligence could be of tremendous value to psychologists and educators. We know that the development of human intelligence requires a rich sensory environment: a baby must be permitted to see, touch, taste, smell, and crawl about his surroundings. Perhaps we can make a computer more intelligent by letting it see and feel the physical world, with its own eye and fingers, instead of filtering all sensory communication through magnetic tape and punched cards.

Integrating Previous Results. We have had some previous success in building automatic visual-perception systems, formal and informal problem-solving systems, and natural-language-understanding systems (see Chapters 4–7). Yet each of these systems seems to require help from some of the others: in order to understand a sentence we frequently need to see what is being talked about; in order to see we frequently need to make logical inferences about partly-hidden objects; in order to solve formal problems we frequently need to understand the subject matter; and so on. Perhaps if we combine all these abilities within the framework of a single system, they can support each other and lead to richer, more-powerful overall capabilities. The problem of developing a robot provides a focusing mechanism for drawing together previous research results and helping to identify key problems for future attention.

Practical Use. Many scientists have no doubt that some day— perhaps in ten years, perhaps not for a hundred, but eventually—robots will be in wide use, helping people carry out their everyday activities. The technology of sensors, effectors, and computers has reached a stage where it is practical now to begin studying how to design the useful intelligent robots of the future.

SIMULATION

One way to approach the task of building a robot system is, first, to build a computer *simulation* of a robot system. Simulation means building and experimenting with an idealized representation (see Chapter 3) of some aspects of a real situation. Many complex situations have been successfully simulated, both with computers and with other representational media. For example, trainer machines called *trainers* simulate an airplane pilot's cockpit, so that student pilots can practice "flying" simulated planes without ever leaving the ground and without endangering any lives. The United States Army Corp of Engineers can simulate a new dam in the San Francisco Bay region by building a scale model of it and seeing how it affects water flow in their scale model of the entire Bay Area. Often, instead of a physical model, the simulation can take place entirely in an imaginary world constructed, with appropriate programs, within a computer's memory. A new traffic-light control system can be tested on a computer by simulating the traffic flow through a simulated portion of a city, and the resulting simulated traffic jams can be ironed out without causing any real drivers to miss appointments or lose their tempers. Similarly, computer simulations have been used to test or study airport operations, factory inventory flow, theories for physiological mechanisms, military strategies, and many more. Why not also simulate robots?

Several simulations of robot systems have been programmed for computers. In some of these systems, the robot and the objects in its environment were imagined to exist on the squares of a grid, like chess pieces. By defining different sets of rules governing the legal moves of the robot—such as which directions it could move, how far away it could "see" obstacles, whether it could "push" obstacles, and so on—researchers have studied the effectiveness and efficiency of various strategies for enabling a robot to solve problems. However, since problem-solving strategies that work well in an artificial chessboard world might not be very good in a more realistic world, more realistic robot simulations were also constructed.

The first generalization of the chessboard world was a continuous two-dimensional world, a kind of Flatland.[4] Here the robot could be a point or a small circle, and the world could be populated with lines and polygons. Now the simulation became more difficult. Messy trigonometric calculations were needed to figure out which obstacles were "visible" when the robot was in a particular position. In one such system,

---

[4]Abbot, E. A., *Flatland,* Dover, New York, 1952. (Originally published in 1884.)

experimenters were surprised to find that their "point" robot kept sneaking out of a sealed room; it seems the lines representing walls did not quite meet at the corners, because of round-off errors in the numbers that told the simulation exactly where the lines ended.

A simulated two-dimensional world can be extended to three dimensions, provided the objects in the world are not very complicated, by adding a height coordinate and perhaps some shape descriptions. Winograd's "blocks world" (Chapter 6) was this kind of simulation. It contained simulated blocks and pyramids, each with a known height, that could be sitting anywhere on a basic two-dimensional plane—or above that plane, if stacked on top of something else or if held up by the robot. The robot itself consisted merely of a simulated disembodied hand that could float to any position in space and could grasp or let go of the objects. This simulation was sufficient to provide the background against which Winograd did some of the most interesting research of the decade on the problem of getting a computer to understand English.

THE TROUBLES WITH SIMULATION

If simulation is so helpful, why isn't it used more widely? Why should anyone go to all the trouble and expense of building real robots, if we can work so much more conveniently with simulations? Two basic answers can be given to these often-raised questions.

Simulating the Real World is Too Difficult. A robot-simulation experiment always consists of two cooperating parts: a simulation of the robot's world, and a simulation of the robot itself. A simulated chessboard robot can never get stuck in a crack between two squares, for example, because the simulated chessboard itself has no representation for such cracks; lines between squares simply do not exist in the simulation, so the robot cannot even contemplate them. Similarly, our simulated Flatland robot cannot climb a hill to look over an obstacle, because the concept of "hill" is missing from any simulation of a two-dimensional world. If we wish to simulate a robot that can perform interesting tasks in the same real, three-dimensional world in which we live, we must first design a simulation of this world so that it can exist in the "mind" of a computer. What form could such a simulation take? How could we design a representation in the computer for every detailed fact about the world that might be needed by a (real or simulated) robot? Suppose, as one small part of the simulated system, we wish to simulate the ability of the robot to see with a TV camera. The world-simulation system would have to produce a picture for the robot's visual system to examine. Imagine pointing a TV camera into the street from a window near where you are now sitting, and think about the picture that would then appear on a monitor's screen. Now, suppose you had to describe how that picture could be produced artificially, in a simulation, from some description of the scene outside the window. How could we describe to the computer everything about the scene—shapes, sizes, colors, textures, shadows, motions, relative positions, perspective, as well as the camera sensitivity, resolution, distortion, and so on—that is needed to produce the picture? Isn't it easier simply to point a real camera at the real scene, and see what comes out? It might be said that this is a "simulation" in which we represent the real world by the real world itself; not only is this the most complete and accurate possible model, but in many cases it is the most convenient model to use.

We Never Know Precisely What to Simulate. Someday I would like to have a little robot that could perform errands for me. I would like to be able to ask it, for example, to please run across the street and buy me a newspaper. Now, I might begin designing such a robot in a simulation system: I could send a simulated robot across a simulated street. But that robot could only simulate that it bought me a simulated newspaper, and I still would not know who won last night's ball games. Let's pursue the simulation idea further; suppose we want to use the simulation to study the behavior of the eventual real robot. How reliably should the simulated robot be designed to perform? Winograd's simulated robot hand performed perfectly: when it was told to move to some position in the simulated world, it went precisely there. Yet I know that a real robot can never go precisely where it is told. The fact that it lives in a real physical world means that no measurements are 100 percent accurate; bearings wear, clutches slip, tapes stretch, screws loosen, and the robot will always end up at least a fraction of an inch away from where it wants to be. Moreover, for similar reasons, it probably will not even know precisely where it ended up. In a sophisticated simulation, we might have the simulated robot make similar errors—but we cannot tell whether errors simulated with, for example, the help of a random-number generator, really have the same character as the errors that might arise in nature. Even if an error-prone simulated robot can cope with its world, I would have doubts about transferring that robot's reasoning mechanisms into my desired real robot.

Moreover, there are catastrophic errors and uncertainties in the real world that could not possibly be anticipated in a simulation. When I send my robot across the street for a newspaper, its batteries might run down on the way, so it should "know" enough to make a side trip to an electric outlet; it has to be careful not to get hit by a truck; it might have to look for another newspaper store, if its favorite one is closed for vacation; it might find the street torn up for subway construction, so another route must be discovered; and so on. The number of possible difficulties that can obstruct the performance of even simple errands, in our modern society, is too enormous to contemplate; and certainly too bewildering to attempt to simulate. Since one major goal of robot research is to invent automatic systems that can cope with the real world, we may as well abandon simulation and plunge right ahead to experiment with real "live" robots.

Components of modern robots

> "What are little boys made of?
> Snakes and snails and puppy-dogs' tails
> That's what little boys are made of!
>
> "What are little girls made of?
> Sugar and spice and everything nice
> That's what little girls are made of!"

What are little robots made of? Surely the nature of the components play a major role in determining the character of the resulting system. At this early stage in the evolution of robot systems, a great many different types of components are being tried out in several different research laboratories. Let's look at the range of current sensors, effectors, and computers being used for robot studies.

Sensors. Many scientists think that vision is the most important sense for human beings, and therefore considerable effort has gone into trying to make robots "see." Most robot-research laboratories have based their automated-vision studies upon the use of high-quality conventional television cameras. At MIT work has also been done with special, ultra-precise, ultra-sensitive cameras. Such work is based upon the premise that, since the first practical robots will have a much poorer store of knowledge and much less reasoning ability than people, they should be given the advantage of better sensory data. At a Mitsubishi research laboratory in Japan, engineers are studying a robot system that has only a rather low-quality TV camera. There they are interested in building robots for industrial use, and are concerned with achieving low cost and small size rather than high intelligence.

Of course, a photoelectric cell—the old-fashioned "electric eye"—is a very simple visual sensor. Groups of photo cells can be arranged to focus over an area and thus sense the silhouettes of objects that move past. Such systems are more rugged and less expensive than TV, and are beginning to be experimented with.

Although black-and-white pictures are sufficient for many purposes, a sense of color can also be very useful. Color TV cameras are still rather expensive and complicated to operate. Instead, several projects have provided their robots with a sense of color by placing different colored filters in front of the black-and-white TV camera. (This makes it possible for robots to see how different the world looks when viewed through red, green, or perhaps rose-colored glasses.)

If a robot is to be able to pick up or move objects, it should have some kind of sense of touch. Several different touch sensors have been developed. The simplest are contact switches: they get pushed shut when the robot touches something. If enough such switches are spread about the robot's fingers, hand, or body, then it can tell fairly accurately what part of it is being touched (Figure 8.12), but it cannot tell whether it is being lightly touched or strongly pressed against. Therefore more complicated switches, which can measure how hard they are being pushed, are often used at key points. Strain gauges or other force-measuring sensors can also be built into various joints in a robot's arm, so that it can tell how much force it is exerting. An appropriate robot arm with both pressure and force sensors should be able, for example, to pick up an egg and then a bowling ball without crushing the first or dropping the second.

Put your left arm behind your back. Now, can you tell whether the fingers on your left hand are extended or curled? How? This kinesthetic sense, by which you know, without looking, where the parts of your body are, is also very important for a robot. Almost every robot system has registers, encoders, or other mechanisms that enable the computer that is a part of the system to find out the current position and status of all the physical parts.

Figure 8.12 A hand with touch sensors. (*Stanford Research Institute.*)

Another sense that we often take for granted is the ability to estimate distance. People do this subconsciously, either from the differences
between what is seen by each of their two eyes or from the sensations in
the muscles that focus the eyes. Scientists at Jet Propulsion Laboratory in
Pasadena, California, are working with a two-eyed, or rather two-
cameraed, robot, in order to compute distances by comparing two
pictures. Some quite different techniques are also being used to sense
distances. At Stanford University, a sheet of light is scanned across a
scene while the camera watches. At SRI, a modulated laser beam shines
at the scene while a special instrument compares its light with the light
of the reflected echo. At IBM, a checkerboard pattern is projected onto
the scene so that the distortions of the pattern can be studied (Figure
8.13). These devices all provide different ways for a machine to figure out
how far away objects are.

The devices mentioned here are the most important sensors for
robots currently being developed. A microphone could be added if we
want the robot to hear anything, but so far research on automatic sound
perception has not been combined with robot systems. Smell and taste
do not seem likely to be important for robots, and to provide them would
require complicated chemical-analysis instruments. On the other hand,
certain nonhuman senses could be important, and would be easy to add
to a robot; e.g., an ultrasensitive heat sensor (such as that used by Prof.
Thring's fire-robot), a compass or other magnetic sensor, a motion detector (that did not require vision), or perhaps atomic-radiation sensors.

Effectors. How do today's laboratory robots exert an effect upon the
physical world around them? Once again, many different systems are in
use in different laboratories.

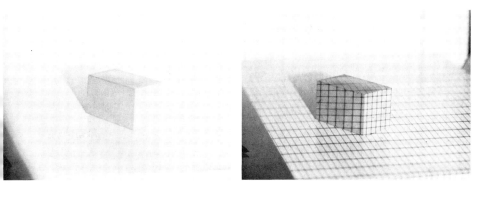

a   *b*

Figure 8.13 Object location aided by projecting a grid. (*a*) Original scene.
(*b*) Grid showing surface orientations. (*Peter Will, International Business
Machines Corporation.*)

First of all, every robot must be able to operate its sensors. Even your eyes would be much less valuable to you if you could not turn your head or open your eyelids. Almost every robot has the ability to turn on its camera, sense where its hand is, or identify which finger is touching something. Usually the robot can aim the camera in a particular direction, change color filters, and adjust the focus. One project at Stanford University showed how, if a robot is given direct control of the delicate electronic adjustments within its TV camera, it can be programmed to "squint" and "strain" to make any interesting parts of its view much clearer.

The next major effector in most systems is the arm. The first arms adopted for robot use, such as MH–1, were originally designed for direct human control, either as remote manipulators or as prosthetic devices. Some were electromechanical: i.e., driven by electric motors that operated cables and levers. These were usually rather weak and imprecise, and since they were often organized as rough imitations of human arm structure, with shoulder, elbow, and wrist joints, they were almost too complicated to analyze in order to direct by a computer. Other remote manipulators, designed for moving heavy loads, were hydraulic, i.e., driven by high-pressure fluids. The motions of these arms were fast, strong, and—when controlled by "undebugged" computer programs—extremely unpredictable. This made them rather dangerous to work near. In fact, at both MIT and Stanford, such arms were kept in special screen cages to prevent them from injuring anyone. Several other arms were invented as trial robot devices. One consisted of a series of separate, strong segments, and resembled an elephant's trunk. Another was a string of circular disks separated by little air bags, and could move into as many strange positions as a snake. However, both these arms were too complicated for the programmers of robot systems to learn how to use. Today's best robot arms are electromechanical devices that are designed especially for control by computers. Their joints are designed to operate in well-understood coordinate systems, and the arms may have useful nonhuman features such as telescoping forearms or wrists that can keep rotating indefinitely, enabling them to do such things as unscrew caps from bottles without letting go.

At the end of every arm is a hand—and the design of robot hands is becoming a specialty field of its own. The first hands had only simple parallel jaws for fingers, so that they could pick up only square boxes or blocks. The hands designed by Professor Thring can pick up many different things with the same simple motions. Hands designed for industrial tasks may themselves be tools, such as screwdrivers or welding guns, or they may just be designed to pick up (or screw into) any of several possible tools. The hand may have suction cups or rubber segments under pressure (Figure 8.14) to help it hold onto things. And the design of almost all robot hands is complicated by the fact that the hand must contain touch and perhaps force sensors.

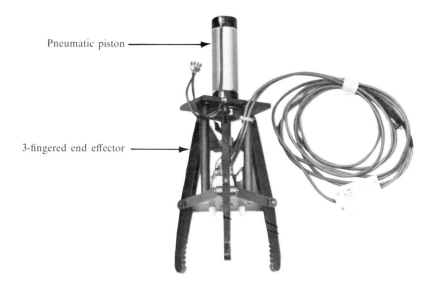

Pneumatic piston

3-fingered end effector

Figure 8.14 Three rubber fingers close when air pressure is applied.

Finally, mobility for both the sensor and the effectors is often a major consideration in the development of robot devices. At MIT, a camera or a robot arm can be suspended from a platform that moves anywhere the computer directs it to around the ceiling. At the University of Edinburgh, although the arm can only go up or down in the center of the room, a large table moves under control of the computer (Figure 8.15); objects of interest can thus be brought within view of the camera or within reach of the arm. At Mitsubishi, a camera is actually built into the center of the hand, so that it gets a good view of anything the arm reaches for. At the Electro-Technical Laboratory in Tokyo, a small one-armed vehicle can move about the floor, dragging its cable-connection to the computer. And at SRI, a wheeled vehicle carries a TV camera as it travels around the laboratory under radio control from the computer (Figure 8.3).

Computer and Software. In early experimental robots such as the Homeostat, the tortoises, and the Hopkins' Beast, special-purpose built-in electronic circuits made all the logical decisions for the machine. Most of today's robot experiments use general-purpose digital computers as the robot "brains." These computers enable researchers to experiment with different control strategies by modifying the computer programs, and thus obviate any slow, expensive reconstruction of the equipment. High-level programming languages and modern program-development

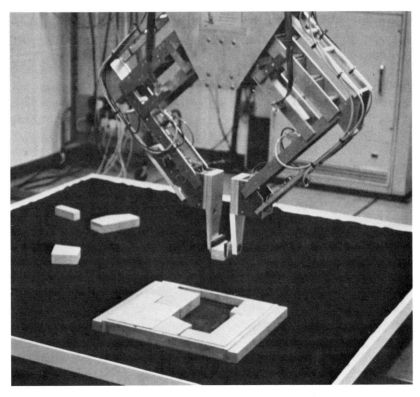

Figure 8.15 Freddy, the Edinburgh robot system. (*Harry Barrow, University of Edinburgh.*)

and program-correction methods have played key roles in the major robot-research projects.

Surprisingly, computers made by such leading manufacturers as IBM, Univac, and Control Data have not been popular for robot research. Although these machines lead the world in efficient performance of arithmetic computations and business accounting operations, many researchers have judged them to be inconvenient both for experimental development of large, frequently changed programs that evaluate knowledge and make decisions, and for continuous, responsive control of sensors and effectors. PDP-10 computers made by Digital Equipment Corporation, Inc., have been chosen for the elaborate robot studies at SRI, Stanford University, and MIT. Large portions of these systems are programmed in high-level symbol-manipulation languages, including languages with important features specifically invented for this type of work. All the systems built around PDP-10's were developed with the aid of direct-access time-sharing monitor systems. The Edinburgh robot system was developed with a much less powerful computer manufactured by ICL, the British computer producer. Until very recently, the Japanese robot projects have had access only to computers, usually of Japanese manufacture, that are extremely small by American standards. Such limited facilities make the successful results of those projects especially impressive. Finally, simple applied systems like the hospital carts and some industrial manipulator arms are controlled by new machines, small in both logical power and physical size, that are called mini-computers. Although such systems are also sometimes referred to as robots, they are much less independent and less capable than the previously mentioned research robots. We shall look at the industrial robots a bit more closely in the next chapter.

Shakey the robot: A case study

At SRI, robot studies were focused on the use of a mobile radio-controlled vehicle called "Shakey." Shakey had a TV camera, touch and distance sensors, and could roll about in a laboratory environment consisting of several interconnected rooms populated with large wooden blocks. Since the problems encountered in assembling the programs that controlled Shakey are typical of those that must be faced in creating any comparable robot system using currently available technology, let us look in some detail at the development of the Shakey system. Over a period of several years, two complete versions of the system evolved.

SHAKEY THE ROBOT: FIRST VERSION

Late in 1969 the first version of the Shakey system was completed. It demonstrated a complete, if somewhat crude, combination of abilities in the fields of perception and problem solving. The control language was a subset of ordinary English, which was translated by the system into first-order predicate calculus. The problem solver was a resolution-type theorem-proving program that used the answer-construction mechanisms discussed in Chapter 4. The scene-analysis component started with television pictures, used Chapter 7 methods to reduce the pictures to line drawings, and then tried to identify significant areas or objects in the scene (as described in Chapter 7). Typical problems that Shakey was then able to solve were **"GO TO POSITION (X,Y)"** and **"PUSH THE THREE BOXES TOGETHER."**

The exercise of assembling Shakey, a complete robot system, was worthwhile for several reasons. First, specific weaknesses were discovered in the scene-analysis component and the problem-solving component. Second, researchers discovered the immense scale of the computing requirements necessary to assemble such a complex of programs. The initial computer, an XDS-940 with 64,000 24-bit words of relatively slow core memory, was just barely large enough for the simplest problems. The housekeeping problems of fitting all the components into that computer and enabling them to communicate with each other eventually required an inordinate amount of effort. Third, and perhaps most important, it was discovered that there were certain necessary components of any complete robot system that had been overlooked in the course of doing research on just the problem-solving and perception components separately. These areas were the problem of data representation and the problem of designing an executive program that could monitor the execution of robot tasks.

Representations. This first version of the Shakey robot system had three different representations (idealizations) of the world. (1) TV pictures were stored and processed in data arrays. (2) the representation of the floor plan of the room was a grid that indicated occupied, unoccupied, and unknown regions of the room. This grid was useful for geometric calculations such as route planning but could not contain symbolic descriptive information. (3) A third description of the world in the form of symbolic axioms of predicate calculus was shared by theorem-proving and problem-solving subsystems, and by the language-analysis subsystem responsible for communication between Shakey and his human bosses.

These multiple representations were awkward to coordinate and to update as the world changed. Changes could not be made simultaneously in all representations because the three representations did not all fit into the computer memory together. On the other hand, the bookkeeping required to remember when the models had gotten out of step with each other soon became intractable.

Executive System. The other difficult area was the design of an executive for the system. In this early version of the robot system a trivial program translated the results of a planning process—the sequence of actions needed to accomplish a task—directly into a sequence of calls to subroutines that actually moved the robot about. Nowhere in this sequence was there any opportunity for using sensors or other means to check progress. Execution of a plan was a completely "open-loop" procedure, which meant that any long complicated plan had virtually no chance of being successful, even if the plan were essentially correct; the slightest inaccuracy or error anywhere during execution would cause the whole system to fall apart.

SHAKEY THE ROBOT: SECOND VERSION

By the end of 1971 a second version of a robot system was completed. The hardware of the robot vehicle itself—a mobile, radio-controlled cart carrying a TV camera and some bumper switches—was virtually unchanged from the first version. However, practically every other component of the entire system was completely replaced.

The controlling computer system for the second version consisted of a PDP-10 with about 200,000 36-bit words of relatively fast core memory and a peripheral computer for control of the robot, an on-line display, and other devices.

The software contained four major levels. At the lowest level we had what were called Low-Level Actions (LLAs). The LLAs are programmatic handles on the robot's physical capabilities such as "roll" and "tilt." They were the building blocks out of which more-complex robot operations could be built.

So that it could exhibit interesting behavior, the Shakey system was then equipped with a library of Intermediate-Level Actions (ILAs). These second-level elements were preprogrammed packages of LLAs embedded in a special interpretive-language framework with various control and error-correction features. Each ILA represented built-in expertise in some significant physical capability such as "push" or "go to." The ILAs might be thought of as instinctive abilities of the robot analogous to such built-in complex animal abilities as "walk" or "eat."

The issue of tradeoffs between preprogrammed expertise and general problem-solving capability is a concern in many problem-solving systems. A special-purpose hand-coded program can certainly solve one well-defined problem better than any general purpose problem-solving system can. On the other hand, a single, general problem solver can solve many different problems, although each of those problems might have to be rather simple and their solutions might not be very efficient. The designers of the second Shakey system drew the line between expertise and generality at the ILA level. Each ILA could be hand coded and could contain as much tricky cleverness as the programmer wished to design into it, but it was intended to solve only a narrow well-defined but widely useful class of problems. At higher levels in the system (discussed below), general planning mechanisms assembled arbitrary sequences and combinations of ILAs to perform a wider variety of possible tasks.

The principal sensor of Shakey's perceptual system was a TV camera. Programs for processing picture data were restricted to a few special "vision" routines that were incorporated into the system at both the ILA and LLA levels.

Above the ILAs we had the third level, which was concerned with planning the solutions to problems. The basic planning mechanism was the STRIPS problem-solving system, which was described in Chapter 5. STRIPS constructed the sequences of ILAs needed to carry out specified tasks. Such a sequence, along with its expected effect, was then represented by a table called a *macro operation* or MACROP.

Finally, the fourth, or top level of the system, was the executive—the program that actually invoked and monitored execution of the ILAs specified in a MACROP. The executive program was called PLANEX (Plan Executor).

Representations. The computer representation for Shakey's world was expressed in the form of a single set of axioms of first-order predicate calculus. It was the responsibility of each LLA that caused changes in the physical world (e.g., "roll") to update the model by making appropriate changes in the axioms—e.g., by modifying the axiom that tells the robot's location. High-level programs could then always assume that the representation—i.e., this set of logical axioms—always described the current state of the world.

The Use of STRIPS. An operator corresponding to each possible physical action of the robot was available to the STRIPS system. As described in Chapter 5, each operator was defined for STRIPS by: a *precondition statement,* a *delete list,* and an *add list.* The precondition statement was a logical theorem that must be provable in the current state of the world in order for the operator to be usable on that state. The delete list and add list contained changes that must be made to the axioms representing the current state in order to transform it into the state that would be produced after the action corresponding to the operator was carried out.

For example, one ILA available in the system was NAVTO (NAvigate TO): a program that first computed the shortest path between any two points in a room while avoiding known obstacles in that room (using the A* algorithm discussed in Chapter 3), and then called the appropriate LLAs to move the robot along that path to its desired target position. The purpose of NAVTO, then, was to enable Shakey to navigate from any point to any other point in the same room. The corresponding STRIPS operator, also called NAVTO, had as its only precondition that the robot be in the same room as the desired destination point. The delete list specified that the current location of the robot, if known, and the possible fact that the robot was next to any known object in the room, must be deleted from the state of the world. The add list specified that the assertion that the robot was at its destination position must be added. Such descriptions provided STRIPS with just the information it needed to determine the effects of various actions and therefore to plan a sequence of actions that would bring about the desired state of the world. The details of how each action was accomplished were left to the ILAs and LLAs that would actually carry out the actions.

An important feature of the system was its ability to generalize and save plans produced by STRIPS. For example, suppose the robot was in room A and STRIPS was given the problem, "produce a state of the world in which the robot is in room B." The specific solution that STRIPS would produce, given a typical set of ILAs and corresponding STRIPS operators, was the two-step plan: "Go to the door between room A and room B, and then go through that door into room B." Observe, however, that this plan has extremely limited utility. Suppose that sometime in the future someone asked the robot to go from room C to room D, or even to go back from room B to room A. Although the particular plan STRIPS had just derived would not be useful for these new tasks, clearly all these tasks are equivalent and a single general plan should work for any of them. Instead of solving the problem of getting the robot from room A to room B, a late version of STRIPS actually constructed the more general plan for getting the robot from one room to another for any two adjacent rooms. That plan would then be used for the current problem, and also stored away as a macro operation, or MACROP, for future reference.

One possibility was that each MACROP be stored and available to the system in exactly the same form as all other operators such as ILAs. This was not done, however, because a MACROP was generally considerably richer than a single operator. For example, suppose STRIPS generated a MACROP consisting of a sequence of five operators. As a side effect of the planning process, STRIPS computed the purpose and effect of each of the five operators separately when they were used in that sequence. This auxiliary information was stored as part of the MACROP, and the complete five-operator generalized plan was available for use in future problems. But STRIPS could also use the auxiliary information to calculate the effects of various subsequences of the five operators and such subsequences could be extracted from the plan when appropriate. The MACROP was thus a concise representation for a family of operators, each of which could be described and used by STRIPS as needed.

PLANEX. When STRIPS completed a plan—a new MACROP— for accomplishing a desired task, it turned the MACROP over to PLANEX, the executive for carrying out plans. Now, PLANEX had available to it all the information in a MACROP, which consisted not only of the names of the action routines to be called in sequence, but also the expected effects of each routine. PLANEX called one routine at a time and, after each routine had finished its task, control returned to PLANEX to decide what to do next. PLANEX did not call the next routine in sequence until it had verified both that the previous routine has accomplished its mission, and that the next routine was still required. If for any reason some routine did not accomplish its intended purpose or accomplished something different, PLANEX was free to rearrange the order in which action routines were called, in order to achieve the desired result more directly. PLANEX could also notice, at an appropriate early point, that the plan was not working and either call STRIPS again or abandon the entire project and ask for help from a human.

Error Recovery. As just mentioned, PLANEX monitored executions of plans and could attempt to adjust progress and recover from errors that it might detect. In addition, each ILA could have a variety of mechanisms for predicting, testing, and recovering from errors that might be produced while the ILA was operating. Such errors were invisible to higher-level routines and PLANEX, for example, would never be aware of them, if the ILA that detected the error was capable of correcting it. If NAVTO had planned a route avoiding all known obstacles and in the course of traversing that route the robot bumped into a new object, NAVTO was smart enough to make the robot back up, add the newly discovered object to the robot's representation of the world, and plan a new route to the goal by going around that object.

Information from the camera could also be very useful for recovering from or avoiding errors. The system kept, in the robot's representation of the world, an estimate of the error in the robot's knowledge of its own position. Every time an LLA moved the robot, that error estimate was increased, and any LLA that made use of the information specifying the robot's current position first checked that the error estimate of that position was within an allowable tolerance. If it were not, the visual-processing routine, LANDMARK, was called. LANDMARK was a special-purpose vision routine that took a picture of the closest "landmark"—i.e., an easily recognizable point in the room such as a corner or the edge of a door jamb—and used measurements made in that picture to determine the robot's current position and then to reduce the error estimate of the knowledge of that position.

Current and future directions

Because of the number of features it encompasses, the Shakey system provides us with one of the best available examples of how computer programs that operate a robot might be organized in the future. Other laboratory robot systems are not divided into software levels as rigid as those of the second Shakey system, they do not contain general problem-solving components similar to STRIPS, and they are primarily systems for controlling mechanical arms, rather than mobile vehicles. However, the designers of all these systems have had to face such problems as how to represent the robot's world, how to recover from errors or uncertainties, how to reconcile the possibly conflicting data from different sensory channels (such as vision and touch), how to communicate with the robot in order to describe the task to be done, and how to organize the executive program that supervised the entire system. Needless to say, these problems have been solved in several different ways at several different places. Because the solutions are available, in the forms of research papers, technical reports, and computer-program listings, other computer scientists can study them and thereby have a head start when they begin developing the next generation of robot systems. Without getting enmeshed in the technical details of how they work, let's look at what some of these systems were capable of doing a few years ago.

At Hitachi Central Research Laboratory a TV camera was aimed at an orthographic projection, resembling a standard engineering plan drawing, of a structure built out of various-shaped blocks. A second camera looked at the blocks themselves, which were spread out on a table. The computer "understood" the drawing, reached towards the blocks with its arm, and built the structure.

At MIT, the camera was not shown a plan; instead, it was shown an example of the actual structure desired. The computer figured out how the structure could be constructed, and then built an exact copy.

At Stanford University, the hand obeyed spoken directions. For example, if someone[5] said into the microphone, "Pick up the small block on the left," that is precisely what the arm would do. An early version of the Stanford system could use its visual ability to overcome the somewhat sloppy work of an inaccurate arm; when one block was stacked on top of another, the camera would look to see whether the blocks lined up properly, and if not, would call the arm back to adjust the stack. In later versions the arm operated more accurately.

At the University of Edinburgh, a jumble of parts for two wooden toys was placed on the movable table near the camera. "Freddy," the Edinburgh hand-eye-table robot system, carefully spread out the parts so that it could see each one clearly, and then, with the help of a vise-like work station at one corner of the table, assembled first the toy car and then the toy boat.

At SRI, Shakey was told to **"PUSH THE BOX OFF THE PLATFORM."** Shakey had no arm, and realized that he could not reach the box unless he was on the platform with it. He looked around, found a ramp, pushed the ramp up against the platform, rolled up the ramp, and then pushed the box onto the floor (Figure 8.16).

Since about 1971, the amount of specific research upon laboratory robot systems has decreased markedly. After a period of inactivity, Shakey gave a final public demonstration during the summer of 1973 and was then permanently retired. Activity with the MIT hand-eye system is sporadic, and Freddy has not been developed much beyond his 1972 level of abilities.

This reduction in the level of visible robot research does not indicate a reduction in people's interest in robots; thousands of years of fascination with the robot concept does not suddenly evaporate. One direct cause of reduced robot research has been a general reduction,

---

[5]Not just anyone could speak to this system. It responded reliably only when spoken to by either of its designers, who both happen to have distinctive foreign accents!

Figure 8.16 Shakey maneuvering to push the box off the platform. (*Stanford Research Institute.*)

since the early 1970's, in the funds available from public agencies that support pure research, especially research that requires such expensive equipment as large computers. (The drastic cutback in proposed space exploration is another result of these funding cuts.) However, most scientists are not so fickle that they can be told, by whoever buys them their equipment, that they should abandon the technical issues they find the most rewarding. Although changes in funding patterns can exert considerable short-term influence, in the long run science selects its own directions.

The principal reason for an apparent decrease in active robot projects is that the recent phase of laboratory research on robot systems is coming to a natural conclusion. Scientists have learned how to build robot systems based upon 1970 computer technology. More important, they have explored the capabilities of such systems, studied their limitations, and identified key problems that must be solved in order to create substantially more-capable robots. Instead of continuing to struggle with existing systems, they are turning their attention to these problems, whose solutions will lead to the next round of laboratory robot systems—five, ten, or twenty years from now. Instead of abandoning their work, robot researchers have been plunging with increasing enthusiasm into new projects in three general areas: hardware, software, and applications. Results from these projects are expected to lead directly toward better robots in the future.

HARDWARE

Much of the robot research of the past decade has been aimed at learning how to patch together complete systems, without sufficient attention to the design of the particular components out of which the systems were built. Thus, for example, early Stanford University and MIT arms sometime oscillated as if they suffered from Parkinson's disease, Freddy required many seconds just to blink his eye, and Shakey's very name is a monument to his mechanical instability. Several current developments will lead to more dependable physical equipment for robots.

Among recently developed sensors, the most important are new sensors for vision and distance. Several distance-measuring devices have recently been invented and are currently being tested and improved. At least one TV-camera manufacturer is offering a well-engineered package consisting of a high-quality TV camera plus mounted color filters, zoom lens, and pan and tilt aiming mechanisms, all instrumented for convenient computer control. A new, much less expensive color TV camera is just now becoming widely available. Solid-state photocell devices are rapidly improving in performance and reducing in cost.

Work on effectors has resulted in the development of several new mechanical arms and hands intended specifically for use in computer-controlled systems at Stanford University, NASA, the Electro Technical Laboratory in Tokyo, and elsewhere. SRI has sketched the design of a next-generation mobile robot vehicle, whose wheeled chassis would be similar to one in use in certain electric wheelchairs. This possible successor to Shakey would have an arm and would carry around a mini-computer, complete with communications terminal, as an integral part of its body. MIT has begun a similar design project for a next-generation, fixed-base, hand–eye robot system. Although these design exercises may not result soon in working hardware, they will provide a wealth of ideas for whatever robot projects do develop in the next few years.

Computer-hardware technology continues to make machines that are faster, cheaper, with larger memories and smaller physical sizes than ever before. Micro-computers the size of your thumbnail are becoming powerful enough to take over responsibility, for example, for the operation of a mechanical wrist joint or a cluster of dozens of photocells. These developments all have obvious implications for the robots of the future. In addition, computers are being used increasingly to monitor and even to cooperate with physical, chemical, and industrial processes as they take place; new data-communications facilities and interactive software capabilities that will be needed for more efficient robot operation are already being designed into many computer systems.

SOFTWARE

The major shortcomings of the recent generation of laboratory robots were not due to hardware; e.g., the amusing fact that Shakey looked as if his head would fall off at any moment did not really limit his apparent intelligence. The principal limitation was one of software. In particular, robot researchers were not able to build into their problem-solving programs sufficient knowledge (or mechanisms for acquiring sufficient knowledge) so that the robot could conduct himself reasonably in a substantially richer problem situation. Experiments with robot systems helped sharpen our understanding of certain research questions, which are now the subjects of intensive study.

Programming Tools. New programming languages and new program-development techniques are being developed to simplify the task of creating more-clever problem-solving and robot-control programs.

Knowledge Bases. As we discussed in previous chapters, if a computer is to understand natural language it must have some advance knowledge of the subject matter being discussed; if a computer is to recognize objects in a visual scene, it must have some advance knowledge of the nature of the objects being percieved. Obviously a robot who must understand, look, see, and act, must first know something about the situations in which he may find himself. We may even hope that a single computer representation of knowledge about the world could serve all the needs of the robot's linguistic, perceptual, and problem-solving subsystems.

Surprisingly, the issues of how to acquire, represent, and make use of a broad store of knowledge has been the most neglected part of past robot research. The developers of the laboratory robot systems were so busy patching together existing capabilities (in vision, language, and problem solving), and filling in essential new areas (representing the physical world, providing for error recovery), that they did not attend to the fundamental issue of knowledge structures.

Now that robot systems have been temporarily put aside, the question of how to represent knowledge has come to the forefront. One group of scientists is studying the level of knowledge that has been acquired by typical six-year-old children, and exploring how that can be placed in a computer. Others are looking at the specialized knowledge of experts in certain narrow specialty fields, attempting to imitate that knowledge base, and then use it in a computer "expert." Still others are concentrating upon studies of possible formal ways of representing general knowledge, such as by predicate-calculus axioms, or by certain complex networks (graphs) of symbolic expressions. Any results from such fundamental research are potentially useful in many possible applications for "smarter" computers, and robots are certainly one such family of applications.

APPLICATIONS

The laboratory robots discussed in this chapter did their jobs in "toy" domains. These systems were of interest because of the research challenges that they raised, because they were the first automatic systems to achieve even their primitive level of capabilities, and because they provided a proving ground for many ideas about how to make better robot systems in the future. Certainly no one would dream of buying one of these machines, at a cost of a million dollars or so, in order to stack up toy blocks, assemble the seven parts of a wooden car, or push a box off a platform. On the other hand, some of the features of even these first complete robot systems might have important commercial application.

In the past decade a generation of machines called *industrial manipulators*[6] has begun to come into use in factories and warehouses. These machines are mechanical arms that can be programmed to go through a sequence of actions—such as unloading a die-casting machine, welding the body of a car, or simply moving a stack of bricks from one location to another. Once a program of actions is defined for such a machine, the arm will follow it repeatedly, with considerable strength, speed, precision, and consistent reliability. Such rugged, versatile machines have already proved their value in thousands of industrial plants.

Unfortunately, the industrial manipulators are blind and dumb. If a foreign object (or a person) passes through the path of such a machine, the machine will smash into the obstacle without being aware of its existence. If the supply line stops and, say, no more bricks arrive to be moved, the brick-moving arm will continue moving imaginary bricks until some person turns it off. If an object to be picked up is more than a small fraction of an inch away from where it should be, the arm is likely to break it or drop it, without knowing that anything has gone wrong.

Now consider the contrast. Robot research has produced demonstration systems that can perceive their environments and solve simple problems on their own, but that are extremely expensive and mechanically unreliable. Industrial engineering has produced economical, practical, mechanical manipulator systems whose usefulness is limited primarily by their lack of perceptual and problem-solving abilities. Isn't it time to try to combine the best features of these complementary technologies? Many robot researchers are therefore turning from the problems of de-

---

[6]Although these machines are also known as "industrial robots," I shall here avoid using the name "robot" in this different limited sense.

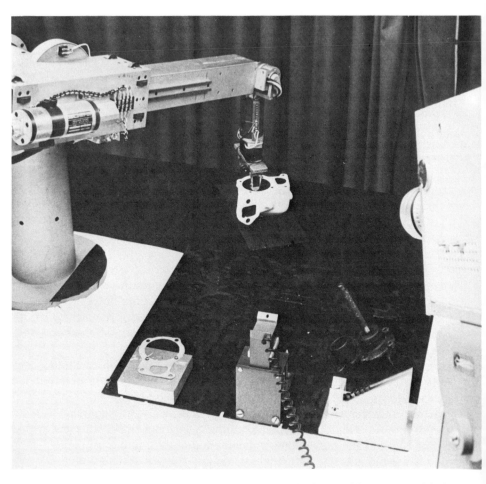

Figure 8.17 A computer-controlled arm at Stanford assembles a pump. (*Artificial Intelligence Laboratory, Stanford University.*)

signing tomorrow's dream robots, to the problems of designing practical systems for today's factories and warehouses. For example:

At Stanford the hand–eye system that used to stack toy blocks can now assemble a real water pump (Fig. 8.17).

At SRI a computer-controlled Unimate arm with touch and force sensors can feel its way as it packs assembled pumps into a case.

At MIT programs are under development to enable a computer to inspect and repair circuit boards for use in computers, TV sets, and other electronic equipment.

These applications are mentioned here briefly to point out one of the directions being taken by robot research. The next chapter takes a more detailed look at applications for the expanding horizons of computer technology presented thus far in this book.

Summary

The term *robot* usually suggests a mechanical device that exhibits nearly human abilities to perform physical tasks. The human-like dexterity and intelligence of some robot devices actually comes from a human who controls the device over a remote communication link. More interesting robots are totally under the control of either special electronic equipment or a general-purpose computer.

Interest in the concept of robots dates back to the dawn of civilization, and clever clockwork devices that give the impression of robot behavior have been built for several hundred years. In the 1940's and 1950's scientists built small, self-contained machines that simulated the instinctive behavior of simple animals. This work culminated in the Hopkins' Beast, a machine whose built-in goal of survival required it to find electric outlets so that it could keep its batteries charged.

In the mid 1960's, as large computers were coming into widespread use, several computer-science laboratories around the world began building robot systems. Each such system generally included sensory equipment such as a TV camera, effector equipment such as a mechanical arm, and a general-purpose digital computer. Reasons for building these robot systems included an interest in studying the basic nature of intelligence, an interest in integrating previously separate automatic perceptual and problem-solving capabilities into richer combined systems, and an interest in developing real, practical, useful robots.

Computer simulation is a useful tool in many problem domains. However, the difficulty of accurately simulating a real robot's environment and physical characteristics limits the usefulness of simulation for robot research. Real robots must be built.

Robot systems consist of sensors, effectors, and computers. Commonly used sensors detect light intensity, color, touch, pressure, distance to obstacles, and the current position and status of all the robot's parts. Effectors include control over the sensors, arms, hands, and wheels or other means of mobility. The controlling computers are medium-scale, time-shared scientific computers for long-range research studies, and smaller mini-computers for prototypes of near-term practical robot systems.

Shakey, the robot developed at SRI, is typical of the major developments of robot research. The software for Shakey evolved through two major systems. The second system had four major levels of software: LLA's (low level actions), ILA's (intermediate level actions), the STRIPS planning and problem-solving system, and an executive program called PLANEX (plan executor). The LLA's operated the direct physical actions of the robot vehicle. ILA's were carefully designed "expert" routines for moderately complex but frequently needed abilities, e.g., route-finding in a room containing obstacles. STRIPS (Chapter 5) was a general mechanism for assembling appropriate sequences of ILA's to solve arbitrary problems. PLANEX monitored the execution of STRIPS plans, and enabled the system to recover gracefully from several types of unexpected difficulties. The complete Shakey system could also "learn" by adding the results of previous STRIPS planning activity to its repertoire of ILA's.

Other robot systems with capabilities of the same general complexity as those of Shakey include systems developed at Hitachi, MIT, Stanford, and Edinburgh. Interest in further elaboration of such complete experimental robot systems has recently decreased. Instead, many researchers have turned to more-specific problems that must be solved in order to create more-powerful robot systems. Major developments coming out of current work include: (1) new hardware technology that is leading to more reliable and less expensive sensors, effectors, and computers; (2) new software technology, in the form of high-level programming tools and studies of how to structure the large knowledge bases that are essential for any intelligent system; and (3) prototypes of simple robot systems that can at least begin to perform truly practical tasks, as will be discussed further in the next chapter.

SUGGESTED READINGS

Abbot, E. A. *Flatland.* Dover Publications, New York, 1952.

Asimov, I. *I, Robot.* Fawcett Crest Publications, Greenwich, Conn., 1970.

Chapuis, A., and E. Droz. *Automata: A Historical and Technological Study.* Editions du Griffon, Neuchatel, Switzerland, 1958.

Heer, E. (ed.). *Proceedings of the First National Conference on Remotely Manned Systems.* Calif. Inst. of Technology, Pasadena, 1973.

McCarthy, J. et al., "A Computer with Hands, Eyes, and Ears," *Proceedings of the American Federation of Information Processing Societies,* Vol. 33, pp. 329–338, Thompson Book Co., Washington, D.C., 1969.

"Shakey: Experiments in Robot Planning and Learning." (Film available for loan from Stanford Research Institute Library, Menlo Park, Calif.)

Winston, P. H. "The MIT Robot." In *Machine Intelligence,* Vol. 7, B. Meltzer and D. Michie (eds.). American Elsevier Publishing Co., 1972.

Frontier Applications 9

The range of abilities computers can be given is steadily increasing. Scientists are learning how to make smarter computers—computers capable of reasoning, understanding, seeing, solving problems, and controlling robots. What significance does the development of intelligent machines have for the future of our society? Should we be delighted, apprehensive, or horrified? How much will these machines influence our day-to-day activities? What form with this influence take?

Such questions can be answered only in time by you, your children, and their children, who will control future society and determine how its technology will be put to use. However, we can at least glimpse some of the possibilities by reviewing experiments and developmental plans being pursued today in some important fields.

Education

When someone mentions the use of computers in education, many people conjure up the image of a machine drilling thousands of students in the same memorization exercises. Such a machine might teach students facts, but it could not teach them to think. It might very well destroy the natural initiative, originality, and creativity that good educational practice should encourage. Luckily, no educator or computer scientist today proposes that such a system should be a major component in anyone's educational process. The image of a drill-master computer proposed a very simple, naive way of using a "stupid" computer: i.e., one that can do only bookkeeping and arithmetic operations exactly the way it is told to do them. The image is wrong for two important reasons: (1) educational researchers have already developed much more clever, stimulating, educationally valid ways of using even stupid computers; and (2) smarter computers, being developed as described throughout this book, open up entirely new avenues for innovation in education. Let us look in more detail at these two complimentary approaches.

SMART USES FOR STUPID COMPUTERS

Computers can play many different roles in education. At the simplest level, computers are already in wide use in colleges, universities, and secondary-school systems in the same ways (and for the same reasons) that they are used in most large business and professional organizations. They assist in the crucial accounting, payroll, and similar record-keeping functions that every organization must carry out. Schools have special problems such as class scheduling and student registration for which computer assistance is often helpful. However, these are still background tasks that are not directly related to the educational process.

The first major direct use of computers in education resulted from a teaching method introduced in the late 1950's called *programmed instruction.* Now, the programming of programmed instruction should not be confused with the programming of computers; the basic concepts of programmed instruction have nothing to do with computers. Instead, these concepts deal with the way instructional material is presented to the student. A conventional textbook usually presents fairly large amounts of material in each section, and it is assumed that the student will study the material under the guidance of a classroom teacher. The programmed instruction concept is that students can learn certain material more effectively without a teacher, if the material to be presented is properly "programmed." This means that the material is logically organized to present only one very elementary idea at a time; each idea builds upon previous ones; and each new piece of information is followed by a series of questions and exercises with their answers, so that the student must constantly integrate and review previous information and keep himself engrossed in his work. With programmed instruction each student may proceed at his own pace, and the teacher is left free to pay extra attention to the especially fast, slow, or otherwise special students.

The tedious job of preparing the instructional material is a major drawback of programmed instruction. The educators who write conventional textbooks often do not have the patience or interest to break down their material into the tiny steps with interspersed drill exercises, that are required. Here is where computers have been a major aid. Special programming languages have been developed to help the course writers. Now the author need only sketch the format in which he wants the elementary facts presented, the logical relationships among the facts, the number and the types of questions and answers to be interspersed, and so on, and the computer does the routine job of laying out the material. Many programmed courses have been developed in this way, especially for introductory courses in technical subjects such as mathematics, physics, and computer science.

So far we have been talking about how administrators or teachers use computers, usually to prepare material for presentation to students. Such material, even if it is "programmed," is still passive, like any book. Communication can take place only in one direction: from the material to the student. But learning often takes place more effectively when two-way communication is possible: discussions, questions and answers, arguments, and so on. Such two-way communication is made possible by taking the next big step: putting the students themselves into direct contact with the computer. Here are some of the ways in which this has already been done.

Computerized Programmed Instruction. One drawback of the programmed instruction method is that material presented in a book must be in fixed order, determined when the book is printed, whereas different students require different amounts and different types of practice exercises. One way around this problem is the so-called "scrambled text." In this system when a student is given a problem that tests his progress, on the next page along with the answer are directions something like, "If you solved the problem, skip to page 103; if you got the wrong answer, continue on page 78; and if you did not know how to attack the problem, go back to page 29." As you may imagine, laying out such a book is quite a chore for the author, and it is not entirely satisfactory because students get distracted and annoyed by the constant page flipping. A better solution is to present the material to the student by means of a computer terminal instead of by means of a printed page. If the student answers questions by typing them on the terminal's keyboard, the computer can match the typed answer with the stored correct answer and automatically present appropriate subsequent material. The student gets a personally tailored presentation without being aware of it, and without being able to cheat by peeking ahead to see the answers. Also, the computer can keep track of what material each student is covering and how many mistakes he is making, in order to prepare summaries for the human teacher.

The experimental use of computerized programmed instruction is increasing. Its wider use is restricted by two major considerations: the cost of the computer equipment needed, and concern about the validity of the basic method of programmed instruction. The cost consideration is diminishing as computers become cheaper and more widely available. Concerns about programmed instruction as a teaching method are usually based upon arguments that the instructor—human, book, or computer—needs to behave intelligently, and of course, computers cannot behave intelligently; or can they? We shall return to this issue a bit later in this section.

Computerized Homework. Instead of trying to automate the entire educational process—e.g., by means of programmed instruction—some researchers are trying first to automate the creation and presentation of homework exercises. Regular teachers run regular classes in the usual way, but the students are given an opportunity to work with computers, instead of just paper and pencil, outside of class. A typical system of this kind drills students in arithemtic. For example, one computer is programmed to create a variety of arithmetic problems, using a random-number generator to select the specific numbers used. The program can compose several types of problems of varying difficulty: single digit addition, addition of large numbers, addition of columns of numbers without or with carries, subtraction without or with "borrowing," and so on. The program makes up problems on the spot as they are needed by each student, and introduces more-difficult problems as the student shows he can handle the easier ones. Thus each student receives his own unique sequence of problems and is constantly challenged without being overwhelmed. In the few experiments of this type that have been conducted, students consistently require less time to achieve a better understanding of their work with computerized homework than with conventional homework—and they consider working with a computer to be fun, too.

Computerized Language Learning. The use of special devices such as records, tapes, and films is an accepted part of current language-training programs. Imitation plays a key role when a student learns to speak a foreign language, and recordings allow many students to imitate the same expert speakers. Computers can add to the effectiveness of language instruction by controlling the presentation of material. In one system, a computer operates a slide projector and a tape recorder; the student sees a randomly generated sequence of pictures of objects, and simultaneously hears their names pronounced. The objects in the collection, the size of the collection, and the speed of presentation, can be changed by the user; or he can let the computer make such changes. If the student types responses to the computer's questions (or dictation test), the computer can check the answers and choose appropriate subsequent problems.

A unique use for computers in language education is based upon the ability of a computer to display visually various representations of phonetic sound patterns. Students and teachers each speak into a microphone and the computer shows, side by side on a screen, the wave forms produced by each one's utterance. By looking at such patterns, students can learn to notice and correct differences in accent that they often otherwise cannot hear. Such a system has even been successfully used to teach deaf children to speak. Here the computer compares the sound produced by the child with the correct sound, and indicates with amusing cartoons on the screen (such as smiling or frowning faces) whether the sound is close enough.

Experimental Mathematics and Physics. By using an appropriately programmed computer and its display screen, students can quickly see the results of experiments that would be difficult or impossible to execute otherwise. If a student is interested in analytic geometry, he can watch how the shape of a graphed curve changes as certain parameters vary; for example, he can see how a circle can be deformed into a parabola or even a hyperbola by smoothly varying the coefficents of quadratic equations. If he is interested in kinetics he can watch collisions between simulated bouncing balls, and he can change their relative mass, or velocity, or elasticity, at the touch of a button; he can even watch how a superball with negative elasticity would move (going higher on each bounce). If he is interested in electricity he can simulate the construction of any circuit, and then measure the currents in it, without worrying about burning out resistors or meters; he can invent components with such special properties as negative resistance, and see how they would affect the circuit. If he is interested in music, a special computer-controlled speaker and suitable software would permit him to invent "instruments" with any sound characteristics he wishes, and hear what they sound like while playing tones at any pitch intervals he wishes. Such computer experiments can give a student considerable insight and understanding of the ways in which classical science has chosen to describe the physical world.

Children Controlling Computers. The most novel and exciting idea for using computers to teach children turns the whole teaching concept around. The children teach the computer. Instead of the computer taking charge of each session by asking all the questions and allowing only simple answers, the student remains firmly in command. He uses the computer with the same kind of authority with which he uses a blackboard or a pencil. In fact, one interesting way in which children use the computer is simply as a very sophisticated pencil. The children learn how to tell the computer to make drawings for them: geometric figures, intricate designs, even rather complicated pictures.

At MIT, a mechanical "turtle" has been designed that can easily be connected to almost any computer (Figure 9.1). A very simple programming language called LOGO has been developed specifically for operating the turtle. Even eight-year olds find it simple and fun to com-

Figure 9.1 Students working with a "turtle." (*General Turtle Inc., Cambridge, Mass.*)

pose LOGO programs. These programs can make the turtle move, turn, blink its headlight, beep its horn, and lower or raise the pen under its stomach, thereby drawing pictures on the floor. The students learn some principles of geometry by observing the drawings that result from various motions of the turtle (Figure 9.2). Even more important, while trying to make the turtle produce a particular drawing they learn how to make their ideas precise (*designing algorithms*), how to divide up a task into manageable chunks (*subroutines*), and how to correct and improve a trial

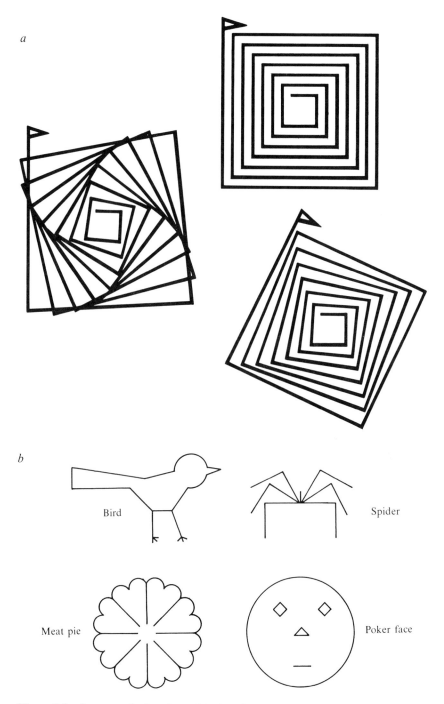

Figure 9.2 Some turtle drawings. (*a*) Test drawings. (*b*) Pictures programmed by fifth graders.

solution progressively. In short, they learn some very general approaches to solving any problem, all while having fun playing with a mechanical turtle.

Another novel teaching technique is related to computerized programmed instruction. However, instead of skilled teachers preparing the course material that the computer will present to the students, the students themselves create their own computerized courses. Every teacher knows that the best way to learn a subject is to try to teach it to a critical audience. Well, why not let everyone learn by teaching? A student who may not be at all interested in, say, geography, is often fascinated by the challenge of creating a series of questions and answers about geography. He can then try out the questions upon his fellow students, and find out how good his presentation is. As usual, the computer provides a nice, flexible medium for experiments of this kind, relieving the teacher (in this case, the student who is doing the teaching) of distracting bookkeeping and paper-handling functions, and the students really love the experience.

PROPOSED USES FOR SMARTER COMPUTERS

The above uses for computers in education all treat the computer merely as an obedient slave. The computer makes choices that have been previously specified; records responses; controls a display screen, a music box, or a turtle; but always acts according to fixed programmed rules. Let us recall some of the prospects discussed in previous chapters. Suppose computers begin to be able to understand English, solve problems, and perceive the world. How can such smarter computers improve education? One major example that is already being tried in some computer-science laboratories is called *mixed-initiative* computerized programmed instruction. As the computer really begins to "know" about the subject matter being taught, it can gradually play a more active role in the teaching process. Instead of either feeding facts to the student, like a big flexible textbook, or being programmed by the student, like a lump of intellectual clay, the computer can become an active partner in the educational process. It can be programmed to behave somewhat like a good private tutor, both asking and answering questions, evaluating student responses, and guiding the course of the teaching session. Such a system might begin a session by asking a preset series of questions, just like an ordinary programmed-instruction machine. However, because of its understanding of English, it could tell from a student's incorrect answers exactly what false ideas the student had, and modify its curriculum accordingly. It could tell whether to proceed faster or more slowly, and might even be able to recognize when the student was becoming bored and needed a joke or some other change of pace. Because of its understanding of the subject matter, it would be able to answer questions raised by the student even when they digressed from the original lesson plan. Either the student, the system, or both alternately, could take the initiative in deciding what to study and how deeply to explore each issue.

Carbonell pioneered a mixed-initiative approach to automated instruction several years ago. The computer's linguistic ability was (and still is) extremely limited, and the computer's "knowledge" was restricted to a rather rigid structure of facts about a narrow subject—in this case, the geography of South America. Still, his experimental system, called SCHOLAR, as demonstrated in the conversation of Table 9.1, illustrates some of the possibilities for interactive teaching systems of the future.

Table 9.1. Conversation with SCHOLAR, 1970. (Lines in capitals are generated by the computer.)

```
WHAT IS CHILE?
A country.
THAT's FINE.

SELECT AN ALTERNATIVE FROM THE LIST:
214000, 864300, 49883, 63698.
FOR THE QUESTION:
APPROX WHAT IS THE AREA OF CHILE?
864300.
YOUR ANSWER IS INCORRECT.
THE CORRECT ANSWER IS 214000.

USE ONE OF THE FOLLOWING:
SUCRE, FRENCH, ARGENTINA, SPANISH.
TO ANSWER THE QUESTION:
WHAT IS THE LANGUAGE IN CHILE?

YOU ARE TAKING TOO MUCH TIME...
Spanich.
YOU SHOULD HAVE WRITTEN "SPANISH."
VERY GOOD.

PLEASE INDICATE IF THE FOLLOWING STATEMENT IS CORRECT
   OR INCORRECT:
THE AREA OF PARAGUAY IS APPROX 47432 SQUARE MILES.
What is the area of Brazil?
THE AREA OF BRAZIL IS APPROX 3600000 SQUARE MILES.
   NOW ANSWER THE QUESTION YOU DIDN'T ANSWER BEFORE.
Incorrect.
VERY GOOD.
THE AREA OF PARAGUAY IS APPROX 157000 SQUARE MILES.

APPROX WHAT IS THE POPULATION IN BRAZIL?
60000000.
APPROXIMATELY TRUE, BUT A MORE EXACT VALUE IS
   70000000.
WHAT IS BRAZIL?
Tell me something about Peru.
PERU IS A COUNTRY. IT IS IN SOUTH AMERICA.
THE POPULATION IS APPROX 7000000 PEOPLE.          (Continued)
```

Table 9.1. *(continued)*

```
NOW ANSWER THE QUESTION YOU DIDN'T ANSWER BEFORE.
Q/A.
DO YOU WANT TO CHANGE THE GENERAL MODE OF THE
  INTERACTION TO Q/A? PLEASE ANSWER Y OR N.
Y
OK, MR. JONES, LET'S GO AHEAD.

Please, Tell me more about Peru.
THE AREA OF PERU IS APPROX 480000 SQUARE MILES.
THE LANGUAGE IS SPANISH.

The principal religion in Peru is ---.
I'M AFRAID I CAN'T ANSWER THAT.
Mixinit.
DO YOU WANT TO CHANGE THE GENERAL MODE OF THE
  INTERACTION TO MIXINIT? PLEASE ANSWER Y OR N.
Y
OK, MR. JONES. LET'S GO AHEAD.

WHERE IS BRAZIL?

PLEASE HURRY UP. I'M WAITING FOR YOUR STATEMENT.
In SouthAmerica.
I BELIEVE YOU MEANT TO TYPE "SOUTH AMERICA."
THAT'S RIGHT.
```

Since 1970, when the demonstration shown in the table was given, work on this type of system has progressed considerably. Systems are being developed with more powerful "understanding" mechanisms, incorporating greater use of semantic networks and associated inference mechanisms. One group is studying how to give the teaching computer knowledge of processes and causal relationships, instead of just static facts. Still others are attacking the technical and economic problems of providing a sufficiently powerful computer that is also sufficiently inexpensive and portable to be feasible for classroom or even home use. And, of course, a truly sophisticated language-understanding system has yet to be embedded into the framework of an educational system.

Note that the system of the future that I have been discussing—which has the imposing name, *mixed-initative computerized programmed instruction system*—is not going to take over the job of teaching children. Instead, it is going to be able to work in conjunction with computerized homework, computer-simulated physics experiments, human teachers, and perhaps computer-controlled "turtles," to help children teach themselves. The "smart" mixed-initiative systems will be able to give complete individual attention, answer any reasonable questions with infinite patience, and keep the lesson moving at just the right pace for each student. Don't you wish you had had such a computer as a tutor? Wouldn't you like your child to have one?

Psychology

Psychology is the branch of science concerned with understanding how the mind works and what determines behavior. The greater the understanding of how the human mind works psychologists can gain, the greater the potential of their contribution to our society becomes. For example:

The major goal of education is to develop the student's mind. As long as we do not know how the mind works, the process of education will be rather haphazard. Teaching methods are now developed on an experimental trial-and-error basis, rather than according to any formal principles. If we understood the mind better, we might be able to use that understanding to devise dramatically better educational techniques.

Psychiatry is the branch of medicine that deals with mental and behavioral problems. A surprisingly large number of otherwise healthy people suffer from depression, neurosis, or other psychological problems. But, psychiatrists cannot develop reliable, consistent methods for helping such people until psychologists produce better explanations for the basic mental functions. Can you expect an automobile mechanic to tell how to fix an engine knock, without knowing whether the engine was rotary, diesel, or steam driven?

Suppose we really understood the mind. This could lead to reliable ways to teach people motivation; patience; will-power; a sense of humor; perhaps even to increase their intelligence. Think of the implications! No wonder the nature of the mind has interested philosophers for thousands of years.

In the past, psychologists have used two major methods for trying to find out how the human mind works.

They conducted experiments on animals: rats, guinea-pigs, monkeys, and so on. With animals, scientists can carefully control such variables as genetic factors, history, and environment, and then carry out all sorts of experiments in areas such as learning ability, social behavior, reactions to stress, and effects of special diets or drugs. Unfortunately such experiments usually wind up teaching us more about the minds of rats, guinea pigs, monkeys, and so on, than about general principles that might also apply to human beings.

They conducted experiments on human beings. Elaborate experiments have been conducted in the same areas as with animals, but these experiments have been carefully regulated so that the subjects suffer no permanent harm—a vital constraint, but one that severely limits the scope of the experiments. Also, such variables as genetic factors and home environment of the subjects cannot be controlled. Such studies occasionally lead to interesting theories about the observable responses, such

as verbal behavior or reaction time, of some people to the particular conditions of the experiment. However, they generally tell very little about
the real internal workings of the mind—the mechanism by which the
experimental conditions as perceived by the subject are translated into
the resulting observable responses.

Recently, a third method has emerged that may result in a major
spurt of progress for psychology. Instead of studying animals in the hope
that strong analogies to human mental behavior can be discovered, or
studying humans with awkward experiments that can gather only indirect
evidence about mental processes, some psychologists are studying computer models of human mental behavior. Such models consist of large
programs that exhibit behavior similar to that of human beings for some
limited domain of tasks. Instead of simply demonstrating one way in
which certain mental tasks can be performed, these programs are designed to perform the tasks in the same way that people do. The more
closely the program's behavior matches that of people, the better model
the program is said to be. The closeness of the model can be tested by
studying behavior at several levels of detail. At the most general level,
the program should certainly be able to perform any task (within the particular domain it is modeling) that most people find easy, and should fail,
or at least take much more time, on a task that people find extremely
difficult. At the most detailed level, no digital-computer program can be
a good model of mental behavior at all; the elementary electrical and
logical mechanisms of the computer bear little resemblance to the chemical, physiological mechanisms of the brain. However, at an intermediate
information-processing level, surprisingly sharp parallels have been developed. By studying the intermediate steps that the program and a person go through while working on the same problem, we can observe how
well the program models the person. We can further test the goodness of
the model by changing the task somewhat, or introducing new factors
during an attempted solution, and observing whether the machine's
modified behavior still parallels that of the human subject. If not, we can
try to change the model to improve the correspondences. Finally, if we
are satisfied with the computer model, we can view the flow chart of its
program as a plausible guide to the logic of the inner workings of the
mind.

At one time, many people would have said that this approach to
psychology was ridiculous; since computers cannot perform human-like
mental tasks at all, how can they perform them in the same way that
people do? But now, as we have seen in previous chapters, computers can
solve problems, perceive, understand, and show common sense, at least
to a limited extent. The development of programming languages and new
representation techniques makes the construction of simple reasoning
programs easy, so that the development of programs that model cognitive behavior is now entirely feasible.

As one example of this new computer-based approach to psychology, we shall briefly examine Newell and Simon's study of human problem solving. In Chapter 5, we examined the General Problem Solver (GPS) system, as a demonstration of how computers could make use of informal problem-solving methods. Actually GPS was developed primarily as a psychological model, rather than just a clever computer program. Its evolution over a period of close to ten years resulted not only in a more-powerful and more-flexible problem-solving ability, but also in more accurate modeling of human mental behavior, which was really the main interest of the developers.

The focus of Newell and Simon's work is admittedly an extremely narrow portion of human mental behavior: namely, the behavior of intelligent adults, of our culture, while engaged in solving short (half-hour) moderately difficult problems of a symbolic nature. For example, the cryptarithmetic problem discussed in Chapter 2 was suggested by Newell and Simon's work. Within this limited field of problem-solving activity, Newell and Simon performed many computer simulation experiments and thereby established certain conclusions that they presented as a theory of human problem solving—a much more precisely formulated theory than any developed by psychologists before the age of computer modeling. Here are some of the elements of this theory.

1.   A human being, when engaged in problem-solving, is an "information-processing system" consisting of an active serial symbol-manipulating processor, input (sensory) and output (motor) systems, internal short-term and long-term memories, and an external memory.

2.   Each type of problem is represented by a symbolic search space, and problem solving consists primarily of search through that space for a solution.

3.   The nature of a class of tasks largely determines the structure of the search space needed for solving those tasks. An effective (human or computer) problem solver constructs a search space appropriate to the type of problem at hand before it begins the detailed job of searching for a solution to a specific problem.

4.   The structure of a search space determines the nature of the possible programs that can be used for problem solving. Moreover, the problem-solver's knowledge—the specific facts, techniques, and experience he has previously acquired—play a central role in determining problem-solving behavior.

The Newell and Simon work on human problem solving is probably the most thorough investigation of its kind thus far. However, other projects such as Anderson and Bower's study of human associative memory, Colby's study of paranoia, and the many smaller efforts focused upon such topics as verbal learning, concept formation, belief systems, mental imagery, and so on, demonstrate that computer modeling has become a vital tool in the development of modern psychological theory.

Medicine

The health-care system of modern American society is now facing a series of fundamental problems. Medical schools are not keeping up with the continuous need for additional physicians. Doctors are increasingly reluctant to practice in rural or depressed urban communities, thereby causing medical care to be desperately inadequate in many localities. The continued accelerating expansion of medical knowledge tends to frustrate even the most conscientious specialist's attempt to keep abreast of his field. Spiraling costs are putting good medical care beyond the reach of a large segment of our population, and placing the whole future of private medicine in the United States in jeopardy. Can the computer help change this dismal picture? Let's see.

Medical care involves vast amounts of paper work. Already "stupid" computers have taken over some of this routine bookkeeping, freeing medical practitioners to concentrate on more significant duties. In many hospitals, the patient's medical history is now collected by a computer. Usually the patient fills out a special form that the computer can read, although in some cases the patient communicates directly with the computer by answering questions on a teletypewriter or other special console. The computer can then route the patient to the appropriate department, in accord with the patient's sex, age, principal complaints, and so on, and can call unusual features of the patient's history to the doctor's attention. The large-scale medical plans that now encourage periodic diagnostic physical examinations might not be feasible without such computer aids.

When a patient is admitted to a hospital, many different hospital staff members become responsible for his care. These usually overworked individuals sometimes do not communicate adequately with one another, and the patient's record file may not be kept completely accurate or up-to-date. Because a surprisingly large number of errors in hospital treatment are made because of human failures in keeping a patient's records, some hospitals have now turned over the job of maintaining these records to computers. In a pioneering system that has been in use for over a decade at Massachusetts General Hospital in Boston, somewhat smarter computer capabilities have gradually been added to the basic bookkeeping operations. Teletypewriter consoles are located throughout the hospital, so that every patient's record may be examined or updated instantly whenever necessary. This computer system has become an active partner in health-care activities. It not only maintains the record files; it also directs the pharmacy to prepare medications, and thinks about the disease, and knowledge about mathematical decision theory, the MIT/New England Medical Center team hopes to build automatic systems that perform in certain areas as well as medical specialists.

2. The vast number of interrelated facts a doctor must acquire and use is an unreasonable burden for most human minds. If an automatic system could integrate each new fact into its memory without needing reprogramming or significant memory reorganization, it would be of tremendous potential value. An experimental system by Ted Shortliffe at Stanford University Hospital has this property. Facts about antibiotic drugs and the treatment of infectious diseases can be inserted or modified at any time, and the system is always ready to answer questions by making logical inferences based upon everything in its memory.

In every walk of life and at every social level, I believe that most people are honest, capable, and conscientious; but you will always be able to find some—whether they are grape pickers, bus drivers, engineers, salesmen, computer scientists, or bank presidents—who are lazy, sloppy, greedy, or just plain incompetent. The same applies to doctors; the only thing special about them is that people's lives are in their hands. Suppose, ten years from now, you move to another city and have to select a doctor at random. Wouldn't you like to find one with a well-educated computer available to help him make critical decisions?

Automation

By the end of the last century industrial development had dramatically changed the character of American manufacturing and, indirectly, the entire American way of life. Some of the effects of industrial expansion were sad, for example the virtual disappearance of skilled artisans, such as blacksmiths and cabinetmakers, who took pride in their custom work. Other effects, such as the widespread exploitation of labor, were downright shocking, and yet decades passed before they were balanced by such forces as unionism and social legislation. In spite of all the negative side effects, however, the primary results of industrialization and mass production were a tremendous increase in the availability of products of all kinds ranging from wheat to automobiles, and a resulting increase in the standard of living of millions of people. On balance, few could seriously advocate a return to a horse-and-buggy culture.

During the past twenty-five years American industry has become relatively stagnant. The average age of factories and factory equipment is increasing. Industrial investment in research into new production methods and new technology has been negligible. The average increase in productivity of United States industry dropped to less than 3 percent per year, and in 1973 was the lowest of the fifteen major industrialized nations in the world. Combined with rising inflation rates this slow-down in productivity resulted in almost no gain in real income for most Americans in 1973, and a definite loss in 1974. Can computers help reverse this trend? Computers are beginning to find their way into factories, warehouses, and offices all over the country. Of course, as stupid computers become cheaper they are called upon to take over the accounting and record-keeping operations of more and more companies. But smarter computers are also finding their places. Laboratory demonstrations have already proved the feasibility of applying the automatic problem-solving, perception, and robot-control capabilities described in previous chapters to practical current industrial problems. The resulting influx of computerized systems into industry, which is now beginning to take place, has already been called "the second industrial revolution." Like the first one, this new industrial revolution can result in a significant improvement in productivity, measured not only in the quantity but also in the quality of goods produced. With a little planning, this second industrial revolution can avoid some of the pitfalls of the first, and result in an improved quality of life and standard of living for all of mankind. Let's look at some of the elements of the coming computerization of industry.

As computer aids gradually creep out of their imprisonment in the bookkeeping departments of American industry, they take on expanded functions throughout the production and distribution systems. The planning and layout of industrial operations is one field in which they have already proved their value. At one time planning and design operations as varied as deciding how to schedule the use of equipment in a machine shop, and how to lay out the electrical wiring in a TV set, were done only by skilled engineers. They generally considered their design work to be an engineering art, performed on the basis of extensive experience; they did not imagine that computers could help them. But now computers are becoming accepted for their symbolic problem-solving abilities as well as their arithmetic speed. Many of the principles used by design experts can be translated into strategies to be incorporated in computer programs. These programs can then employ some of the search and problem-solving methods described in previous chapters to produce solutions that are frequently better than solutions produced by purely human methods. Programs developed in this way have been used, for example, to plan the use of space—the placement of walls, heating ducts, furniture, and so on—in office buildings; to specify the arrangement of cutting knives and the routing of stock material in paper, cardboard, and box-making factories in order to minimize the amount of scrap produced; and to design the layout of wiring paths on printed circuit boards. In most cases the importance of such programs is not that they produce solutions to their problems quickly, but rather that the solutions they produce are somewhat better than the purely human solution and result in substantial savings.

When we move from planning to actual factory operations, we should first consider the problem of quality control—perhaps the biggest satellite would ever have been launched without the availability of computers to calculate orbital corrections and fuel expenditures. However, such activities are the traditional jobs of "stupid" computers. Now let's look at just a few of the ways in which smarter computers are beginning to promote the advance of science.

MATHEMATICS

Mathematics provides basic tools for much of science, as well as being a fascinating field for research in its own right. Arithmetic, an elementary branch of mathematics, has long been considered most natural for computers. However, since about 1960, several nonnumeric branches of mathematics have succumbed to computerization.

Next to arithmetic, algebra is probably the most widely used branch of mathematics. The automatic solution of symbolic algebraic equations was one of the first applications for symbol-manipulation programming techniques. Strategies were developed for simplifying, factoring, and otherwise rearranging algebraic expressions, and for solving sets of dozens or even hundreds of simultaneous algebraic equations. Today physicists and engineers have available special programming languages, subroutines, and interactive computer aids enabling them to perform high-speed, error-free, algebraic calculations far beyond their former manual abilities.

Integral calculus was once the first branch of higher mathematics faced by students that forced them to use their ingenuity, rather than cook-book solution algorithms. Since "stupid" computers solve problems only according to strictly algorithmic rules, they could not do integrals. Yet in 1962 James Slagle at MIT developed a program that did do integrals about as well as MIT freshmen; in fact it scored 88% on an MIT calculus final exam. This smarter computer worked largely by modelling the students' approach to solving calculus problems, much as Newell and Simon modelled other kinds of problem-solving behavior. The only reason Slagle's program did not score 100% was that it did not "know" the method of partial fractions, which was needed for some of the problems. The computer's memory was not large enough to hold programs for applying that method along with all its other programs.

Later, Joel Moses and other MIT computer scientists improved upon Slagle's program by replacing the techniques used by naive students with new methods developed by expert mathematicians. Now the calculus program has been combined with the algebra-manipulation system, equation solvers, and other mathematical aids, into a system called MACSYMA, a system for mathematics and symbolic algebra. This system is available as a working tool for thousands of scientists who have access to it at any time by means of a network of computers that extends from Hawaii across the United States to England and Norway.

Chapter 4 explained some of the basic ideas of mathematical logic, in particular the resolution approach to proving theorems in predicate calculus. At that time we were interested in how such formal deductive methods could be applied to automatic methods for solving a variety of different common-sense reasoning problems. Here, though, I want to point out the principal reason such methods were developed: to automate the use of mathematical logic itself. Mathematicians are continuing to improve predicate-calculus proof procedures and are beginning to use them as working tools, just as they use calculus and algebra systems. Versions of automatic theorem-proving systems have been tailored for use in various specialized branches of mathematics such as set theory, and have already helped mathematicians develop new results.

CHEMISTRY

Can smarter computers help with the intellectual work of professional scientists? One program has already achieved an impressive degree of competence on an important problem of analytic chemistry: the DENDRAL system, developed by Feigenbaum and Lederberg at Stanford University, is a computer program written to solve problems of inductive inference in organic chemistry. The system identifies the chemical composition and the organic structure of various chemical compounds, when given as data the results of certain standard tests such as the "mass spectrograph." For some families of molecules the program is an expert, even when compared with the best human scientists. It has solved problems that caused difficulty for professional chemists, and has even found errors in published chemical tables.

The DENDRAL system, which is the result of years of development effort by a joint team of computer scientists and chemists, has several key components.

1. Pattern classification ability, used for extracting key features from the experimental data.

2. An understanding of basic rules of chemistry, such as how chemical structures join together and what determines unstable compounds.

3. A model of the theory of operation of the mass spectrometer, so that trial answers may be tested by simulating the instrument and comparing its simulated results with the actual data.

4. Packages of special empirical rules, given to the system by human experts that apply only to limited classes of compounds.

The last of these components is the most important. DENDRAL generally performs extremely well when it has much specialized knowledge that is applicable to its current problem, and often performs rather poorly when it must fall back upon its knowledge of general principles. (Of course, the same can be said about almost any human problem solver.)

Therefore the current continuing DENDRAL research program is studying how different types of expert knowledge may be acquired by a computer and combined, in a DENDRAL-like framework, into future automatic experts for other branches of science.

COMPUTER SCIENCE

How can smarter computers be applied to the problems of computer science itself? An exciting new example of computer science helping itself is the research area called *automatic programming.*

Twenty years ago the major problem of computer science was to build a reliable computer. In comparison to the design, construction, and maintenance of the hardware, the problem of *programming*—the design, construction, and maintenance of the "software"—was considered to be so easy and unimportant that it received very little attention.

Today in most computer installations programming costs have caught up with the hardware costs, and experts predict that by 1980 the value of the software typically will be double the value of the hardware. Although high-level languages and interactive systems have improved programming methodology considerably, the process of creating a large error-free program is still a slow, frustrating, largely trial-and-error activity. Most programs can never be thoroughly tested; they are designed to be able to work with literally millions of possible inputs, only a tiny fraction of which can ever be tried out. Generally the programmer chooses a few test cases that he hopes are typical, makes the program work properly on them, and then crosses his fingers and puts the program—e.g., an automatic billing system—into general use. Later, when errors turn up, and Mr. Raphael's credit-card bills continue to be sent to Vienna months after the billing system was notified that he had moved to San Francisco, the programmer must be called back for a job peculiarly called "maintaining" his program—and Mr. Raphael is tempted to swear at the "stupid computer."

Scientists are now developing methods to avoid such problems by using smarter computer programs to test and correct other programs. Instead of testing a program by trying some test cases, this new approach is to try to *prove* that a program will do what it is supposed to. If the proof fails, then the testing program can often figure out, from the way the proof failed, what's wrong with the program. These smarter program-proving programs may make use of a combination of formal logical proof methods, special-purpose knowledge about the particular task and programming language being tested, and perhaps even a model of the way a skilled programmer thinks.

Another approach to the automatic programming task is to develop a program that can actually create other programs. If such a program-writing program is good enough it will produce nothing but absolutely correct programs, and the problems of program testing and correction will just disappear.

Automatic program-testing and program-writing programs are still in their earliest developmental stages. It will be years before such systems can be put to practical use, but the work that has been done on them has given us confidence that such a day will come. Someday we shall be able to describe to a computer in English what task we want it to do, and a language-understanding system will call upon an automatic programming system to create a new program especially tailored for the desired task.

Other areas

What else can smarter computers do for mankind? Think about the growing automatic capabilities discussed in this book—problem solving, perception, language understanding, representation of knowledge, expert performance in science and mathematics, and so on—and dream a little. Here are a few suggestions, to get you started.

Service Information. Our society seems to be desperately short of skilled technicians and repairmen. The cost of hiring a plumber, carpenter, auto mechanic, or electrician, has skyrocketed. We have been forced to become a nation of do-it-yourselfers. And yet, "doing it yourself" is often nearly impossible because of the absence of good information. Think of the last time you tried to fix a toaster, lawn mower, or faucet. Did you wonder which screw to take off first? Did you take apart more than you really needed to? Did you have parts left over when you were through? Direction sheets and how-to-do-it books are sometimes helpful, but even if you have exactly the right one for your job (which is rare) it is usually hard to figure out and doesn't answer your particular questions. Now suppose that a smart computer had all the information about the thing you wanted to fix, and all the knowledge needed about how to go about fixing it. All you would have to do is telephone the computer and ask for its advice.

Entertainment Center. Recreation is a rapidly growing industry. Although people have enjoyed the challenge of games of cards, darts, or backgammon for hundreds of years, it is not always possible to find an interested opponent at the appropriate level of skill, and many would occasionally like more varied, challenging games. Once again, think about calling up your friendly computer. It could certainly carry on an interesting game of chess or checkers. It might play scrabble, at whatever skill level you choose to specify, either two-handed or with as many simulated additional players as you wish. Plugged into your home TV system, the computer would be glad to play a simulated game of ping-pong, or imitate a pin-ball machine with as many bumpers and flippers as you care to specify.

Music and Art. Computers have long been used to compose musical pieces and to create novel drawings: usually to the ridicule of the critics. They have not yet been programmed to create works that appeal to the esthetic sensibilities of human connoisseurs. However, they certainly provide new tools, new media, for the human artist. A computer-controlled sound synthesizer can create any sound or combination of sounds the composer can imagine, including many that are not possible with any existing musical instrument. A computer-controlled plotter can draw geometric patterns with greater precision and patience than a human artist. As the computer becomes smarter, it can begin to collaborate with the composer or artist, instead of just following orders. It can fill in or modify passages according to general guidelines, combining its innovative abilities with those of the human, and produce compositions that neither the human nor the computer could have conceived of independently.

Actually, significant steps have already been taken toward using smarter computers in each of the above ways. But, even if they hadn't been yet, they soon would be. Thinking computers are here, waiting to be still further educated and then put to good use. All it takes is your ideas about where to use them.

Summary

As computers become less expensive and more widely available, society is becoming more dependent upon them to perform conventional book-keeping functions. More important, however, is that as computers become more intelligent they can take on valuable new roles in the service of society. In education, computers constitute a rich new medium for a student's creative expression and experimentation. They can be used to demonstrate laws of physics on a dynamic display screen, to illustrate mathematical principles through the design of algorithms, and to carry on tutorial conversations. In psychology, computer models of mental behavior provide knowledge of how the mind works. In medicine, computers can model physiological and biochemical processes, and both store and deduce large numbers of facts about diseases, drugs, and treatments. In industry, computers can help both in the front office, scheduling activities and monitoring progress, and on the factory floor, directing automatic inspection, materials handling, and assembly systems. Such activities can both increase productivity and improve the quality of the goods produced. In mathematics and science, computers are beginning to function as intelligent assistants to professional scientists, performing such jobs as solving and simplifying symbolic equations, analyzing chemical compounds, and verifying the correctness of simple computer programs. Other roles for intelligent computers pervade our daily life; as novel sources of information, amusement, or artistic experiences, the potential for us to benefit from such machines is limited only by our imaginations.

SUGGESTED READINGS

Allen, John R. "Current Trends in Computer-Assisted Instruction." *Computers and the Humanities,* Vol. 7, no. 1, 1972.

Anderson, J. R., and G. H. Bower. *Human Associative Memory.* John Wiley & Sons, New York, 1973.

Elspas, B., et al. "An Assessment of Techniques for Proving Program Correctness." *ACM Computing Surveys,* Vol. 4, no. 2, Association for Computing Machinery, New York, 1972.

New Educational Technology. General Turtle, Inc., P. O. Box 33, Cambridge, Mass., 1973.

Newell, A., and H. A. Simon. *Human Problem Solving.* Prentice Hall, Englewood Cliffs, N.J., 1972.

Proceedings of the 1st Conference on Industrial Robot Technology. (University of Nottingham, U.K.) International Fluidics Services Ltd., Felmersham, Bedford, England, 1973.

Schwartz, W. B., et al. "Decision Analysis and Clinical Judgment." *Amer. J. of Med.,* Vol. 55, pp. 459, 1973.

Shortliffe, E. H., et al. "An Artificial Intelligence Program to Advise Physicians Regarding Antimicrobial Therapy." *Computers and Biomedical Research,* Vol. 6, pp. 544–560, 1973.

Epilogue

Some of the readers of this book will be upset. They will think, "If this book is true, computers are going to replace teachers, doctors, laborers, mechanics, even computer programmers. We are going to be taught and guided by computers, diagnosed and treated by computers, play games with computers, and be subjected to computer-composed music and art. Society will be dehumanized! Computers will take over!"

I believe such forecasts of doom are incredibly misleading, even though they contain a kernel of truth. Listen to the same voices a hundred years ago: "Machines are going to replace ditch-diggers, lumberjacks, coachmen, hay-balers, even blacksmiths. Machines will take over!" Or, a hundred thousand years ago: "Fire will cook our food, heat our caves, even provide light at night. Fire will take over!" Each prediction true, but each truth turned into an essential benefit, rather than a threat, for mankind.

Yes, computers, if misused, can possibly "dehumanize" society; but they can, and I believe they will, have just the opposite effect. Computers in education can free human teachers of drudgery, and allow them to devote the bulk of their time to personal guidance of those students who most need it. Computers in medicine can raise the level of health care to a decent minimum for all, and allow doctors to concentrate on giving vital emotional support when needed, and dealing with novel problems at the forefront of their specialties. Computers in industry can free laborers from mindless jobs in unpleasant and dangerous environments, and can raise the average standard of living (and reduce inflation) by increasing productivity.

As computers become more intelligent, they will certainly cause some problems in society, and may force us to devise new ways to distribute our jobs, our wealth, and our time. Such problems and their possible solutions are well beyond the scope of this book. In the long run, however, I am confident that computers are here to stay, to the immense benefit of mankind. We must learn to understand them and to live with them. I hope this book has made some contribution toward that understanding.

Index